American Spaces
of Conversion

AMERICAN SPACES OF CONVERSION

*The Conductive Imaginaries of
Edwards, Emerson, and James*

ANDREA KNUTSON

OXFORD
UNIVERSITY PRESS
2011

OXFORD
UNIVERSITY PRESS

Oxford University Press, Inc., publishes works that further
Oxford University's objective of excellence
in research, scholarship, and education.

Oxford   New York

Auckland   Cape Town   Dar es Salaam   Hong Kong   Karachi
Kuala Lumpur   Madrid   Melbourne   Mexico City   Nairobi
New Delhi   Shanghai   Taipei   Toronto

With offices in

Argentina   Austria   Brazil   Chile   Czech Republic   France   Greece
Guatemala   Hungary   Italy   Japan   Poland   Portugal   Singapore
South Korea   Switzerland   Thailand   Turkey   Ukraine   Vietnam

Copyright © 2011 by Oxford University Press, Inc.

Published by Oxford University Press, Inc.
198 Madison Avenue, New York, NY 10016

www.oup.com

Library of Congress Cataloging-in-Publication Data
Knutson, Andrea.
American spaces of conversion : the conductive imaginaries of Edwards,
Emerson, and James / Andrea Knutson.
p.   cm.
ISBN 978-0-19-537092-8
1. Conversion—Christianity. 2. Puritans—Doctrines.
3. Puritans—Influence. 4. Edwards, Jonathan, 1703–1758.
5. Emerson, Ralph Waldo, 1803–1882.
6. James, William, 1842–1910. I. Title.
BX9323.K58 2011
248.2'40973—dc22
2010009160

1 3 5 7 9 8 6 4 2

Printed in the United States of America
on acid-free paper

Contents

Acknowledgments

—————

Acknowledging all who have supported me during the writing of this book seems like a small gesture in relation to the gratitude that I feel. At The Graduate Center of The City University of New York I had the good fortune to find an exciting and supportive intellectual community and to study with remarkable scholars. William Kelly's questions shaped the way I envisioned the project. He broadened my perspective by asking me to think about conversion in relation to figures and events outside the confines of my chapters. David Reynolds's feedback helped me clarify my ideas. He challenged me to find the right word, phrase, or sentence to capture them and did so with enthusiasm and kindness. My deepest thanks go to Joan Richardson. Her intellectual curiosity and rigor have been an inspiration for me throughout. Her course "Doers of the Word" introduced me to scholarship in American theology, literature, and philosophy, and it was in that seminar that the idea for this book developed and that my intellectual interests crystallized. It was a conversion in every sense of the word. The book also received financial support from The Graduate Center's English Department. I am grateful for having won a Morton Cohen Dissertation Year Award, which allowed me to make the transition from years of research to writing.

At Oakland University I have found dedicated teachers and scholars in Robert Anderson, Gladys Cardiff, Jeff Chapman, Natalie Cole, Brian Connery, Kyle Edwards, Annie Gilson, Kevin Grimm, Susan Hawkins, Niels Herold, Edward Haworth Hoeppner, Jeffrey Insko, Nancy Joseph, Kevin Laam, Jim McClure, L. Bailey McDaniel, Kathleen Pfeiffer, and Joshua Yumibe. It's a privilege and a pleasure to be among colleagues who are committed to student life and learning and whose thoughtfulness and supportiveness are the backbone of the department. In particular I'd like to thank Jeffrey Insko, a valuable reader whose thorough feedback was a considerate and much appreciated gesture toward this junior colleague. Kathleen Pfeiffer organized a writing workshop that supported me through the early stages of revisions. Gladys Cardiff's counsel on all matters was instrumental in moving this project into completion. I am especially grateful to Phyllis Rooney, who generously organized a brown-bag meeting with her colleagues in the Philosophy Department to discuss my ideas. This book benefited from that discussion with Oakland philosophers Fritz McDonald, Paul Graves, and John Halpin. Finally, Susan Hawkins offered guidance in too many ways to enumerate. She made the transition to a new department, university, and city as smooth as it could be while making it possible to finish the book in practical ways that cannot be underestimated.

Transforming a manuscript into a book also takes dedicated and insightful readers who are sensitive to an author's objectives and personal vision. I found such readers in Vincent Colapietro, Roger Ward, Andrés Páez, and the anonymous readers at Oxford University Press. Their attention to and enthusiasm for this project shaped the content of the chapters and the trajectory of the book, and their insights have directed me beyond this project into new areas of research. Finally, I am so grateful to Shannon McLachlan, Brendan O'Neill, Mark LaFlaur, and Joellyn Ausanka at Oxford University Press, whose kindness and astute handling of the manuscript have made the complicated process of making a book enjoyable.

I cannot imagine the years it has taken to write this book without friendships old and new. I thank Diana Polley, Christopher Bruhn, Tina Meyerhoff, Jennifer Bernstein, Robert Kaplan, James King, S. J. Rozan, Jennifer Gurley, Tom Knutson, Anne Vattendahl, Therese Simmons, Peter Spitzform, Jeff Chapman, Kyle and Laura Edwards, Natalie Cole, Andy Henry, Kathy Battles, Rachel Andrews, L. Bailey McDaniel, Todd Estes, Natasha Vaubel, and Ellen Dahl. Our conversations have supported life and work. I would also like to thank Ben and Nancy Aibel whose retreat in Vermont was made available to me on several occasions. Much of the early stages of making connections and drafting happened in the Green Mountains. This book is a product of their generosity.

Finally, I owe the greatest length and breadth and depth and height of gratitude to my family, especially to my parents, Linda and Bob Luna. They are my closest, most enthusiastic supporters. I learn from them every day that love is unbounded perception, and to them I dedicate this book.

Abbreviations

The following abbreviations are used in the text and notes for frequently cited works. Full citations are provided on first use in the text.

EL Ralph Waldo Emerson, *Ralph Waldo Emerson: Essays and Lectures*

MIND Jonathan Edwards, *"The Mind" of Jonathan Edwards: A Reconstructed Text*

NEM Perry Miller, *The New England Mind: The Seventeenth Century*

PP William James, *The Principles of Psychology*

PTV Thomas Shepard, *The Parable of the Ten Virgins Opened and Applied*

RA Jonathan Edwards, *Religious Affections*

SB Thomas Shepard, *The Sound Believer*

TSC Thomas Shepard, *Thomas Shepard's Confessions*

VRE William James, *The Varieties of Religious Experience*

American Spaces
of Conversion

Introduction

In *Religious Affections*, Jonathan Edwards explains the fourth sign of what he calls the "spiritual sense" having been laid in the foundation of the soul by claiming that gracious affections arise from a new understanding of divine things. He states that "the change made by this spiritual opening of the eyes in conversion, would be much greater, and more remarkable, every way, than if a man, who had been born blind . . . then at once should have the sense of seeing imparted to him, in the midst of the clear light of the sun, discovering a world of visible objects."[1] The ecstatic nature of vision described here is only one result of conversion, which transforms an individual through the saving operations of grace in such a way that motives, choices, and actions all become signs of holy inclinations that guide conduct in the world. Aligned with the will of God, the individual is granted the ability to discern a new "world of visible objects," an experience analogous to Ralph Waldo Emerson's when he crosses the "bare common" and claims "I am nothing; I see all." However, the centrality of these ecstatic imaginings of new visual acuity to American literature must be considered alongside their less ecstatic but no less important correlative—the incremental process of what Emerson calls at the end of *Nature* "the advancing spirit," whose slow progress is assured to the extent that an individual can detect a pattern of development in how the world is perceived.[2]

Though *Nature* begins with an image of ecstatic transformation through the metaphor of the transparent eyeball, that image is contrasted with, or balanced by, the succession of chapters that follow which represent the stages of "spiritual advancement" he claims will realize "the kingdom of man over nature."[3] In addition, at the end of "Compensation"

Emerson reiterates the centrality of his idea of transparency as the necessary condition for perception that fosters the experience and sight of ever-evolving regenerating and regenerative relations to the world. This image, however, conveys a different experience of transparency:

> The changes which break up at short intervals the prosperity of men are advertisements of a nature whose law is growth. Every soul is by this intrinsic necessity quitting its whole system of things, its friends, and home, and laws, and faith, as the shell-fish crawls out of its beautiful but stony case, because it no longer admits of its growth, and slowly forms a new house. In proportion to the vigor of the individual, these revolutions are frequent, until in some happier mind they are incessant, and all worldly relations hang very loosely about him, becoming, as it were, a transparent fluid membrane through which the living form is seen.[4]

In this passage, the incessant but slow growth of perception and, therefore, consciousness is the result of a certain transparency, but it is imagined as a "fluid membrane" that is energized in proportion to an individual's vigor and commitment to seeking revolutions in worldly relations, rather than ecstatically. The two kinds of transparencies, therefore, are very different, and their qualities arise specifically from within their immediate contexts. The power of the "transparent eyeball" arises from the context of a "bare common" and is activated in a moment of solitude. In contrast, the "transparent fluid membrane" is integral to a dense context of friends, home, laws and faith. Because of this density, like "shell-fish" we crawl slowly through experience, yet with vigor, to each succeeding context, which is as dense as the previous one. We don't fully transcend the defining nature of these contexts, but the relations are fluid and permeable, shifting and morphing as we seek revolutions.

Emerson's "advancing spirit" moves through the world in a way that is as powerful and steady and life-affirming as the cyclic process of nature's regenerative seasons: "As when the summer comes from the south; the snow-banks melt, and the face of the earth becomes green before it," the advancing spirit shall "create its ornaments along its path, and carry with it the beauty it visits, and the song which enchants it."[5] In contrast to the immediacy and intensity of transformation conveyed in Edwards's image of a blind man restored to perfect sight in the "clear light of the sun," Emerson goes on to describe the quality of sight associated with a spiritual process that is gradient, that creates enough ornaments until "evil is seen no more." It is a kind of vision that creates the "kingdom of man over nature" because an individual discerns degrees of progressive difference, prompting man to "enter [the kingdom] without more wonder than a blind man feels who is *gradually* restored to perfect sight."[6] In contrast to the ecstatic nature of perception symbolized by the transparent eyeball, Emerson offers these alternative, quotidian moments of perception, which provide a more ordinary context for perceptual advances but which Emerson claims "draw around its way" such greatness associated with "heroic acts."

In turn, Edwards's image of a blind man's vision being instantly restored to reveal a new "world of visible objects" serves to express the potency of the gift of the Spirit because it "makes a great change in a man," but it is likewise offered as an instance best understood within the wider context of a pattern of perceptual advances. For Edwards, in fact, the image serves to foreground the "preparatory" activity associated with the Puritan Reformed process of conversion. As he writes, the effects of "God's implanting that spiritual supernatural sense" would be as though a man born blind could suddenly see in the "clear light of the sun" *if it were not for* "the very imperfect degree, in which this sense is commonly given at first, or the small degree of this glorious light that first dawns upon the soul."[7] We know from Edwards's "miscellanies" that his own conversion experience did not follow the strict order of preparatory stages enforced by such ministers as Thomas Shepard of the previous generation, and his *Religious Affections* is a testament to his need to theorize a new perceptual approach for detecting the "advance" of the spirit. In contrast to imposing a predetermined grid of preparatory stages onto experience as a way to manage and chart one's spiritual progress, Edwards offers in his descriptions of the signs of religious affections an emphasis on the individual's powers of discerning a pattern of affective, intellectual, and outward changes that indicate continual, progressive growth in consciousness. Instead of relying on a codified framework of marks to hit indicating a "correct" path, Edwards proposes that a saint's (an elect's) unique experience in the world, the personal manifestation of faith, demands that he or she understand what Emerson calls in "Compensation" the "crack[s] in every thing God has made" as opportunities for spiritual regeneration.[8] These "cracks" do not signify, as they would in preparatory theology, regressions to an earlier stage of the preparatory scheme; instead, they are "preparatory" because they offer opportunities for conscious growth and spiritual advancement. To the extent that saints can convert these circumstances, or "cracks," into truth, they become signs of growth and contribute to a pattern of progressive differences in perspective evidencing renewed relations to the world and, therefore, to

God. As a result, discerning these "degrees" of "glorious light" becomes the hallmark of realizing God's will on earth because one's spiritual growth is both the cause and effect of these advancing degrees.

This study is an examination of the "advancing spirit" in American literature. It explores how the concept of conversion and specifically the legacy of the doctrine of preparation, as articulated in Puritan Reformed theology and transplanted to the Massachusetts Bay Colony, remained a vital cultural force shaping developments in American literature and philosophy. Testimonies of conversion recorded by the Puritan divine Thomas Shepard reveal an active pursuit of belief by prospective church members occurring at the intersection of experience, perception, doctrine, affections, and intellect. This pursuit of belief, codified in the *ordo salutis* (the "order of salvation"), and originally undertaken by the Puritans as a way to conceptualize redemption in a fallen state, established the epistemological contours for what Jonathan Edwards, Ralph Waldo Emerson, and William James would theorize as a conductive imaginary: a conscious space organized, or that self-organizes, around the dynamics and tensions between emergent and stored up truth, uncertainty and certainty, and perception and objects perceived. As a result, each author offers a picture of consciousness as both a receptive and active force responsible for translating the effects of experience—they offer a description of the mental space wherein what William James calls a person's "collection of ideas" is reorganized by new information into action guided by a new "habitual centre of . . . personal energy."[9] By virtue of an individual's willingness and consistent effort to exercise the conductive nature of consciousness, the new "habitual centre" reflects the spirit's advancement in the world, and the "heroic acts" that Emerson refers to reveal the "possibilities of character" these "inner alterations" indicate.[10]

I hope to provide an intellectual history that takes as its point of departure what Perry Miller calls the "one fissure in the impregnable walls of systematic theology"—the site of daily experience for the Puritans.[11] This fissure becomes an infinite, powerful resource for thinkers such as Edwards, Emerson, and James precisely because of its ordinariness. The ordinary serves as the site for adaptations in belief structures that define and bind and energize the relations between an individual, the divine (or incalculable), and evolving notions of the environment. Puritans understood their experimental faith as occurring at the intersection of God's hidden will (their daily lives) and his declared will (the Bible), and their efforts to interpret experience against doctrine determined the course of their spiritual advancement in conversion. As an epistemological process where a perceiver is linked to an infinite potential, the "morphology" of conversion remained of deep interest to Edwards, Emerson, and James, each of whom developed philosophies celebrating the perception and translation of experience through an affective relation to the environment.[12] As such, the experience of belief, framing the dynamics between an individual and history, society, nature, and language, served as a central trope for theological, philosophical, and literary expression in America. The idea of conversion, therefore, provides a conceptual framework for examining the fluidity that persists between the specialized fields of literary, philosophical, and religious studies, extending as it does from Reformed Christian piety to pragmatism. Shifting from religious doctrine, to literary style, to philosophical premise, the subjects of this study present conversion as a driving force in individual and cultural identity, guiding constantly renewed definitions of the world.

Controversy over the formulations of the dynamics of conversion has its roots in the Bible because operations of grace are as varied as the manifold experiences of each regenerate individual. Scripture offers conversion as an experience that foregrounds an individual's relation to God as one of his elect, but it also conveys conflicting messages about the workings of grace. Hence, regeneration is possible within a broadly defined spectrum of spiritual experience that emerges from two primary and opposing descriptions of conversion presented in the Bible: man's voluntary return to God and God's turning of man to him. This template first gave rise within the continental Reformed tradition to a mystical understanding of grace conceived as an arbitrary gift bestowed at the will of God, wrenching man out of his depravity and exemplified in Paul's conversion on the road to Damascus. However, around 1570, during the reign of Elizabeth, certain English divines began to speculate about an individual's ability to respond to God's promises as set forth in the covenant of grace. Challenging Paul's conversion experience as normative, they claimed that natural man, though only in "external covenant" by virtue of baptism, might be able to predispose himself to saving grace. This was the attitude that took hold within English divinity, became the defining force within Puritanism, and would eventually become an integral part of the New England Way.

The earliest Puritan pastors such as Richard Greenham, Richard Rogers, Arthur Hildersam, and William Perkins held that grace was not an external element that descended from God but that it dwelled in the heart: one need only search for signs of its evidence. This understanding gave rise to an experiential piety that was not viewed as separate from biblical religion but as one and the same. The practice within this new experiential tradition was to correlate personal experience with the most appropriate scriptural passage because the Holy Spirit was believed to be at work while an individual read scripture, shedding light on one's sin, serving as a guide in one's examination of his or her state of grace, and perhaps providing the right passage that would offer assurance of one's eternal salvation. The result was a piety dependent on protracted meditation upon experience with the goal of discovering signs of election. Experiential piety granted natural man the ability to respond to God's grace, but in doing so, it created a space between man and God that saints were expected to navigate in their desire to know or establish their relation to God. Out of these new conditions requiring saints to search for evidence of grace, preparationism emerged as an articulation of covenantal theology in New England. Janice Knight has noted that

> it was the founders' ingenious invention to harness the remote power of the Godhead. . . . This contract mitigated the problem of assurance while providing for God's actions through secondary means in the world of time. Conditions of the covenant afforded a human sphere of action—if one could believe, he or she could lay claim to God's mercy. By means of the covenant, then, the unknowable God was tamed and the saint was made in some measure responsible for his or her salvation. Voluntarism and the doctrine of preparationism were born.[13]

The "human sphere of action" opened up by the idea that one could search for signs of election paved the way for developments in Puritan doctrine which attempted to account for the "stages" of spiritual experience that one could expect to reach in the journey toward assurance, hence William Perkins's ten-step morphology of conversion. Though the Puritans retained the integrity of a predestined universe, they held that natural man could "entertain" grace because the elect had received the "seed" of faith, and this notion placed a new emphasis on human potential manifested within the interpretive imperative embedded within preparatory activity.

Puritan theology, therefore, placed natural man, with all his postlapsarian faults, in the position of finding assurance of eternal salvation equipped only with the cracked lenses and broken tools he was left with after the Fall. In addition, addressing this sphere of action and "closing with Christ," was tied to a saint's ability to sustain an interpretive mode within experience, the imperative being to maintain, coordinately, receptivity to the workings of grace. Because a saint could not trust his or her intellectual, affective, or perceptual faculties to interpret experience correctly, the preparatory stages associated with the morphology of conversion provided a way to organize experience into units that conformed to doctrine. Yet, using the preparatory stages as a way to chart one's spiritual progress was, as the chapter on the Puritan conversion narratives will show, one element of the cultural movement toward fostering spiritual discipline enforced through a ministerial emphasis on reason's primacy in determining what constitutes evidence of grace. Preparationist ministers such as Thomas Shepard cultivated a strong distrust in the affective dimension of the conversion process among congregants, fostering, instead, a habit of thinking that reflected the influence of Ramist logic and faculty psychology on preparation theology. By placing man in the position of discovering the will of God, Puritan experimental faith thrust man to the edge of experience in search of signs, and preparationist ministers provided a methodology for approaching the uncertainty and chaos found there in order to convert it into truth.

It is this central role of a habit of thinking in discovering truth and how it contributes to a definition of piety or active consciousness that each of the subjects of this study takes as his life's work. William James, in fact, concludes his chapter on habit from *The Principles of Psychology* by claiming, "the physiological study of mental conditions is . . . the most powerful ally of hortatory ethics. The hell to be endured hereafter, of which theology tells, is no worse than the hell we make for ourselves in this world by habitually fashioning our characters in the wrong way. . . . We are spinning our own fates, good or evil, and never to be undone."[14] Indeed, Shepard, Edwards, Emerson, and James are all preoccupied with the "mental conditions" of their respective audiences. Each of them is responding to what James calls in *The Varieties of Religious Experience* the problem of the "sick soul." In this sense, each writer understands his role as ministerial in that his work is meant to foster a sense of personal regeneration through a change in mental or spiritual "conditions." Yet, each also understands his work as performing cultural revision, specifically as it foregrounds the intersubjective nature of that revision process. We see this aspect most overtly in the first chapter because of the Puritan migration to the Massachusetts Bay.

The narratives of conversion Shepard recorded for church membership reveal that the majority of his congregation felt disappointment in New England as a means to grace when they arrived. Saints, in fact, testify to having had confidence in the premigration preparatory scheme that contained the idea of New England as a means to grace, but then they admit that experiencing the reality of the New World context could not be contained by the old morphology. Shepard's response to the crisis in faith caused by the migration is evident in his sermon series on the parable of the ten virgins. In it he performs a theological resurrection of New England as a means to grace by recontextualizing the idea of New England in a newly adapted morphology. The testimonies demonstrate the confessors' adoption and internalization of New England's revived place in the morphology because they follow the pattern identified by Patricia Caldwell in her book *The Puritan Conversion Narrative: The Beginnings of American Expression*. Identified by Caldwell as a "since-I-came-hither-dead-hearted-but-I-have-been-revived" convention, she argues that the migrants understood their disappointment caused by the migration as an insurmountable sin that inaugurates a legacy of "open-endedness" in American literature.[15] I argue that this pattern demonstrates a different relationship to the New World, that it expresses the newly conceived *promise* of America as it has been reconstructed in Ramist fashion through a new axiomatic rendering of the *idea* of New England. The confessions demonstrate the provisional nature of the idea of New England, that its meaning is contextual—grounded in experience and history. In Chapter 1 I argue that we see the axiomatic rehearsals of New England's reconceived place in Puritan experiential faith. In their collective stuttering they testify to the rebracketing of New England in the morphology and demonstrate a modern expression of the mind as a constructive force. And though the morphology remains intact as an organizing template for experience, the re-placement of New England within its classificatory structure illustrates Shepard's awareness that in order to revive his congregants' faith, he needed to create an original relation to their new context by redefining its value for them. In doing so, he resurrected their faith in a new geographical location whose spiritual potential was realized through the conscious space opened up by the new meaning attached to it.

As a discursive force fostering the new conceptual understanding of New England's place in the morphology, the sermons on the parable of the ten virgins enforce a rigorous intellectualized experience of conversion. As a result, Shepard's saints do not testify to the transcendent, felt dimension of conversion, which is, in fact, the moment of justification in the process. Though many of the confessors testify to reaching the moment just before they feel the urge to turn their will over to God, they inevitably fall back on the prescribed form of experience dictated by Shepard—that of conviction, compunction, despair, and humiliation—the aspects related to the disciplined stages of the conversion process fueled by the work of conscience. I examine the interstices, expressed through the saints' descriptions of their progress, between what they feel they believe, and how they subject that feeling of belief (what should be the joyous moment of consummation) to what they know they should feel. Because Shepard's saints exhibit a specific anxiety surrounding the moment of transcendence, their confessions expose the frustrating but dynamic process of interpreting what one experiences as belief against the giant forces of doctrine and rhetoric.

The second chapter presents the ways that grace and the conversion experience become reinterpreted, through Edwards's reading of Locke, as "simple" sensory impressions on par with natural man's other sensory experiences but instilled with a new principle in the perceptual realm called by Edwards the "sense of the heart." His idea of the "sense of the heart" allowed him to maintain a mysticism that prevented his theology from sinking into philosophical materialism: with it, the mind retained an unaccountable element that prevented the reduction of experience into a synthesis of data and systems of thought as Locke had configured. His works explore the matrix of thought, feeling, and perception that is consciousness, characterizing it as expansive, and, therefore, redemptive, only insofar as an individual continually exercises its potential. Conversion for Edwards, then, grounds one's redemptive path within a web of relations, his "room of the idea" infused with God's will, of course, but experienced as the thoughtful dynamic between receptivity, perception, and interpretation that enlivens the bond between natural man and God. The "room of the idea" emerges as a precursor to Emerson's and James's renderings of consciousness as an ever-evolving, originating process whose continual production of perceptual truths patterns the operations of grace.

I explore the ways that Edwards, without sacrificing the integrity of doctrines central to Calvinism, theorized conversion and a new "Logick" (a new method of perception) by adopting the idea of consciousness as an active, creative force bringing God's world into being. Edwards's concept of the "sense of the heart" and focus on "conviction" as the feeling structuring our spiritual, scientific, and philosophical beliefs about the world foregrounded spontaneity and immediacy in the perception of truth, thereby freeing his congregation from a preexisting, generic pattern of experience. In addition, I demonstrate how Edwards's idealism allowed him to conceptualize what James would later call a space of the "vague" within consciousness. By theorizing consciousness as a boundary phenomenon between abstract truths and concrete reality, Edwards was able to advocate what he called "attention of the mind in thinking" as a form of piety. Instead of using the method of technologia to establish the objective truths of God's universe (as was the case with the previous generation of preparationists), Edwards claimed that "intelligent beings are created to be the consciousness of the universe, that they may perceive what God is and does," thereby equating piety with an active, lively consciousness ever attuned to the "degrees" of divine truth emerging from the horizon of consciousness.[16] Moreover, I interpret *Religious Affections* as a treatise about perception. Whereas Shepard would claim that saints "see things in another manner" after conversion, his adherence to an intellectual tradition in Puritan piety did not permit him to explain how. In contrast, *Religious Affections* attempts to provide that description of *how* saints see things anew when what he calls the "new spiritual sense" is laid in the foundation of the soul. In doing so, Edwards firmly establishes gracious *affections* as the dynamic mediating relations between a saint, God, and the world.

The legacy of conversion in American literature is in many ways the reflection of an intellectual history of what William James calls the "physiological study of mental conditions." James's lifework is, indeed, an outgrowth of this interest, which, I would argue, descends from a long-standing preoccupation on the part of these writers with the experiential aspects of conversion. In *The Varieties of Religious Experience* he states regarding conversion that "neither an outside observer nor the Subject who understands the process can explain fully how particular experiences are able to change one's centre of energy so decisively." This is the mystery that preoccupies Edwards and Emerson and culminates in James's *Principles of Psychology*, providing, much like *Religious Affections* and *Nature*, ways of understanding the dynamics of consciousness. James, of course, is the most "scientific" in his adherence to a specialized field of study; nevertheless, we see in Edwards's and Emerson's descriptions of the nexus of experience, perception, and interpretation a concern over "mental conditions" that comprise consciousness. Remarkably, though Edwards's explanations are contained within theological discourse (and are, therefore, perhaps the most overtly "powerful ally of hortatory ethics"), his efforts at using language to capture the effects of the "changes" in mental conditions after conversion come very close to characterizing an actual physiological process. His description of the effects of the supernatural are represented as a new spiritual "sense" that results in what he attempts to frame in terms of physical manifestations of transformation. Having had the spiritual "sense" laid in the foundation of the soul, a saint acquires new habits that are evidenced in physical ways: natural man's senses and perceptions are altered permanently, and the physiology, once changed, cannot be changed back.

Discussions surrounding Emerson's work often emerge out of the most distinguishing effect of his sentences—disorientation. This disorientation, though frustrating to experience, is always attributed to what is generally understood to be Emerson's project of provoking the search for meaning and "original thought" or "original relations" in his audience. Chapter 3 historicizes this quality of disorientation and the accompanying search for meaning by situating it within the Puritan Reformed tradition of experiential piety. In drawing parallels between Shepard, Edwards, and Emerson, I show that Emerson inherited the ministerial imperative to guide his audience into a "saving" experience with the world that Shepard described as "wrapped up in words." In line with Shepard's and Edwards's sermons, Emerson's essays and *Nature* work to habituate his readers to a method of thinking that moves them into experiencing the feeling of transcending the world of fact and the forces of doctrine, language, and history. This chapter builds on the scholarship of Richard Poirier and Stanley Cavell, who have clarified the coordinately repellent and attractive aspects of Emerson's style that challenge the reader's experience with language. In Emerson's essays, as Poirier points out, circles represent the fluidity of his sentences because within their structures there is always movement from the text and movement toward the text enacted in the reader, what William James would call the "turnings-toward" and "turnings-from" experienced in the process of discovering meaning. The disorientation felt in the process signals the active role consciousness plays while in search of truths, which, Emerson emphasizes, are always in a state of "perpetual inchoation." In reading Emerson's sentences we experience what James describes as the space of the "vague," the liminal space on the horizon of consciousness on the border between concrete reality and abstract ideas. The polar dynamic that results establishes a pattern of perspectival transitions that Emerson symbolizes in his image of the staircase in "Experience." His question for the reader standing on the staircase, "Where do we find ourselves?" is no longer an obstacle, as it was for the Puritans, but a moment of receptivity and meditation. Edwards's "room of the idea" now includes a staircase, as it were, and the "steps" mediating the experience of grace find representation in a solidly "ordinary" figure.

It is also in such figures as Emerson's eyeball and "fluid membrane" that we see his interest in representing the mysterious, but real, physiological changes of conversion. They serve as literary tropes symbolizing the "vigor," or "currents" according to James, associated with consciousness in the ideal state of active passivity, a mode of consciousness that is at once receptive and creative, obeying the law of its own "universal impulse to believe." This impulse is universal because it is physiological, but it is also "impulsive," a term adopted later by James to characterize the motion of thought and feeling occurring within consciousness. In the chapter on will in *The Principles of Psychology*, James describes the relationship between feeling and movement in the currents of conscious activity, the very relationship that Emerson provokes in the experience of his sentences:

> Consciousness is *in its very nature impulsive*. We do not have a sensation or a thought, and then have to *add* something dynamic to it to get a movement. Every pulse of feeling which we have is the correlate of some neural activity that is already on its way to instigate a movement. Our sensations and thoughts are but cross-sections, as it were, of currents whose essential consequence is motion, and which no sooner run in at one nerve than they run out again at another.[17]

Emerson's sentence style is, indeed, nothing if not impulsive, and the topical nature of his sentences is closely aligned with this pulsating energy. They are, in their containment of ideas, cross-sections of Emerson's own currents of thought, and to the extent that a reader is "vigorous" in his or her efforts at activating the dynamics of transparency in relation to Emerson's sentences, they serve as platforms for the reader to launch into his or her own interpretative work. In this way, they represent both the effect and cause of the growth of consciousness and contribute to the work of generating looser, less technical descriptions of the world through which the "living form" can be seen. Moreover, Emerson's claim that "the preamble of thought, the transition through which it passes from the unconscious to the conscious, is action," and his commitment, manifested in his literary style, to provoking the movement of a reader's thought demonstrates a recognition of the idea articulated by James that, because thoughts are actions, consciousness is impulsive.[18] The train of thought and feeling, occurring within experience translates automatically into movement, and each of these writers, in the spirit of "hortatory ethics" writes in order to articulate the process and advantages of conscious growth for their time in the effort to energize the "advancement" of spirit. Thoughts are actions in American literature, and the impulsive or spontaneous aspect of consciousness's translation of thought and feeling into movement necessitates, for these writers, the articulation of a habit of thinking in order to guide that movement which results in cultural revision.

The natural philosophy of Emerson's time esteemed the active power of consciousness—the role of reason—and in Chapter 3 I show how this cultural force allowed Emerson to adopt this method of science as the method of perception he inculcates in his audience through his sentences. As such, we become natural philosophers of the soul, continually troping our definitions of the world and self as we engage in the project of incessant regeneration. In this way Emerson compels his audience to become conscious of what Lee Rust Brown calls the "edge of experience" which "cuts its way through the world at a point beyond the direct grasp of knowledge," translating what was for the Puritans the discomfort of feeling lost into a saving disorientation that means one has not stagnated in one's worldview.[19]

Chapter 4 explores how *The Varieties of Religious Experience* manifests James's project to conceptualize the structure of belief during an age overshadowed by what Paul Jerome Croce calls "the eclipse of uncertainty" precipitated by Darwin. *The Varieties of Religious Experience* reflects James's challenge to the absolutism of science and dogmatic religion that marked his era through a sustained rendering of the process by which one experiences the gap between a fact and its interpretation, what James would term the "transmarginal" field of consciousness. James argues for an epistemology that would embrace the uncertainty of human inquiry and provide a methodology that meliorates this uncertainty by writing a text requiring its audience to employ the methodology of probabilistic thinking that James found compelling in Darwin. This method, the pragmatic hermeneutic, fosters the experience of "tendency" central to the empiricism James conceptualized. In doing so, he advocated a psychology of religious experience that integrates the indeterminate and disorienting nature of an individual's relation to the environment, celebrating what happens to an idea in the course of experience. Conversion finds a conceptual home in modern philosophy as James's pragmatic hermeneutic, which is tied to the process that characterizes and drives consciousness. As a sustained rendering of this process, *The Varieties of Religious Experience* embodies an Edwardsean "room of the idea" or depicts the "living form" of loose ideational relations seen through Emerson's "transparent fluid membrane."

In addition to characterizing the space of perception and receptivity in consciousness, the amassing of countless spiritual testimonies grounds the process of conversion in the formation of discursive communities. His situating of beliefs or bodies of knowledge in discourse leads him to propose that we arrive at these "stages" by coordinate methodological paths—theoretical and theological—both of which he argues are "founded in feeling." In effect, scientific and religious inquiries confirm consciousness as a space always verging on the unknown, but hinging on a relation to one's own thinking and thriving on the incalculable/divine. James advocates, therefore, a psychology of religious experience that (as the Puritans had a hard time accepting) celebrates the indeterminate and disorienting nature of an individual's relation to the environment. This characterization

of experience as highly unstable deems establishing conceptual frameworks for approaching the world seemingly impossible as well as a strange
sort of fate: caught up in indetermination, we are never sure of what we
are conscious of until the invisible, underlying processes of transformation are made visible by the actions that result—the "fruits" as James puts
it. In this experiential indeterminacy, the fruits never prove anything
about the cause; rather, they legitimate belief in the face of uncertainty,
and to be religious in this sense means approaching the world as a place
where theories and beliefs are tested and realized through the fruits of
action and behavior. Justification, in fact, continues to order our world,
but truth can be found in every corner of experience.

CHAPTER 1

―――――◆―――――

A Believing Attitude

As scholarship addressing the Great Migration has shown, Puritan dissenters had many reasons for leaving England, but launching an exemplary Puritan "errand" wasn't one of them. Revisions to Perry Miller's thesis of the "errand" demonstrate that instead of imagining themselves as being on a world-saving mission, Puritans saw themselves primarily as exiles in flight from the oppressive reign of Charles I.[1] With the rise of the Stuarts, Puritans witnessed a powerful Arminian, High Church party gain ecclesiastical control, and, as Theodore Dwight Bozeman explains, its members were "militantly anti-Puritan," and "pledged not only to secure 'thorough' accord with the church's established ritual, government, and canons but also further to embellish the liturgy and to make the whole more imposing, complex, colorful, and magnificent. Their program was intolerable to Puritans sensitive both to theological innovation and to elements in English worship lacking biblical authorization."[2] The sense of a Catholic incursion was deepened as well through Charles I's threats to traditional county and local privileges, and little hope remained for founders such as Richard Mather in terms of overcoming barriers to England's reformation and return to the ordinances of the apostolic era. The mother country was becoming a Babylon, and the Puritans' "real aim was, instead, to fulfill the role of the 'woman in the wilderness' (Revelation 12:6) and seek an asylum in which the fight against the Antichrist could be carried on."[3]

These revisions to Miller's thesis of the "errand" are also supported by the trail of debate over migration left behind by founders such as John Cotton, Edward Johnson, Peter Bulkeley, and John Winthrop. Referring to Winthrop's larger body of writing, Bozeman notes that among the reasons he provides for removal, the notion of an "errand" is absent. Instead, Winthrop focuses on problems such as overpopulation and corruption of schools and universities by anti-Puritan elements. In addition to presenting New England as a place of refuge, Winthrop offers it as the site of a missionary enterprise. Devoted to the spread of Protestantism, the missionary effort would not only uphold the Reformed tradition and preserve the covenanted church; it would thwart the advancing work of the antichrist represented by the Jesuit presence in North America. Moreover, the missionary effort would entail the conversion of native inhabitants, an integral aspect of the theory of colonization found in the leaders' promotional literature, in which there is no appeal to the "errand."

Andrew Delbanco extends these revisions by emphasizing the moral confusion suffered not under any particular tyranny, but caused by England's new economic potency. As Delbanco explains, Shepard did not celebrate the economic advantages his parishioners enjoyed; he lamented an emerging "self-interested reciprocity—of material exchange—as the governing structure of experience."[4] The rationale for migration is born out of the desire to escape the decline in social unity because, as Delbanco argues, "nothing pains Shepard more than the spectacle of collapse in human relations; his heaven is a place of human contact, his hell a place of loneliness."[5] Delbanco's *The Puritan Ordeal* revises Miller's "errand" in such a way as to discredit Miller's account of first-generation Puritans' determination. Instead, he stresses the experience of emotional and psychic revolution and uncertainty inherent in the act of migrating. Congruent to the following analysis of the conversion narratives collected by Thomas Shepard, Delbanco's revision emphasizes the idea that the migration caused a semiotic upheaval as well:

> We can begin to apprehend the manifold complexity of this immigrant experience only if we bend close to the words with which the Puritans recorded it. Theirs was a language under terrible stress, threatened by the migration itself. How could one continue to speak convincingly of the "suburbs of salvation" (a common metaphor for the preparatory stages) in a land without cities? How could one press home the reality of evil through its old (now foreign) associations—mumbling Catholics, or prelates with golden goblets and scarlet robes?[6]

The subject of this chapter draws on and is an extension of various threads in the scholarly conversation surrounding the Puritan experience in New England. It is not only an outgrowth of the ideas behind Perry Miller's thesis of the "errand" and meticulous construction of the New England "mind"; it is a product of the various revisions to these influential propositions. The following analysis of conversion narratives develops the line of Puritan scholarship seeking to challenge Miller's notion that the Puritans who emigrated to New England were a zealous group embarking on a grand mission to found an exemplary society, but it does so with the purpose of articulating the ideological contours of an uncertain project whose legacy can be traced to later concerns and figures in American literature and philosophy. The emotional and psychic uncertainty Delbanco argues for can be heard in the testimonies of Shepard's congregants as they rehearse the new words and sentences necessary for retaining social cohesion in the new semiotic terrain that is New England.

The Problem of the Will

Before Perry Miller begins his examination of Puritan thought in *The New England Mind: The Seventeenth Century*, he devotes some time in the first chapter to explaining his intent: "I am here endeavoring to portray the piety rather than the abstract theology in which it was embodied. . . . I shall undoubtedly do the material a certain violence by speaking of the sharply defined concepts of systematic divinity in the looser and vaguer language of human passion."[7] This "passionate" piety, Miller argues, doesn't actually run counter to abstract theology in the Puritan mind. It is instead the "one fissure in the impregnable walls of systematic theology; from the point of view of history, it was the portal through which ran the highway of intellectual development."[8] This fissure is the site of daily experience for the Puritans. Located in the space between God's declared will in scripture and his secret will, experience provided all the accidents of time and place that exerted pressures on theology, shaping interpretation and doctrine. Decades after Miller's declaration, the conversion narratives collected by Thomas Shepard would be published, offering the kind of testament to what Miller terms the "living reality of the spirit" that he claimed to be erecting.[9] They answer Miller's call to hear the "looser and vaguer language of human passion" in a way that his study, comprehensive as it is, could not achieve solely through the texts produced by Puritan ministers. The narratives do so by framing, through the voices of the congregants themselves, the problem of the will in the discovery of a believing attitude.

I borrow these words from Miller, however, to begin my own tracing of the "intellectual development" that he claims proceeds from this passionate piety. In fact, the title for this chapter is taken from William James's essay "The Will to Believe," in which he argues, *"our passional nature not only lawfully may, but must, decide an option between proposi-tions, whenever it is a genuine option that cannot by its nature be decided on intellectual grounds.*"[10] Describing faith as a "believing attitude," James states it is the "passional" grounds on which we adopt new truths, not only regarding religious matters but also about all "living options which the intellect of the individual cannot by itself resolve."[11] It is this issue of maintaining a "believing attitude," and the role it plays in adopting new truths that preoccupied Shepard's congregants and structures the narra-tives, giving voice to Miller's "living reality of the spirit." The concept of the will was, for the Puritans, the locus of discussions attempting to exact a theory about perception and identify the nature of knowing, and in a Calvinist universe, this demanded a description of the soul's operations that could accommodate not only an individual's experiences but God's actions as well. As such, it served as the discursive point of departure for theological ventures into characterizing and determining the ontological boundaries between a saint and God that became confused in the course of experience. This chapter examines the narratives of confession Thomas Shepard collected as tests for church membership in order to uncover how congregants understood their pursuit of belief in the process of con-version, specifically as it is conceived in the New World. As essentially narrative reconstructions of the movement of the will toward truth, the confessions present the workings of consciousness as each saint moves through experience. Therefore, the tacit descriptions of the will's opera-tions characterize it as a kind of nerve that registers such dynamics of consciousness as the tensions between codified knowledge and indetermi-nate or vague truth, certainty and uncertainty, or objects encountered in experience and the perception of those objects. Because the will acts like a conductive channel connecting the saints' souls to God and his universe, it serves as the main trope around which they organize their descriptions of how they interpret the dynamics of consciousness.

According to Norman S. Fiering, not only did two very different understandings of the role and power of the will and its relation to the intellect coexist in Puritan reasoning in the seventeenth century, but they were often present in some combination.[12] As a consequence, the problem of the will was the focus of intense debate at seventeenth-century Har-vard, and is the topic from which Fiering's analysis departs. His compar-isons between theories of the will's operations historicize it as a concept and make some important distinctions that complicate the reasons why the nature of the will was so central to Puritan theology. Simply put, the "question was not whether or not man is free but wherein his freedom lies," and it is this same question that echoes throughout the conversion narratives of Shepard's congregants.[13] Identifying William Ames as the theologian "most highly esteemed in New England," Fiering frames his analysis by quoting Ames from the *Medulla Theologiae*: "The will is the true subject of theology since it is the true beginning of life and of moral and spiritual action."[14] In Fiering's analysis, Ames stands as an important figure because his theology synthesized ideas about the will in that it contained aspects of Augustinian voluntarism that stood in opposition to predominantly held views. As Fiering explains, the established view in Ames's day, reflecting faculty psychology, was the intellectualist position, granting a dual-faceted nature to the rational soul; the understanding first judges objects and ideas of experience as good or bad, and the will, as the "rational appetite," either embraces or rejects what the understanding presents to it. Therefore, the will "is itself never culpable in the case of moral error, since it invariably follows the judgment of the intellect."[15]

Ames, however, espoused a view of the will's relation to the intellect that was also in line with the Augustinian tradition, one that granted the will the same kind of power as the affections to sway or even undermine reason. In this way, Fiering explains, the will gained "cognitive as well as active power" to the extent that it could "*suspend*" action.[16] Ames's own reasoning about why the will has the power to act independently of the intellect was articulated in his *De Conscientia*:

> The *Will* can at pleasure *suspend* its act about that which is *apprehended* and *judged* to be good; without any *foregoing act of judgment* that it should do so; for if to *suspend* an act, and to leave off acting, an act of judgment be necessarily required; then to suspend that judgment, another judgment is requisite, and to suspend that, another, and so *in infinitum*.[17]

In this view, actions, which lead an individual not only through the world of objects but also through the world of ideas, are not necessarily anchored to judgment. They are not, in other words, determined by the bodies of knowledge from which the imposition of judgment originates. The will, therefore, can carry a subject through experience, blazing an affective trail in the discovery of truth. In the midst of the dominant, intellectualist view of the will, Ames's voluntarist definition was considered radical even though, as Fiering asserts, it actually has its roots in a Puritan religious sensibility that "insisted on a dichotomous struggle between good and evil in the soul which swept the intellect along rather than was guided by it."[18] Informing even intellectualist doctrine, such as Shepard's, this mainstay of reformed Protestantism made the will the "supreme faculty of the soul because it is within the will that the decisive movement takes place which determines man's final relation to God."[19] However, Ames's definition is essentially antithetical to the intellectualist position, and powerfully so, because it characterizes the will as a conduit to God that is immune or resistant to codified knowledge:

> Because the will cannot be compelled, even by the force of logic as is the case with the intellect, it is the center of that free choice by which man determines his eternal condition. The will is the apex of the soul; or better, the free act of willing is the climactic movement of the soul.[20]

In both conceptualizations of the will, therefore, it is responsible for a subject's acting in the world. Whether guided by understanding or working freely, it is the channel of grace, and the narratives of conversion that Shepard transcribed chronicle his congregants' attempts to determine whether it was God's will or their own that was the source of their actions, feelings, and thoughts. Knowing this, and identifying a pattern of the work of the Spirit led them to belief in Christ and salvation. Consequently, observing the "actions" of the will was a way to chart and measure the distance between a sinful saint and God, shaping how the saints understood their place in God's universe. As a disciple of Ames, Shepard would also inherit Ames's intellectual investment in Ramist logic and the doctrines of conditional covenant and preparation, and it was through this preparatory process in conversion that his congregants detected whether or not they possessed a will to believe. In turn, discipleship such as Shepard's was responsible for securing Ames's legacy in New England.[21]

Thomas Shepard's Response to the Crisis of the Migration

The Puritan minister Thomas Shepard has remained a compelling figure in American Puritan studies because he left behind a variety of authorship serving different personal and public purposes. His *Journal, Autobiography*, and sermons offer a picture of a complicated and conflicted man who continues to intrigue present-day readers because he played significant roles in the settlement of New England and because of his striking modernity. His works, as Andrew Delbanco has demonstrated, not only allow us to "reconstruct Shepard's mental life," they also show "the identity of idea and feeling for the Puritan sensibility."[22] In addition to his sermons, memoir, and journal, however, Shepard transcribed the testimonies of conversion that were given as tests of church membership at the First Church at Newtown (now Cambridge). There is consensus among scholars of American Puritanism about how Shepard's preparation theology impacted the quality of his congregants' conversion experiences, producing testimonies that reflect the "anxiety of living this side of justification" and the "joy of union continually deferred."[23] Yet, their expressions of a will to believe, rather than union with Christ, draw into relief dimensions of the conversion experience, prior to regeneration, that remained as important to thinkers such as Jonathan Edwards, Ralph Waldo Emerson, and William James as the aspects associated with the ecstatic moment. Instead of narrating testimonies of assurance, Shepard's congregants elaborate a habit of thinking that he fostered to enforce spiritual discipline, ensure the purity of the congregation, and further the "policies of the emerging orthodoxy," but they are also America's first articulations of an architectonics of the will to believe.[24]

The conversion narratives overwhelmingly attest to the fact that the Puritans understood their migration to New England as one of the stages of their spiritual progress. Patricia Caldwell's analysis of the narratives in her book *The Puritan Conversion Narrative: The Beginnings of American Expression* demonstrates that within the cardinal stages of William Perkins's ten-stage theology of conversion, the movement to New England was associated with the early preparatory stages in the Puritan imagination, casting New England as a "means" to grace rather than an "effect" of grace.[25] She goes on in that study to show how the migration did not meet those expectations and how the resulting disappointment the Puritans felt inaugurated a uniquely American form of expression marked by open-endedness. In what follows I hope to elaborate on this distinctive feature of the narratives by recognizing other aspects of the Puritan immigrants' piety that might account for the open-endedness. Building from Caldwell's analysis, I would argue that Shepard's preparatory theology, given new urgency by his postmigration rational faith, necessitated, for the sake of building a society of visible saints, a re-placement of New England within the stages of preparation. In terms of Ramist logic, this would entail a kind of reimagining of the morphology of conversion to accommodate New England's reestablished place as a means.[26] The migration's unexpected effects demanded that New England be conceptually relocated within a Ramist-inspired scheme from a premigration understanding of it as a means to Christ to a newly bracketed, postmigration place as means, representing, in Ramist terms, a new "content of consciousness." The congregants' narratives of a will to believe, therefore, express the imaginative effort to re-place New England within the stages of preparation, a sort of rebirth for America itself as a new idea. And for Shepard, as one of the "Intellectual Fathers," this would have been the first, most important step in the operations of faith in the new land; for, in a preparatory scheme of the operations of grace, the re-bracketing of New England conceptually would have been understood to be the guiding force of the affective process of growth in grace.[27] The narratives express a profound disappointment because the saints' expectations for New England betray a kind of hope suggestive of the immediate, sensational effect experienced in a Pauline conversion. Eventually contained in their narratives by the regulatory force of preparatory theology, their admissions of hope for the migration's effects serve as a kind of defunct emotional marker of grace to be subsumed in an ever-expanding, newly established distance from God.

That distance from God is cognitively and affectively mapped by Shepard's doctrine of preparation, and is often represented by the spatial arrangement of a Ramist-inspired diagram. Conceived as a universal logic, the dialectic of Petrus Ramus, could be applied to any subject, from physics to theology, as a way for its practitioners to become proficient in a certain body of knowledge. In addition, having emerged out of the pedagogical practice of discourse as a process that creates conviction within a subject matter, this form of reasoning was understood as an acquired skill, a mental art or habit that one could master. That Ramist logic influenced the Puritans, especially New England's preparationist ministers, is well recognized, but a thoroughgoing consideration of the testimonies of Shepard's congregants in light of that Ramism has not been undertaken. The fundamental principle behind the force of Ramist logic was not simply that one could master an art through an acquired habit or method of thinking, but that the habit was conceived in spatial terms; this form of reasoning not only considered an external world in terms of the "real," but it objectified ideas and organized the "contents" of consciousness by dispersing and arranging them on a *visual* surface. Adrian Johns notes that each Ramist schema "was a 'cartography of the mind,' a printed map the tracing of which revealed logical paths to desired conclusions."[28] Organized in the form of dichotomies, these bracketed openings, or containers of thought, were "designed to be heuristic: they belong to the part of logic known as 'invention,' that is, finding."[29] In this way, Ramism concerns itself with "the data of common experience, more or less critically processed."[30]

The spatial arrangement of this common data lends the "contents of consciousness" the cultural value of being as "real" as the objects of the external world, and as in the case with the data of the "real" world, organizing it into patterns and storing it made it easy to be observed and controlled. The doctrine of preparation reflects the Ramist idea that a fund of common experience can be organized into heuristic units that impose order on the confusion of experiential piety. So, when an event that carries such an immense emotional weight as the migration slips out of its bracket, as it did when it did not meet the immigrants' expectations, it must be reincorporated, as the data of experience would be manipulated in a Ramist scheme, back into the morphology and, therefore, back into the discourse of salvation. Caldwell's argument is that the saints' feelings of isolation after the migration are caused by the unavailability of a communal expression for their individual experiences; therefore, they rely on what she terms a "since-I-came-hither-dead-hearted-but-I-have-been-revived" convention "not so much to provide a literal description of their emotions . . . as to symbolize the inner deadlock over the problem of expression itself. Thus the attempt to 'find feelings' in the new place *became* the attempt to find an adequate expression for them."[31] In this connection, Caldwell's analysis comes close to explicitly stating the interdependent relationship between the language that the preparatory scheme offers and the affective guidance that that discursive context makes possible. With this in mind, I would offer that the conventional expression Caldwell identifies emerges, in Ramist terms, *as* the new expression of the dialectic undertaken to mediate between the overarching dichotomy that brackets the experience of the migration and the pattern of isolation—that is, the move from old England to New England. The convention, therefore, *becomes* the communal expression of a will to believe, an expression of the saints' understanding of New England's reintroduction as a means postmigration, thereby transforming their isolation, discursively, into membership. In this way, New England has been "re-invented" (found once again) within a kind of communally understood Ramist axiom whose terms have been modified to express the new meaning of New England. As the bedrock of the testimonies, the convention inheres within the momentum, albeit halting, of the saints' declared intents to discover a will to believe *in America*—understood as both the geographic location of that search and as the promise that the newly iterated idea of America offers.

The Revival of a Community of Saints

By revisiting Shepard's preparation theology and its impact on his congregants' expressions of spiritual experience, I do not intend a return to the paradigm of American Puritan studies offered by Miller's *The New England Mind: The Seventeenth Century*. Though Miller is credited with rescuing New England Puritans from Progressivist contempt in the 1930s, scholarship in social and cultural history, work in new historicism, and the retrieval of a transatlantic perspective have challenged what Janice Knight has called Miller's "imagined homogeneous Puritan origin," a univocality she argues does not obtain in subsequent studies of emergent or contested social and ideological formations within Puritan culture.[32] In fact, the confessions recorded by Shepard, though they reflect his emphasis on spiritual discipline, force cracks into Miller's monolithic model of culture as well. Though the ministry was a significant source of inspiration and practical guidance, the spiritual challenges the confessions contain suggest that these were people who had needs and interests of their own and made demands on their ministers.[33] The confessions contain moments where we can witness New England Puritanism in the making because they document conversations between minister and congregant in which faith is unstable but negotiated. We see ministers unable to ease their flock's spiritual pain, and we see times when parishioners seek each other out for spiritual guidance. Shepard's saints were, in fact, "makers of their faith" in the ordinary course of their lives."[34]

The confessions, in fact, exhibit one of the earliest examples of New England Puritanism in the making because they are records of the saints' physical and spiritual arrivals to America. Of central importance to our deepening understanding of Puritan culture has been the fact of the Puritans' experience in the New World as immigrants. Andrew Delbanco's *The Puritan Ordeal*, published in 1989, goes a long way in clarifying how the impact of this "psychic upheaval" manifested a new imagining of sin as threatening enemy, shaping not only the immediate future of New England society, culture, and theology but also the future of generations of Americans to come. His project follows how, in the New World, the idea of sin as entity (rather than as privative in the Augustinian tradition) "leads directly to a very high valuation of psychological and political control, and thereby puts a premium on socially approved behavior (what the Puritans called sanctification) as the best measure of virtue."[35] Arguing that the effects of this idea's force in the New World can be traced straight to the heart of middle-class culture and its constitutive aversion to deviance, Delbanco wonders if it is even possible for us to imagine the kind of social world envisioned by such "ecstatic writers" as Jonathan Edwards, Ralph Waldo Emerson, Herman Melville, Walt Whitman, and Henry Adams.[36]

In the introduction to that book, Delbanco recognizes Caldwell's study of the Puritan testimonies, published in 1983, as an important contribution to articulating the effects of the migration on the life of the Puritan mind. To this end, Caldwell, like Delbanco, is interested in exploring the literary quality of Puritan texts, in her case the conversion testimonies

Shepard collected, as a way of recovering the inner experiences of first-generation Puritans and of making her argument that the conversion narrative marks the "beginnings of American expression." Though published six years earlier than Delbanco's book, Caldwell's project unearths the very psychological and emotional effects that the immigration experience has on the Puritans, identifying, as Delbanco does, the new relationship to sin that results from this "psychic upheaval" as a salient feature of their conversion narratives. While Delbanco's study is primarily concerned with examining the historical context of the migration and the subsequent social and ideological formations that result from the immigrant experience, he identifies and traces the emergence of a new strain of sin within the Puritan imagination that influences those formations. Interestingly, Caldwell's analysis of the disruptive effects of the migration on the Puritans' sense of spiritual progress leads her to claim that their overwhelming reliance on the rhetoric of "dead-heartedness" stands in for what she argues is a problem of expression attributed to the new, "overwhelming awareness of sin—an awareness so painful and fearsome that it produces a short circuit of the verbal faculties."[37] Consequently, these two analyses speak to one another in complimentary ways. Taken together they show how remarkably immediate was the collective response to life in the New World, specifically to the newly conceived, threatening nature of sin that ministers such as Shepard and Thomas Hooker fostered and the new "awareness" of this sin that Shepard's congregants express.

Yet, the role that sin takes on in the wake of the migration can be complicated further when we consider its integral role in the adaptations Shepard made to his preparatory scheme in response to the migration, a role that helps to explain more fully the quality and dynamics, not to mention the legacy, of the new habit of mind practiced by Shepard's congregants as a will to believe. As the architectonic element of their testimonies, professing a will to believe, instead, plots the anti-conversion narrative Delbanco identifies as a persistent ideological force in America—the roundly recognized concomitant attentiveness to sin that precedes the ecstasy of closing with Christ. It shapes the immigrants' narratives in ways that can only be understood as a response to the demands that Shepard's preparation theology made, not only on the confessors to express an understanding of New England's reimagined place in that theology, but on Shepard himself.[38] The rational expressions of faith that result, which shape the inner logic of each individual testimony and lend the collection as a whole coherence, demonstrate the saints' adoption of a habit of mind necessary for their new life in America: they represent the conscious effort to root out and contain the sin newly conceived as rampant. In effect, the stability of the new meaning of America in their spiritual lives is inextricably bound to, in fact leads out from, their collective commitment to the spiritual discipline and social order associated with the preparatory work of conviction, compunction, and humiliation. The crisis of the migration forces Shepard to reconfigure the idea of America within the structure of the morphology, a revision in his theology that culminates in the "open-endedness" that Caldwell asserts marks the testimonies. However, it is also a rhetorical move, one that demands a "confession" of his congregants' understanding and adoption of America as a new means.

Caldwell's study develops the argument that there is something "genuinely American" about the Massachusetts Bay Puritan imagination, that it inaugurated an "American tone of voice" found hence in American literature. This tone, she argues, emerges from a majority of the narratives in which an immigrant's expectations that New England would serve as a means for closing with Christ are painfully derailed. In her comparison of English Puritan narratives to New England's, she argues that the disruption the immigrants felt in their conversion experience upon arrival in New England signaled an "American tendency to open-endedness":

> The problem seems to be at least one of temperament—as if a certain strain of the collective personality is trying to work itself out in the conversion narrative: a personality that, unlike the English, with its drive toward completion and resolution, is more comfortable with ambivalence and open-endedness. The Englishman ends his conversion narrative with one foot in heaven; his brother starts out for heaven but gets sidetracked in New England, where he continues his seeking but somehow needs to postpone his final salvation.[39]

Caldwell argues that this open-endedness resulted from the saints' endowing America with a divine power to affect grace, thereby making their disappointment in America's facility to close the rift between man and God a sin. America, therefore, became a "foggy limbo of broken promises" forcing a saint to accommodate this unexpected chain of events by inaugurating a unique American expression of conversion adhering to a "since-I-came-hither-dead-hearted-but-I-have-been-revived" convention.[40] The relationship Caldwell traces in this insight very usefully identifies the isolation the saints felt as a circumstance of the absence of a communal expression to represent their individual migration experiences. In the passage above, she identifies a "personality" that "somehow" postpones salvation, and in doing so she suggests the interdependence of the vitality of the saints' faith, their ability to express that faith, and the vitality of a ministry. The postponement she identifies, however, I would describe as the saints' collective efforts to profess the newly conceived promise of America. Their testimonies of a will to believe, therefore, ironically bind the saints together in their covenantal corporate identity and, simultaneously, reflect the newly American obsession with self, their new "object of meditation" in the search for sin.[41]

Caldwell's theory about the open-endedness found in the confessions rests on the idea that the disappointment resulting from the migration created a new, insurmountable sin because as a means to grace it failed to deliver them to assurance. Indeed, the migration, as a means to grace, failed to live up to the expectations of many of Shepard's congregants, but I would offer that its failure to meet those expectations is not *the* sin that ultimately stands in the way of closing with Christ. A saint's life was spent seeking means to grace. The confessions are replete with descriptions of attempts to find the right means to stay on course, and the saints openly admit that often the means they encounter do not come at an opportune time, or, for one reason or another, do not have the effect they anticipated. Means were inherently unpredictable and often had the opposite effect anticipated. Moreover, the doctrine of election stressed that saints would continue to undergo conversion throughout their lives. One moment of grace did not necessarily provide assurance of salvation. As a continual process demanded by the tenets of a living faith, it inherently eschewed a "completion" of the process. Instead, the disappointment the saints feel must be converted into hope by the re-bracketing of New England as a means in the morphology of conversion.

Legitimizing New England as a Means to Grace

As a preparationist minister who preached a doctrine of means, Shepard believed that grace was "received mediately, through a chain of second causes [such as man's faculties, the ordinances, or hearing the Word] . . . which forms the 'middle term' between God's intent and man's condition."[42] Yet Shepard's ministry also evidences a theology aligned with that strain in Puritanism that regards Christ as the "one true center of activity and efficiency" and holds that "in spiritual things, including divine commands, activity in and from the creature is as inadmissible after regeneration as before it."[43] At the heart of this difference lay the issues of whether an individual was passive or active in the reception of grace and how one interpreted Paul's claim that "a man is justified by faith." These doctrinal

issues surrounding human agency manifested themselves in an epistemological conundrum for Shepard's congregants: how they would know
whether their wills had undergone regeneration. Though preparationist
ministers reminded their congregants to keep converting, the force behind
their message kept the focus of their spiritual progress on the delineated
stages and rational figurations of the process of faith, in other words, the
conceptual resting places that helped make sense of an unpredictable,
chaotic experience. What the morphology couldn't contain or predict
were the daily experiences of God's hidden will, the ordinary currents
infusing saints' lives with the divine. The migration carries such a heavy
cognitive and emotional weight in the confessions because it tests the
Puritans' faith. Although the migration was by no means an "ordinary"
experience, it became an event demanding a new interpretation, a new
home in language, when the reality of the experience failed to affirm that
it was a means, or channel, for grace's operations. Many of the saints claim
to have heard a "call" to go to New England, an experience they interpreted as the will of God. Because discipline was at the heart of Shepard's
ministry, his congregation was magnetized around the earlier stages of
conversion such as conviction, compunction, and humiliation, which provoked an awareness of sin. These are the stages that are more easily captured and contained in language, and it becomes imperative after the
migration that New England, as a failed means, find a new conceptual
home, a new meaning for the will to move toward, through its re-contain-
ment within the discourse of preparation. And Shepard's congregants
needed to be able to express that they understood the difference.

George Selement makes an important distinction between Shepard's
ministerial soteriology and the lay understanding and expression of that
soteriology in his study of the narratives. He finds that saints reveal their
understanding of Shepard's doctrine of preparation without using doctrinal terminology; in other words, they generally don't use the terms
"conviction," "compunction," or "humiliation" to describe their experience even though in the rendering of their experience they demonstrate a
clear understanding of these concepts.[44] Selement attributes this to a distinction central to the ministration of Shepard's doctrine of grace instruct-
ing congregants to heed the difference between "heart" knowledge and
"head" knowledge of every aspect and stage of the conversion process:

> Shepard had warned his congregation against relying on a know-
> ledge of the intricacies of formal theology for salvation. He encouraged
> them to cultivate a "heart" knowledge, that is, one that transformed the
> affections, rather than a mere . . . intellectual understanding of

redemption. Thus, Shepard's parishioners, heeding their minister's exhortations, quite naturally avoided an exposition of formal soteriology and devoted their relations to explaining the way in which God personally dealt with them.[45]

As personal expressions of Shepard's ministerial soteriology, we can expect the saints to focus their narratives on the stages associated with conviction, compunction, and humiliation. Accordingly, because New England becomes reconceived as a means within that soteriology, we can expect to find a lay understanding and expression of New England's place within that doctrine of preparation. Shepard was aware of the power that language had to bind a community of saints together and to prevent isolation from that group identity, and he was aware of that same power to also inhibit grace. He uses a variety of adjectives in his works to describe an intellectual understanding of the operations of the Holy Spirit, for example "literal," "discursive," and "notional," and when speaking about the kind of knowledge that affects the heart in conversion he calls it "saving." Though the saints relate their testimonies in personal terms, reflecting "heart" knowledge of Christ, their new identities as members of Shepard's church depended on their ability to communicate their adoption of New England as a new means. As a result, their rhetorical performances affirm New England as the context for their revived faith at the same time that they affirm New England's revived identification as means within the context of the doctrine of preparation. Fueling these rational figurations of the promise of America were the saints' meditations on experience and the focus on rooting out sin, which provided the cognitive and emotional markers to chart the movement of the will in the search for belief.

Shepard's intellectualism is the subject of "Thomas Shepard's America: The Biography of an Idea," in which Andrew Delbanco traces the evolving nature of Shepard's struggle with the idea of depravity found in *The Parable of the Ten Virgins* and the *Theses Sabbaticae*. He concludes that in the effort to secure the will of the Bay Colony's infant society, each member had to practice the "revelation of the context of sin."[46] As noted previously, in New England the concept of sin had shifted, becoming what Delbanco describes as "invasive."[47] As the regnant force of Shepard's post-migration homiletics, this message placed the burden of the godliness and health of society on each individual and located the origins of societal order in the regenerate will of the saint. Shepard's homiletics obviated complacency and was proscriptive of self-deceptive assurances of grace and empty professions of faith, and the confessions recorded in Shepard's notebook reflect his doctrine. Therefore, I would argue, the sense of open-endedness that Caldwell attributes to the disruption caused by the migration results from a deeply felt awareness of the stakes of salvation: a regenerate will that denoted belief in Christ and hence a holy society of visible saints. Members of Shepard's congregation would have been committed to professing a faith that did not implicate them as complacent sinners or as saints who felt they had accurate knowledge about the state of their souls. Instead, the re-placement of New England as a means within the stages of Shepard's preparatory theology, in effect, rhetorically subsumes the disappointment caused by its original meaning. By reincorporating New England as a place of means, it gains fresh theological grounding, effectively transforming it into a new, doctrinal context for the emergent obsession with sin and self. The re-placement thereby reinstates the saints' distance from God but carries with it the new promise of America.

In this effort to reveal to his congregation the sin that infused their lives and threatened the future success of the colony, Shepard warned against the false sense of security a saint could feel in New England. Therefore, it was not necessarily a sin to feel a disruption in the course of salvation upon arrival to New England but rather a prelude, an acknowledgment that America, as Shepard feared, held the potential to become a social landscape like England. More likely, members of Shepard's congregation would have been wary of the hollowness of their own profession that New England *was* the means to close with Christ. They would have heeded Shepard's warning found in *The Parable of the Ten Virgins*:

> There is no place in all the world where there is such expectation to find the Lord as here; and hence men bless the Lord for our rising sun when it is setting every where else. Here, therefore, they come and find it not; hence not considering the great and last temptation of this place, whereby God tries his friends before he will trust them with more of himself.[48]

According to this passage, arrival to New England actually marked a kind of initiation of their spiritual journey, and New England became the testing ground that may or may not have yielded signs of a regenerate will. The disruptions in the morphology expressed in the testimonies exhibit a moment of crisis in a saint's lived process of faith that was not contained by any standard doctrine of election. Some thought they would "find grace," because of the "certainty of things here." One immigrant felt that "one sermon [in New England] might do me more good than a hundred there [in England]," and another thought that "here the Lord might be found" because New England is not "an ignorant place, with little means." But almost without exception, these expectations are over-shadowed by the disappointing reality of the migration.[49] What the testimonies reveal is the test of a saint's ability to keep the idea of salvation alive, to have it exist as a possibility for their souls. They contain the most deciding moments of the conversion process—the culmination of personal history and God's will in which belief becomes a possibility—and these moments reveal a spiritual life that ultimately turned on the saints' ability to interpret their experience in light of God's will, allowing them to trust that the intersection of means and free grace had brought them to a legitimate moment of belief willed by God.

Determining that legitimacy is the central aspect of the testimonies. Forged at a unique historical moment by the discourse of Shepard's preparatory theology and the disappointment of the migration, they convey the urgency of establishing a communal habit of thinking to cement a new society. As Delbanco argues in "Thomas Shepard's America," Shepard's ideas about the role a regenerate will plays in society were the force behind a vision that inspired his life's work. He writes that

> Shepard would be sad, but not surprised, to know that historians have called the great migration a flight from a depressed wool industry, an adventure in fur trade, an expression of land hunger. He would not grant the sway of economic need over the human will. This is not to say that he thought material motives irrelevant to the reading of history; in fact, his plea that New Englanders remember and relive the demands of a harsh past is nothing else than a call for the will of a new society to oppose the record of the old—to break the precedent of "progress." It is a recognition that thought can govern action, that assumptions about the nature of man can generate their own truth.[50]

As the central human faculty in Puritan psychology and therefore in conversion, the will served as a conductor between experience in and knowledge about the world and the muscles, powers, and passions that constituted action. The fact that the will acted as an affective agent in moving a saint to and from an object meant that though an intellectual understanding of doctrine and law was important to conversion, conversion was not possible without the affective dimension, without the will's effect on the heart. It was the "crucial aspect of faith, as the soul's movement into union with Christ, is an act of will, carrying with it the whole man, soul and body."[51] Yet, covenant theology held that God's covenant of grace works coordinately through nature and grace; God remains an absolute power but he works on man through second causes, such as man's rational faculties, his heart, and his will. Covenant theology relies on the notion that man can consent to the promises that God offers.[52] As stated earlier, the intellectualist position held that the will serves in this active role because it either accepts or rejects what the understanding presents to it as a course of action. William K. B. Stoever explains, "entry into the covenant of grace requires an act of consent from man because such an act belongs to the nature of a covenant," and "to deny that the will is active in closing with Christ is to suggest that the covenant of grace is not truly a covenant."[53] So the will not only carries the soul to Christ; in its regenerative state, God moves the soul as he intends, binding the saint to God in a covenantal agreement of mutual respect and integrity.

However, union with Christ—a saint's conversion—depended on the messages received about the soul's activity or passivity during the moment of grace. According to the covenant, God works through second causes, making the will the seat of action in that it consents to Christ. It must for that is the nature of the covenant, and yet doctrine maintained that man is wholly passive, that a saint is overwhelmed by the Holy Spirit. According to Shepard, a saint is passive and Christ does all in causing belief, even as he couches the experience in terms of the covenant: one experiences conversion "in the beholding of the Lord as he comes and appears in the glory of his covenant; for when the Lord reveals himself so as to cause the soul to believe, and thereby to make it one of his people, he never makes any people, but by entering into covenant with them."[54] The conceptual line that distinguishes the saints' active or passive roles in conversion becomes problematic when the moment arrives and they feel a movement toward Christ. The saints had to distinguish whether the movement was caused by the Holy Spirit or by their own faculties and sense of self-preservation, and Shepard's saints understood that their limited perception, a consequence of the Fall, prevented certainty about the cause. Afflicted with damaged faculties with which to comprehend the world, congregants could never be completely confident in their assurances of grace because they prohibited them from gaining pure insight into God's workings. Because a regenerate will was responsible for realizing a society of visible saints (it was the channel connecting God to a saint and a saint to the world), it was the focus of attention for any individual interested in the fate of his or her soul. Shepard's "call for the will of a new society" gathered his congregation around the idea that their commitment to a living faith would ensure a society free from the oppressions they had fled.

Shepard's doctrine on the newly American nature of sin and his lessons about remaining vigilant against complacency created a discursive community fostering the constant interrogation of belief as a way to keep members' sinful natures in check. This emphasis on humanity's sinful nature in fact guides saints in the process of conversion through the paradoxical reasoning that the "law serves, not to justify, but to make men aware of their absolute inability to achieve justification, thus preparing them to receive the grace of God in Christ."[55] The morphology of conversion categorized and ordered the entire process, from preparation to justification, to vocation and sanctification. The stages served as a map so that saints knew where they stood in the process and what to expect; they described an emotional and psychological landscape and clarified obstacles that saints might encounter in their daily progress. These stages made it possible for saints to locate what they were feeling and thinking within a spiritual framework. Moreover, the discursive world that a minister shaped for his parishioners created the ways in which they would comprehend their conversion; it was a perceptive lens aimed at correcting the limited and distorting faculties that were their curse. In effect, the discursive space opened by a divine's ministry formed the affective receptors permitting the will of God to take effect. It shaped a conductive imaginary that made a life of faith and conversion possible because it determined the affective and epistemological shapes of knowing. Indeed, the confessions reveal the discursive nature of the will.[56]

Even though the Bible was the lens through which a saint viewed the world, each divine determined what the edges and contours of that world would be. Faith, and therefore justification by faith, came from hearing the Word. The spoken Word was, according to Miller, "the one means above all others which was perfectly adapted to working upon all faculties, that simultaneously could carry phantasms to both reason and affection, that would impress the species of Gospel theorems upon the understanding and at the same time plunge them deep into the heart."[57] In order to be successful, the means of grace that a saint undertook, from attending to the Word, to introspection, to observing the ordinances, needed to be effective in both penetrating the understanding and exciting the passions, and hearing the Word was the most effective (and affective). During conversion, the Holy Spirit acted through the epistemological channels or sections in the brain according to faculty psychology by first enlightening the understanding and permitting a saint to see the truths of scripture. These "phantasms," however, "are not to rest in the brain as disembodied objects of contemplation" (*NEM*, 294). Because they are products of the Holy Spirit, they attract the will, thereby exciting true spiritual passion and action. As the linchpin between a saint's body of knowledge about the world (and the discursive realm that engenders that knowledge) and the acting on that knowledge, the will's attraction to or rejection of objects that cross the horizon of a saint's experience creates new perspectives and leaves old worldviews in its wake. Conversion, the influx of grace, transformed a saint entirely from the inside (through the faculties) out (through behavior), and in order to understand the necessity of re-placing New England within the morphology in order to revive this process, it is important to explore the impact of Shepard's intellectualism on his congregants' interpretations of the movement of their wills.

Shepard's message to his congregants characterizing the kind of knowledge of Christ necessary to closing with him falls directly in line with the rational approach to conversion, informed by the method of logic and technologia he inherited from Ramus via Alexander Richardson and William Ames. In Ramist logic the function of thinking was to enact a method of "discerning and disposing, not investigating or deducing," applicable to theology for the purposes of discerning truth in the Bible (*NEM*, 134). Through this method, perception of truth could be unquestionably established because it prevented a saint from arriving at truth via emotions such as fear, love, greed, or envy. As Miller shows, logic originates in the Bible wherein God transcribed the divine order, and then "the laws of God found in the Bible were hypostatized by the logic of Ramus into never-failing realities, as endurable as facts" (*NEM*, 148). Therefore, when a saint uses the method of logic, the thinking process mirrors or reenacts the divine order as it is set down in the Bible and found in the universe.

Technologia, a method based on logic for discerning truth in the natural cosmos, described the theory and practice behind what a saint could know about the world and how a saint knew it. The universe is the "embodiment" of God's mind, and in his mind the "plan is single." An observer of God's cosmos, however, can only perceive God's plan as "reflected through concrete objects," which limits apprehension of the divine order to a series of temporal and diverse "segments" which are "various arts." Through natural abilities, namely reason and the method of analysis, an observer may extract and assemble the principles of the particular arts, allowing them to distinguish the "particulars within the synthesis." Technologia was a "science of distinguishing and defining both their [the arts'] contents and relations—in reality the wisdom of God—and their purpose—which was identical with the will of God" (*NEM*, 162). A saint's limited faculties, however, could never apprehend God's infinite wisdom; though ideas "radiate from the divine mind and into the human mind," they must be "filtered" through the objective world. God's "white radiance of eternity" would "blind" a saint's finite intelligence (*NEM*, 169). Therefore, humanity must attempt to understand the rules and patterns governing God's ideas—the arts—as they are reflected, or refracted, through matter. The doctrine of technologia was a stabilizing force in Puritan intellectualism. It upheld the theory that though saints cannot know the divine mind, they can, through the proper method, discover the pattern of God's ideas reflected in his creation. It stated that though the "visible world is but a veil or a screen between the intellect and the true and perfect ideas" and despite human fallibility, a saint has access to the essence of things, the pure ideas of God (*NEM*, 179).

Alexander Richardson, who adapted Ramus's logic to suit Puritanism, claimed that comprehension of the visible world, and therefore the wisdom of God, is by analysis because "things are first in themselves, then they come unto the senses of men, and then to the understanding."[58] This highly intellectualized strain of Puritan epistemology fueled the energetically rationalized teachings on grace and the conversion process in Shepard's ministry. Yet, his countless exhortations to see the Lord in his glory "as he is" and to perceive Christ's glory "really" constitute an integrative discourse, allowing Shepard a middle way that accommodates both his spiritism and his intellectualism.[59] Though logic itself was not redemptive, both grace and logic were divine gifts that through either supernatural or natural means led to truth. Shepard would lead his congregation, as an intellectualist preacher would, on a spiritual path using the methodology of logic and technologia to illuminate the truths found in scripture, indoctrinating his flock into a methodological mode for discerning the work of the Spirit in their hearts. This mode of perception thus fostered a habit of thinking that both contained the promise of grace and dilated the distance between sinful man and God at once.

When he explains in *The Parable of the Ten Virgins* how a saint can come to have love for the Lord, he quotes 1 John 3:1–3 which states, "we shall love him as he is." Shepard goes on to argue that this knowledge or seeing of Christ "as he is" which serves as a conduit for his love, is "the saving knowledge of Christ, to see the Lord in his glory as he is; not perfectly, for that is in heaven" (*PTV*, 123). This fact, he continues is apparent on certain grounds:

1. That knowledge the saints have of Christ, it is not by bare word only, but also by the Spirit. The word relates Christ, but the Spirit is the interpreter of the word. . . . Now, the Spirit ever shows us things

as they are, even though they be deep things and mysteries, it makes them plain. . . .

2. Because the sight of the knowledge of Christ, it is as the knowledge of a thing in a glass. . . . Now, though you see not the man face to face, yet if you see him in a glass, there you see him as he is. . . .

3. Because that estate of the saints is translated into a state of glory. Hence, when justified, then glorified. Hence, as that sanctification that is in the will is the beginning of the life of glory, so that light God puts into their mind is the beginning of the light of glory. Hence, as in heaven, the soul sees Christ by the full light of glory perfectly, face to face, so in this life the soul sees Christ really as he is, yet, as in a glass, imperfectly. (*PTV*, 123–124)

Though Shepard speaks here of a saving sight of Christ, one which suggests the workings of the Holy Spirit, he has couched the project in a discourse of technologia, establishing a reliable epistemological foundation grounded in an analytic process of seeing the knowledge of Christ as reflected or refracted through a glass. Attempts to discern God's wisdom, as always, can only be known in part and mediately despite the efforts to penetrate the veil that obscures the view and experience an immediate relation to the universe and God. The later Shepard's intellectualism drove him to write sermons that emphasized preparationism, the need for saints to understand the doctrine behind the piety, to, in effect, be able to "close" with an idea as the means to receive grace.

As a result, his later works established a ministry urging parishioners to deal with their doubts through further examination, to make use of all the means to grace but not to trust them, and to employ a lay technologia in discerning matters of the heart, such as the moment a saint feels the fullness of God's love or when there is an influx of saving knowledge. His advice to his congregants, explaining the methodology for knowing if they love Christ in a gracious way adheres to an intellectual tradition: "It is a question whether the beams of the sun are fire. Some demonstrate it thus: Take a glass and gather together the beams, it burns. Therefore so, if you would see so as to be affected, gather together the beams of his glory and love; thus you see the means to get fit love" (*PTV*, 95). Shepard's idea of perception as informed by logic is clear here. All saints need to do to see if they love Christ is to collect the beams and detect the truth of the knowledge of love. In the analogy of the glass, the methodology leads to a truth, or in this case an effect. The *effect* of the glass is transformed into an *affect* in the spiritual experiment. In Shepard's example one can "see" the workings of natural law as easily as one can "see" the workings of one's love for

God. A saint need only use the method of perception informed by techno-logia.

Shepard's embrace of method reflects his preparationism and his fa-miliarity with logic and the doctrine of technologia; as a form of means, developing as full an understanding of the Lord was prudent, for the will cannot consent to an object without understanding it. The means in this way was a method of collecting as much information as possible not only about the state of one's soul, but also about Christ, the Holy Spirit, and God's divine plan. Anything that could be subjected to the method of technologia could provide knowledge that led to belief. Saints operated under the theory that they could be one of the elect, trusting that God's promise applied to them while they gathered as much knowledge as they could to realize that theory. Quoting Samuel Willard, the author of *A Compleat Body of Divinity*, Perry Miller relates the function of reason in a Puritan's worldview: "I must needs have some Idea in my mind of the thing believed to be, or else I believe, I know not what, which is ridicu-lous."[60]

But it is through the Puritan theory of regeneration that "head" and "heart" piety occurred simultaneously in conversion's moment of belief, for it was not solely rational understandings of doctrine that were the avenues to grace. Grace was a supernatural force, a wholly arbitrary, un-reasonable operation of the Holy Spirit causing a collapse between the subject and object, and it was characterized by the divines, Shepard in-cluded, as an irresistible force. It was, finally, a felt relation to the divine, grounded in rationality—but not a rational event—that signaled consent and belief. Closing with Christ entailed a "coming out of oneself," a joy in the union with Christ, and yet Shepard's discourse on Puritan ways of knowing continually blurs the line between a saint's natural abilities, through reason, to see things "as they are," or in Ramist terms "really," and the necessary intervention of the Spirit to help a saint see things "as they are." Shepard acknowledges that a saving knowledge of Christ can-not be experienced through discursive means or, more specifically, under-stood through doctrinal frameworks such as tradition or works. It is, he explains, the "Spirit [that] ever shows us things as they are, even though they be deep things and mysteries, it makes them plain." Shepard describes the kind of perception he attributes to the work of the Spirit by using the phrase "as they are" to describe the Spirit's ability to give human experi-ence immediacy, not only with Christ, but with the world and all of the disconnecting ways it is comprehended. This perceptive immediacy, this getting closer to things *as they are*, is figured as possible through intellect and through the heart, as perception felt immediately, rather than as mediated to describe the penetrating apprehension available to a saint either through the method of technologia or through the Holy Spirit. Both lead to belief through the consent of the will to an idea. Logic, technologia, and the Holy Spirit were all avenues to truth and knowledge of the fixed and immutable laws of God's divine wisdom. Because it was believed that one could approach truth with certainty through the method logic afforded, a saint actively sought the truth under the guise of "receptivity" to God's grace. This paradox is at the heart of Puritan piety because it reveals the irony behind the belief that reception to truth was a result of grasping it intellectually.

As a preparationist, Shepard placed the role of God's love within the realm of means that prepared a saint for conversion. Shepard reasoned, "for though Christ will convey rich grace to his people, yet it shall be by love" (*PTV*, 62). Yet, in *The Parable of the Ten Virgins*, in addition to figuring God's love as a means to grace, Shepard places it at one more remove by describing it for the purposes of "seeing" it. Couched in terms of measurement and organized by a list, God's love, which is infinite, must be "seen" in these terms in order to be understood. Shepard packages God's love in a way that accentuates the distance between sinner and God and stresses the inherent problem that a saint faces in the conversion process when in possession of damaged faculties and limited perception:

Quest. How shall I comprehend [God's love]?

Ans. First, the apostle prays for it. Secondly, see what it is by his description, and meditate on it.

1. The breadth, i.e., the same love wherewith the Lord comprehends all saints, as Abraham, etc.: thou art as dear to the Lord as he or any in heaven; nay, it may be, did cost more: not a cross, not a mercy, but it is common (for substance) unto all saints.
2. The length, from eternity to eternity, nothing can part, nothing shall part; all other things are but summer swallows, that build with us for a time.
3. The depth, that the Lord should look upon thee when in thy pesthouse, when no eye pitied thee, when as low as the grave, nay, as low as hell, nay, lower; for they in hell would come out, thou wouldst not. Never think to see what infinite love is, till thou seest infinite wrath.
4. The hight, to be as happy angels, and more so; nay, to be all one with Christ, and in Christ, and loved with the same love Christ is. John xvii. 23, 26.

5. When thou seest it thus, yet it is the love of Christ that passeth knowledge. (*PTV*, 62)

In containing the idea of God's love in a list and through terms of measurement, Shepard believes he has made it available to be understood by his congregation. Yet, only a few lines later Shepard qualifies the mechanistic process of perception he has just described with what has the tone of an apology—and spiritism—of a sort of longing for immediacy in a felt relation to the divine: "The eye is but little, yet can comprehend a mighty world quickly; man's mind is but little, yet can comprehend, though not the infiniteness, yet an infinite" (63). Immediacy erupts as an issue in conversion here in that though he has stressed the difficulty of comprehending God's love, he reassures his listeners that closing with Christ (or closing with the idea of God's love) can happen "quickly," betraying the part of his piety that, as Delbanco claims, "Shepard's heart feels . . . [but] his intellect resists."[61]

The intellectualized framing of God's love in the above passage is in contrast to his much earlier use of this familiar idea found in *The Sound Believer*:

Oh, come, come therefore unto the Lord Jesus for Christ himself, and for all his benefits; I say for all his benefits. This is that which the apostle prays for with bended knees for the Ephesians, that they might—not take in a little, but—comprehend the height, depth, length, breadth of Christ's love, that so they might be filled with all the fullness of God.[62]

One issue remains the same in both versions of the passage and that is Shepard's faith that though the eye and mind are "little," and can only take in a "little," a saint can still comprehend the fullness of Christ's love, the channel of grace. In *The Parable of the Ten Virgins* it comes in as more of an afterthought, as though the saints, and perhaps Shepard himself, shouldn't forget, after all the rationalizing, how union with Christ feels. The difference is in the apparent delivery of the sermon. The first version emphasizes the rational comprehension of God's love and frames the faculties (man's small eye and mind) as a significant barrier to God's grace, though it does remain possible for a saint to receive it. *The Sound Believer*, however, is a display of converting ministry in action. The fact that a saint's mind is little is only a small matter, contained by the dashes. In addition, his sermon puts his congregation in the place of the Ephesians, urging them to "not take in a little," and proceeds with a rhetorical momentum that allows the fullness of Christ to be felt with each measurement of Christ's encompassing love tripping, immediately, one upon the other.

Though a saint's conversion experience depended almost entirely upon hearing the Word, there is a constant tension, as we've seen here, in Shepard's theology between the efficacy of the Word, and of the discursive community that embodies his ministry, and the limitations of words in representing faith, grace, and spiritual experience. Regeneration led a saint into a divine existence, permitting access to a realm beyond mere representations of reality fixed in language and known only through language and report. This movement beyond words thought of as "actual" deliverance by the Holy Spirit did not simply increase one's knowledge or tweak the perceptive powers. The message of Puritanism was one of rebirth that, indeed, could not be described:

> Now, there is a light of glory, whereby the elect see things in another manner; to tell you how, they can not; it is the beginning of light in heaven, and the same Spirit that fills Christ filling their minds, that they know by the anointing all things, which if ever you have, you must become babes and fools in your own eyes. (*PTV*, 235)

Yet, though a saint cannot describe how they see "things in another manner," Shepard offers the answers for how a saint can know with "certainty" whether there is the work of grace in their soul. The light that discovers things *as they are* shines through the Word because the light of the Spirit goes with the Word. It also shines through the light of experience and sense that is the "experimental knowledge of the work of grace." We know this light, he explains, as "certainly" as "by feeling heat, we know fire is hot; by tasting honey, we know it is sweet" (*PTV*, 222). This sense, he continues, is "diversely apparent to experience," at which point he defines experience in three important ways, reminding his congregants that he "never knew yet a *thinking* Christian deceived" (222, 223; italics added). Shepard's conceptualization of experience maintains that experience happens in the thinking process, but it is a process reflecting a piety governed by reason. Though Shepard claims that the experimental knowledge of grace involves an immediate taste or sense that cannot be mistaken, he looks to the orderly, rational processes of thinking understood in faculty psychology to provide the tools for judging the sensations. Defined three ways, experience is first described as judging one's "act[s] of life" as spiritual by which one compares an act to the "rule." Second, experience is described as seeing and feeling "the operation of love" by which one judges if they possess virtue. Finally, one may understand experience as "temptations and trials" by which one may know what is in the heart. A thinking saint, according to faculty psychology, is a judging saint and one who understands his or her experiential piety as a series of judgments made by reason applied to a sensual apprehension of the world. Therefore, at the same time that Shepard's ministry could offer the discursive and doctrinal support to his parishioners for interpreting the work of the Spirit, it performed the coordinate imaginative function of reinforcing their distance from God, fueled by the role that attentiveness to sin played.

In his essay "Thomas Shepard's America," Delbanco characterizes Shepard's theology as one that "cries the fiendishness of sin but feels it as a bridgeable gap, a space, between man and God."[63] Faith was necessary for overcoming this distance, but sometimes it couldn't be supported because of the nature of the faculties, which were distorted by the limits of language and perception. Yet, saints had to use all of the means necessary to grapple with sin if they were to keep alive any chance of conversion and the gift of a regenerate will. The testimonies contain the records of each saint's struggle to create a receptive space for grace and the re-placement of New England within the morphology was necessary for defining the contours of that space and making belief possible. It was a conscious space where saints searched out and meditated on their sins and attempted to take control of them through the process of framing and containing them with the theological doctrine propounded by their minister. This attempt at the constant destruction of sin and self performed a coordinate task: by clearing out the obstacles to salvation, the saints opened that space for the reception of grace and a regenerate will.

To this end, Shepard encouraged his congregants, "resign up thyself to him to give thee a will, (put it into his hand, as bad as it is; this is spouse-like,) and to take away that will to sin, so thou shalt have him; 'I am my beloved's, he is mine'" (*PTV*, 136). Only through self-destruction could a saint receive grace and a regenerate will, and it was the foundational act that made conversion possible. Notably, it is a saint's struggle with the concept of the will that stands out in the confessions as the epistemological and spiritual barrier to grace. The will played the most complex role in the process of conversion because saints knew they had a corrupt one, so that their relation to the environment was damaged. A corrupt will caused a disconnection between the reason (which sorted sensory information into categories of either "dangerous" or "good") and the will, which converted reason's judgments on an object into reactions of either choosing or refusing the object. It was the mechanism that converted spontaneous and sensory perception of the environment into action. Shepard would warn in *The Parable of the Ten Virgins*, "before conversion, the main wound of men is their will" (100). Puritans had an epistemological problem to face because there were always two wills at work in their spiritual and mental universes: their own corrupt ones and God's. This created the difficult situation of having to discern whose will was prompting the affections to choose or refuse an object. In Puritan epistemology, an individual's responses to the objects encountered in their environment, whether the Word of God, a bear, or ideas were the result of the same process; the affections were aroused by the will, which carried an individual to the object or away from it.

Testifying to America's Promise

Because they are testifying about their conversion process, the saints' narratives unfold a story specifically about their wills' encounters with the idea of belief. What is interesting, however, is how, in the progress toward belief, whether it is spoken of as a feeling or as a thought, it is objectified. It exists within their environment as an object to be encountered and judged in its reception in the same way a bear would be. The moment of truth came for saints when the object of belief (the idea of belief) was presented by God within their purview. Choosing belief would mean conversion and refusing belief would halt the process. Because a saint battled against the sin of "unbelief" as a regular part of the preparatory process involving conviction, compunction, and humiliation, one would think that when God made real the possibility of believing, a saint wouldn't think twice. Until the moment when a saint felt close to Christ, the introspective work was mostly the work of conscience and the meditation on sin and depravity in order to clear the way for grace. Ironically, this stage was meant to soften a stony heart so that a saint would be willing to entertain God. Yet the confessions demonstrate that this rarely happened. Sir Starr's testimony exemplifies the typical Puritan experience when a saint is faced with the choice to believe: "And if sin be continued in, no salvation, and hence no use to believe out of conscience, and all belief unworthiness. [I] heard when the Lord then carried my heart after Christ, and I could say, Lord I believe, help my unbelief, but I feared to presume."[64] Starr knows that he cannot "believe" if it is motivated by conscience because his belief would have resulted from the impulse toward self-preservation. Then he relates a moment when he feels his heart "carried" after Christ, a description of his will acting as a channel for grace. Described as an act of God, this transcendent moment leads him to a clear statement about being given an option. He states, "I could say, Lord I believe."

However, the transcendence is short-lived because his conscience and his reason intervene to ignite fear that his "heart" has masked his urge for self-preservation as virtue.

Starr rejects accepting a believing attitude out of fear even though it means rejecting the reception of grace. He, in fact, undergoes conversion when he feels "carried" to Christ, but then he quashes it. His rejection comes at the moment when he is faced with the actuality of the phrase "Lord I believe." He feels carried to Christ, which is a transcendent moment, but when the time comes to state his belief, he cannot. Fear interrupts it, as though the act of capturing the moment in language creates a crisis. In effect, "closing with Christ" cannot be accomplished successfully unless Starr can "close" with the idea of belief by realizing it in language. Starr's confession then moves immediately into a recitation of references from the Bible which follow one upon another, demonstrating the quality and tone of being back in his discursive "comfort zone." Starr's moment of being "carried" to Christ should have been interpreted as the will of God, but he immediately mistrusts his "heart" when he has the option to claim that he believes and he suspects that the claim cannot be true. Faced with the option of determining the idea of belief as either dangerous or good, he reacts with fear and rejects it.

Starr closes his confession by describing the state of his soul as teetering on the edge of conversion:

> And so Mr. S[hepard] on Romans 8:penult., When we [have] clear knowledge of our justification, and a principal [ ] of [ ] persuasion, and I saw Christ freely offered and would have received Christ. And the soul should be brought to that [ ], Wilt receive Christ or reject him [?] I found a desire to receive him, and I was afraid to reject him, but Lord carries my heart after him and to help me against some sins, which encourageth me still to seek after the Lord.[65]

Starr lingers over what is persistently for the confessors the problem of consent. The soul is brought to the moment of conversion, but when faced with having to select either rejection of the Lord or reception of the Lord, they consistently choose to keep "seeking" after him for fear that the will to believe is their own corrupt one. And, as noted previously, the confessions conclude with statements emphasizing their humbled, sinful nature. These feelings of unworthiness were an effective and affective reality that could be easily attached to a wealth of ideas about human depravity familiar to Puritans. Acknowledging one's sinful nature did not seem to imply any act of the will on the saint's part. Choosing to believe in Christ without certain knowledge that God, through his providence, had willed it would have been too presumptuous (as Starr described it) for members of Shepard's congregation; we see the influence of Shepard's teachings against hollow professions clearly in Starr's testimony. Shepard's call for the "will of a new society" put the saints in the position of having to distinguish between their own will to believe and God's grace, and when faced with having to select one of the options, they chose the one that reflected Shepard's doctrine, fulfilling the goals and lessons of his ministry, and ultimately serving to induct them into a society of visible saints. Their testimonies not only acknowledge the tightly woven discursive nature of membership in this society, but the inherently discursive nature of the will.

Barbary Cutter illustrates the same barrier to conversion when she uses the story of Balaam to describe the problem of the will, specifically that portion of the story in Numbers 22:24–26, when Balaam's donkey, unbeknownst to Balaam, reacts to an angel of God that Balaam cannot see. The road they are on narrows and becomes enclosed by vineyards on either side, so that when the angel appears to the donkey, the donkey has no room to go around it. Balaam beats his trusty donkey because he doesn't understand the cause for the animal's behavior. Verse 26 presents the image that Cutter uses to illustrate her situation: "The angel of the Lord moved on farther and stood in a narrow place where there was no room to turn to either right or left."[66] Cutter's testimony highlights the anxiety saints felt when the moment of belief was upon them: "Yet hearing sin of unbelief to bring heart to strait, either to receive or reject Him, and so heard as Balaam then stopped in a straight so found sweetness. But I lost that which I found in the Lord" (*TSC*, 91). This passage, though difficult to decipher because it is fragmented, communicates a similar crisis to Starr's in that she reaches a moment when she must choose to "receive" or "reject" the Lord, and, like Starr, her heart is brought to a "strait." Cutter, however, refers to the story of Balaam (to whom the angel finally reveals itself and solves the mystery of the donkey's behavior) to express a relief she feels from this passage in scripture about Balaam's experience with the Lord. When the Lord reveals himself to Balaam, Balaam is able to reconcile his relation to the Lord, who has been testing his obedience to God. It is typical for a saint to refer to Bible passages as a way to demonstrate knowledge of scripture, but in this instance, Cutter testifies that this passage offered relief when she felt that she too had reached a "strait." Her testimony recalls that when she reached that moment of conversion (when she must "receive" or "reject" the Lord) she found relief from her distress in a passage from scripture, but this is apparently all. In the next breath she claims to have "lost that which [she] found in the Lord." The only true relief Cutter finds is in doubts. Her confession ends by taking up the discourse of human depravity, finding real comfort in her identity as a sinner: "I saw and was convinced of my sin especially the last out of 35 Isaiah—say to them that be fearful be strong your God comes" (*TSC*, 92).

Typical of Shepard's congregants, Starr and Cutter reach potential moments of conversion but ultimately defer consummation and take up the discourse associated with the early stages of preparation and the continual labor of addressing the containment of sin. As the work leading up to conversion, the destruction of man's nature entailed the emptying of six "rooms" of things a saint is full of to make way for grace. They include sin, darkness, unbelief, Satan, self, and the world. Emptying these rooms was the preparatory work that called upon the saints to maintain a state of active passivity; the destruction of man's nature, through the meditation on sin, created the receptive space in which saints could be overwhelmed by the work of the Spirit. Yet, the saints' inability to consummate union with Christ was a crisis of consent because the choice to accept Christ entailed a perceptive act pressured by judgment and a stressing of the role of the understanding. When the moment arrived to close, they expected to feel passive, as though their wills were acting freely and were being "carried" after Christ; but they could not feel passive because all the work that had gone into preparing for Christ had demanded highly active uses of the mind involving intense introspection and impossible feats of conception such as "comprehending" the fullness of God's love or "understanding" the work of the Spirit. Though the doctrine of means was preached as the way to Christ, it established a perceptive mode that undermined the passivity a saint understood to be his or her proper "activity." The saints' retreat back into the discourse of helplessness and doubting is a retreat back into a perceptual mode that can accommodate the acceptable active work of a pietistic mind.

Because the moment of belief was a definitive experience in the life of a saint, the ability to prove whether self-deception was avoided became paramount, challenging their ability to make a statement about the reception of grace confidently. Shepard's confessors stop short of testifying to assurance, so the narratives end on virtually the same note of helplessness or submission before the Lord. There are many terms for this sentiment, from claims of "emptiness" and "doubting" to being "humbled" and able to "apply nothing." The saints were humbled by the countless sins they had to account for and "unbelief" could be lumped in with all the rest that they felt powerless over. Yet, the sin of "unbelief" played a special role in the process of conversion because the only way saints knew their souls were saved was experiencing the moment *they believed* that God had granted *the will to believe* in his determination to save. Essentially, they had to *judge* whether they believed that they believed—the problem Ames identifies when the intellect determines the movement of the will. They knew that only God granted the will to believe in Christ, but when the moment arrived in which they had to determine whether it was the result of grace (as they had to do with any aspect of their spiritual lives) they were faced with the inevitable problem of trusting that their search for this knowledge had been undertaken in good faith and whether they had been dutiful enough in seeking means.

The confessions evidence open-endedness because they seem frozen at the stage in the process of conversion just *before* the reception of grace—the moment of submission to God's will. This moment is often expressed by feelings much like what Goodwife Champney testified to: "I thought I was lost and unsupported and I thought Lord had left me to be so" (*TSC*, 191). In many instances saints concluded their testimonies simply by acknowledging that God's promise exists, yet they were unable to say whether it exists for them, as expressed in Sizar Jones' final words: "Lord helped me to hope and so desire to hope still" (*TSC*, 202). Shepard's confessors framed their narratives in a way that foregrounded their sinful natures and hence their dependency on God, and by ending their confessions at the moment just before the reception of grace, they made a new kind of sainthood visible, legitimizing the *potential* for a regenerate will and not full conversion as the criterion for church membership.

Because the moment of belief signaled the transition, through the operations of the Holy Spirit, from sinner to saint, it represented the realization of potential into actuality, of preparation into deliverance. In *The Sound Believer*, Shepard's exposition on his soteriology, he explains why saints are unable to believe through any ability of their own:

> Faith is a gracious work of the Spirit of Christ; the Spirit, therefore, is the efficient cause or principal workman of faith; the Spirit doth not believe, but causeth us to believe; . . . the souls of all the elect (especially when humbled) are, of all other things, most unable to believe: nay, look, as, before compunction and humiliation, Satan held the soul captive chiefly by its lusts and sins, so now, when the Lord hath burnt those cords, and broken those chains, all the powers of darkness strengthen themselves, and keep the soul under mightily, by unbelief. (*SB*, 194)

Shepard's confessions are a collection of vivid stories of the saints' experiences with this stage of conversion, the period of potential. Congregants narrate their struggle with the sin of unbelief and their attempts to discern the moment when the Spirit fills the "room" of unbelief with grace, causing union with Christ, but they stop short of expressing what Shepard calls "man's actual deliverance" (*SB*, 115). A saint's conversion is made *actual* by the "efficacy and power of the Spirit of Christ" because "the Spirit therefore takes fast hold of the souls of all the elect, [and] draws them unto Christ," doing so through an "omnipotent and irresistible" power (*SB*, 115, 194). This is the moment of faith whereby "the whole soul cometh out of itself to Christ, for Christ and all his benefits, upon the call of Christ in his word" (*SB*, 190).

Yet, closing their narratives with doubt and self-loathing did not signal a dead-end in the conversion process. These feelings were, in fact, the channels for faith. Barbary Cutter's testimony, for example, describes the important role doubt played in a saint's relationship with God: "And . . . Lord hath let me see more of Himself as in doubtings. That Lord did leave saints doubting as to remove lightness and frothiness, hence doubtings, and to cause for fresh evidence and by this means kept them from falling" (*TSC*, 92). Feelings of doubt meant that a saint's faith was alive because they reinforced a saint's potential to receive a regenerate will. These feelings, in fact, were the most profitable ones a saint could have under Shepard's later ministry, and feelings such as confidence, joy, and relief were considered suspect because they flirted too strongly with assurance. This affective dimension to conversion legitimized feeling as a basis for judgment; every felt relation to the divine, whether it was doubt and helplessness or hope and relief, served to give them a reading as to their alignment with God's will. Indeed, it was an *attitudinal* positioning that sustained a potent relationship with God.

What actually proved to be a threat to their conversions was feeling nothing, what many saints described as "dead-heartedness," the language Caldwell identifies as an expression of their sense of isolation. A dead frame meant that one was disconnected from God and unmoored from a life of faith. It was a space in which saints became "confused," or knocked off course in the regular apprehensions of their experience. These moments in the confessions are described in images of desperate loneliness where saints do not simply feel helpless before God (for this would denote a right relationship with him); instead, these are moments of isolation arising out of a temporary disconnection from an interpretive community, the discursive space that ordinarily provides the conceptual and descriptive means to understand and orient their spiritual lives. For

Goodwife Jackson, this disconnection is caused by the migration, and it manifests in an image of desertion and even paranoia: "And when I was come to New England, I did look on myself as cast in the open field, and so saw myself in a sad condition, and though[t] others thought ill and meanly of me, and I thought worst of myself, and I was in a sad condition, and my sleep did depart away from [me], so that I did not know what to do."[67] For William Manning, the isolation arises after he questions

> whether there was a God or the Scripture true or no. And being gross I was loathe and ashamed to make my condition known, yet the minister showing out of Psalms 14:1 that there was a God by Scripture and by reason; but fain would I put off these temptations. Now I found hardness, unbelief, deadness to lie very heavy upon my soul. And another minister handling the affections of the soul, he met with my corruptions. I was burdened with them in a confused manner and did strive against them with my own strength and not the Lord's, or else I believe I might have had help before now. (*TSC*, 95–96)

In these instances, caused by the migration, the saints speak of circumstances that brought them to a gap in the familiar structure of faith that they weren't able to traverse. But the effect is rather profound: the very foundations of everything they believe seem to fall away. Golden Moore described it thus: "And I coming hither I found my heart in a worse frame than ever, not a heart so much as to desire help from the Lord. And hence called all into question" (*TSC*, 123). These reflections are not simply doubts about one's election or meditations on sin; these moments reveal the fragility of a living faith and the inherent instability of the worldviews that sustain that faith. In these particular instances confusion and loss of direction and complete insecurity were not tied to any recognizable stage of the morphology or any other part of faith. As a matter of fact, these moments take the saints by surprise because they find themselves in the position of feeling the ground under their feet give way, unable to know what to do about it, and they temporarily lose the ability to keep the possibility of salvation alive. Overcome, Golden Moore became resigned: "hence [I] feared time was passed" (*TSC*, 123).

These ruptures in the fabric of faith expose the unstable layers beneath, which, when tested, seem to tear very easily. The discursive life a divine gave to his worldview shaped and lent stability to the saints' faith. It was an environment of words essential to the success of the colony, providing an alternative, no less sensible environment, to the new and harsh realities they found themselves in. This discursive space was the material of experience, providing temporal, recognizable signs that made sense out of their lives. For Shepard, faith was the imagined borderland between the self and God. It was the "motion of the soul between these extremes, throughout that vast and infinite distance that is between a sinful, wretched man and a blessed Saviour" (*SB*, 202). In effect, it was the soul's energy that bound and energized the space between an individual and the Savior. David D. Hall describes it in more succinct terms: "Faith depends upon the promise of free grace and God's initiative. Yet faith emerges from energetic use of all the 'means,' including . . . self scrutiny."[68] It is no wonder then why a saint never uses the word "faith" itself to characterize their conversion process. Faith happened between the words, in the spaces that carried a saint to each description and clarification of their spiritual experience. Faith may lead a saint to new epistemological and theological truths, but ultimately it cannot be captured by language itself because it is constantly in "motion," as Shepard described it. As an interdependence between a saint's use of means and the promise of free grace, faith was a constant, but ever-changing and unpredictable relationship with God, creating new paths and radiations in the Puritan consciousness. One of those new paths, and certainly a new radiation in the Puritan conscious-ness, is best represented by the migration itself. Having had the expecta-tion of getting one step closer to closing the "vast and infinite distance that is between a sinful, wretched man and a blessed Saviour," the saints' faith is tested when, upon arrival, they find themselves lost and unsupported in what amounts to both a real and imaginary unknown horizon in their regular apprehensions of faith, what William James calls the space of the "vague."

The confessions of Shepard's saints record this life of faith. They record the trials associated with living up to the doctrines and lessons propound-ed by a minister. They also record the times when circumstances were so overpowering that saints lost faith, became isolated and cut off from the interpretive community and found themselves unable to evolve in the conversion process. These moments when faith appears dead, in fact, speak to the "saving" properties of one's discursive community. Granted, a Puritan believed that grace was given freely by God. Yet, these confes-sions reveal conversion experiences that cannot be compared to Paul's, where the moment was distinct and immediate, unfettered by conditions or circumstances. The confessions in Shepard's notebook present a com-munity of saints whose conversions are wholly mediated by language and the discursive community of which they are a part.

When discursive structures fail to represent their experience, the effect is the collapse of the grounds of knowledge, isolation, and in the extreme case, loss of identity. Faith was the web connecting a saint to all parts of experience. As the "motion of the soul" between God and the saints it carried them through their spiritual lives, leading them to new truths about God, the world, and themselves. It was the intersection of lived and living truth forming a conscious space, a conductive imaginary, where salvation was in constant negotiation, bringing to bear God's will and a saint's attending on the signs and means available: as such, it was a dynamic nexus not simply enlivening the bond between Savior and saint, but serving to ground and realize the divine and spiritual in the ordinary world of their daily lives. That grounding occurs in the material reality that language and discourse offered. In effect, the soul's motion between Savior and saint occurs within the realm of consciousness understood as a discursive medium, and conversion is that process that registers the movement of the soul through a life of faith. When faith is alive and potent, (because language is representing reality) the soul is able to move fluidly between Savior and saint, circulating between the two "extremes" and closing the "infinite" gap. When a saint's experience cannot be understood and described by the available language, that "infinite" distance becomes impassable.

When Jane Palfrey gives her confession, she expresses the nature of a typical saint's reaction to the New World as a new "content of consciousness" with a stunning image of having everything familiar to her suddenly become obsolete: "I had a mind for New England and I thought I should know more of my own heart. So I came and thought *I saw more than ever I could have believed* that I wondered earth swallowed me not up" (*TSC*, 151; italics added). Her initial confidence that New England would be, as most of the congregants state, a place to "find power" is echoed by William Manning, who explains his own intentions for New England: "having at last thoughts of this place in New England, my wife and I hearing some *certainty* of things here, I desired to come hither" (*TSC*, 97; italics added). Manning, then, inevitably testifies to a "discontented mind," but then he refers to a sermon he hears Shepard deliver. He recalls:

> But hearing Mr. Shepard speaking upon a text to encourage them that newly came to land, that *it may be had that which I expected not* (though troubled). . . . It began to revive me and then I considered I had forgotten the mercies of *old* much more those *new* mercies. And showing the great means I had there [in New England] for the present which the whole world had not, which all saints, though with straits and wants, yet might support their hearts and strength. (*TSC*, 98; italics added)

In addition, we see the "psychic upheaval" in Nathaniel Sparrowhawk's testimony, which also contains the reimagined place of New England in the discourse of salvation emerging from Shepard's ministry:

> [I] had thought to find power and thought to prize means here; but the Lord hath helped me to see my own heart reaching after things of this world. But the Lord hath let me see the insufficiency of means; and the Lord hath let me see I must look to the Lord Jesus in it and in *all* means. But the assurance of the Lord's love I have not found. (*TSC*, 64; italics added)

In these passages, the "psychic upheaval" the Puritan immigrants suffer revolves specifically around coming to a new understanding of what role New England will play in their spiritual progress. In Sparrowhawk's case, it takes the form of a new measurement being taken. He weighs the "insufficiency" of means, presumably in old England, with the new, more thorough understanding of "all" means he has gained in New England. The measurement he takes indicates that there are more means available in New England, an idea introduced by Shepard. In William Manning's case, we also see the movement of faith occurring in the mediation between a recently acquired understanding of the difference between old and new "mercies," and the discourse of measurement applies as well because he testifies to having forgotten the "new mercies" more than the old. Like Sparrowhawk, Manning takes care to demonstrate his understanding of New England's reimagined role in his salvation by making a distinction between what old and New England mean to his preparatory work. In both cases the measurements they take serve to widen the already "vast and infinite distance" between themselves and God but in doing so, they convert New England into a revived means.

All of the progress that the saints will achieve in their salvation in New England depends on their ability to mediate the dichotomy that frames every other aspect of their experience: the distinction between the place of old England and New England in their preparatory work. That mediation results in the rhetorical convention that emerges in one way or another throughout the majority of the testimonies, identified by Caldwell as the expressive pattern, "since-I-came-hither-dead-hearted-but-I-have-been-revived." What emerges in these mediations is a kind of Ramist axiom within which New England has been reborn as a new "argument" or term, the building blocks, in Ramist logic with which discourses are constructed. In many of the confessions the actual situating or arranging of New England's place in the morphology becomes an expression that sounds more like a tentative "finding" of oneself situated in a new geography, a discursively constructed "arrival" to not only a new geographic space, but a newly bracketed place for New England in the morphology. This arrival to a new place sounds more like a stutter in Golden Moore's testimony, but in the end he "invents" the axiom:

> I set myself to seek Christ and to get more acquainted with Christ and hence used means to *come hither*. Hence [I] did think to enjoy more of the Lord, and so *coming hither* and being in fears of my estate and that if my life was gone I had no promise to support. And I *coming hither* I found my heart in a worse frame than ever, not a heart so much as to desire help from the Lord. (*TSC*, 123; italics added)

By the end of his testimony Moore has professed to feeling revived and having hope, thereby reflecting the pattern. However, Moore's confession poignantly demonstrates what the saints struggle most with in constructing the new axiom, that is, the part of the dialectic called "invention" in which the terms are arranged. The rebirth of New England conceptually requires a new arrangement of terms: In the premigration axiom New England was a means. Then that axiom proved untrue, unreflective of God's divine order because it failed as a means. In the new axiom, New England has been converted back to a place of means.

Through Shepard's ministry, the members of his church were bound together by a new, communally recognized axiomatic expression demonstrating America's place as a revived means to grace. However, the spiritual impact of America as a new means has yet to unfold. The migration to New England brings the saints not only to a new geographic horizon, it brings them to the horizons of their spiritual and discursive lives, requiring a new theological conception of America to accommodate the expanse of feeling that needed space to evolve. Having no language to describe the fact that America lost its meaning when they arrived, the saints testify to being temporarily lost amid the signs of grace. They suffer isolation and disappointment, and yet the geographical move to America also stimulates an original relation to the morphology, to language, and to America. We see in the move to a geographically unknown territory, a necessary imaginative effort to discover a new truth about America's place in consciousness. These efforts are usually described in Puritan scholarship as the formulaic or staid recitations of the morphology. Indeed, they reflect the morphology, but they are also imaginative efforts to convert New England into a place of salvation. The new axiom not only resurrects New England as a means, but it also resurrects the saints' spiritual progress by offering a revived *ordo salutis*, and in the traditional Ramist role of dialectic, the new axiom generates conviction, a new confidence in or, ironically, an *assurance* of America's promise. That promise, in turn, is instantiated by their demonstrations of a habit of thinking to ensure social order—a focus on the darker recesses of the soul where sin hides.

In the same way that America was in need of a new semantic context, the saints' own spiritual identities relied on the semantic context provided by Shepard's ministry, and the identity that emerges from the confessions reflects a ministry that defines the will as, very specifically, ruled by intellect. Though the saints relate moments wherein they seem to have the experience of being "carried" to Christ, they testify to practicing the habit of thinking that enforced spiritual discipline. As the confessions show, by controlling the actions of the will through judgment, discreet moments in the thinking process seem to be brought to the fore of consciousness for observation, and in these moments of attention to the mind in thinking options for belief present themselves for consideration. The saints don't choose "belief," for in the context of Shepard's ministry this would mean further isolation. They choose, instead, to keep searching and by doing so, they choose community. Their faith is revived in their expressions of a will to *defer* belief in Christ, but in doing so they *profess* to believe in the promise of America. The confessions are, in the end, conversion narratives: the saints testify to having converted America into a new meaning, and that new meaning is maintained in a process of thinking that opens to a person's view the various relations or contexts of a certain idea. When they choose to defer belief in Christ, they choose to sustain the thought of America.

CHAPTER **2**

"Something That Is Seen, That Is Wonderful"

Jonathan Edwards and the Feeling of Conviction

Instead of the image of a zealous, determined group on a founding "errand," therefore, we have individuals hoping to overcome their feelings of isolation and doubt on a far-flung strand, working to resurrect their faith in a new land and achieve the necessary social cohesion of a covenanted church. The fragility of that social cohesion is what stands out in the congregants' testimonies, and whatever unity they achieve depends on the ability of each member to respond to the new context with a common language adapted to their circumstances. Inherent in their rehearsals is a communal assent to the kind of growth in grace that makes explicit and radicalizes the relationship between an individual's pursuit of conversion and membership in the covenanted church. Like Thomas Shepard, Jonathan Edwards believed that life was a matter of relations, so membership in that community was a necessary part of growth in grace. Yet, as Gerald McDermott shows, Edwards's concern over the communal life of the regenerate is tied to what he calls Edwards's "obsession" with the millennium. McDermott argues, "Edwards's eschatology is dominated by an unyielding concentration on the coming *global* community that implicitly relativizes all merely national concerns and condemns all egoistic nationalism."[1] Therefore, Edwards's emphasis on the millennium is also at odds with Perry Miller's notion that New England retained special meaning in a global community: "Before the majestic dimensions of the 'one holy and happy society' that is to come, New England and America fade into insignificance."[2] Although McDermott distinguishes between Shepard's and Edwards's theology by noting that Shepard's was focused on Christ's Second Coming and Edwards's was millennial, they worked toward the same end—to advance "the good community," which was "always the terminus on the edge of the horizon, toward which all is progressing."[3]

Edwards's sense of himself as a world citizen and his desire to become an international figure and leader in a global Reformed evangelical movement was an outgrowth of facing what Sang Hyun Lee describes as the "basic problem that seventeenth-century thought bequeathed to Jonathan Edwards's generation," that of "revising the Aristotelian-Scholastic world view so as to come up with a perspective that could accommodate the new methods and categories of thought presented by mechanicoexperimental science."[4] Edwards's response to the intellectual trends of his day would result in a reconceptualization of piety, and the shift in Edwards's vision, stimulated by new horizons in science and philosophy, permitted new possibilities for understanding and describing conversion. As George Marsden notes, Edwards was influenced early on in his thinking by these cultural developments. He was an enthusiastic reader of *The Spectator* and at Yale he had access to the Dummer collection, which contained works by Isaac Newton and Richard Steele. In addition, Yale was in the process of updating its curriculum while Edwards was there and began to include Locke and Newton by 1718–19 while phasing out the logic of Petrus Ramus and Aristotelian science. Even so, as Marsden explains, "to understand Edwards throughout his career, we must appreciate the premium that he and other educated eighteenth-century people placed on logic. Along with the study of language and classics, logic was the bedrock of the educational system. Every schoolboy was trained in the basics of dialectic."[5] Indeed, revising the preparatory theology of the previous generation in light of revolutionary scientific and philosophical thought would mean conceiving of a new logic that could accommodate natural philosophy's investment in observation of the natural world. Yet, even as he was "determined to know everything," he remained equally grounded in the Calvinist doctrine of his forefathers and, therefore, "felt called to use the new learning in defense of God's eternal word."[6]

Modifying the Structure of Belief

Edwards scholars recognize that one of the most influential people in Edwards's spiritual and intellectual life was the Puritan divine Thomas Shepard. Conversion remained a doctrinal challenge for Edwards, and it remained an experiential challenge for his parishioners, and though both Shepard and Edwards faced these same issues, one hundred years of science and philosophy separated their ideas and influenced their theological conceptions of conversion. For Edwards, this would mean allowing his religious beliefs to inform a new theory of knowledge and his scientific interests to generate new possibilities for religious experience. For both Shepard's and Edwards's congregants the conversion experience consummated an essential process in the social and pietistic life of an individual, and central to both pastors' theology was the idea that a saving knowledge of Christ was necessary for assurance of election. The distinction between a discursive or rational knowledge of Christ and a saving knowledge of Christ is the theme of Shepard's sermon series on the parable of the ten virgins, and Edwards would adopt it as the central issue in his *Religious Affections*.[7] As John E. Smith notes in his introduction to *Religious Affections*, in preparing the treatise "Edwards quoted more from Shepard than from any other writer, depending chiefly upon *The Parable of the Ten Virgins*."[8] Though Edwards retained the tenets of evangelical Calvinism, his theories about the human mind transformed notions of how one came to know the divine mind and, therefore, the state of one's soul. He explored the matrix of thought, feeling, and perception, characterizing it as an ever-expansive, and, as such, redemptive conscious space only insofar as an individual exercises its potential for approaching degrees of divine truths that God excited therein. For Edwards, conversion would ground one's redemptive path within the web of relations he called the "room of the idea," a conscious space infused with God's will, but experienced as the ordinary, thoughtful dynamic between receptivity, perception, and interpretation enlivening the bond between humanity and God.

The previous chapter aimed to contextualize the confessions of Thomas Shepard's congregants in order to understand more fully how aspects of Shepard's ministry resulted in the open-ended character of the testimonies. This chapter extends the analysis of the dimensions of conversion introduced in the first chapter in order to examine how Edwards modified the Calvinist belief structure reflected in Shepard's theology and the confessions. Although Edwards, as we shall see, was critical of the limitations that Ramist logic and the doctrine of preparation imposed on the pursuit of belief and conversion, he was as interested as Shepard was in describing the efforts of thinking, perception, and imagination in those pursuits. Whereas Shepard's descriptions of the kind of piety necessary to revive the saints' faith emphasize the thinking process as one that maintained spiritual discipline and prevented self-deception—but also deferred conversion—Edwards would theorize a different kind of mental habit, one he called "attention of the mind in thinking," which he believed had the potential to be a saint's most powerful act in glorifying God as well as the conductive force behind conversion. In this way Edwards, just as Shepard did, emphasizes the role of what William James would call a "strenuous mood" in living.[9] Edwards's descriptions of these mental and affective efforts culminate in stunning characterizations of individual consciousness, the imagined space in which the will, as it did in Shepard's theology, registers the boundaries, or lack thereof, between the spontaneous and sensory perception of the environment and the bodies of knowledge that inevitably inform that perception.

As discussed in the previous chapter, although Shepard preached the difference between "heart" knowledge of Christ and "head" knowledge of Christ, explaining to his congregants that mere notional familiarity with doctrine, though necessary for an influx of grace, was not itself the experience of grace, the intellectualism his ministry fostered undermined the spontaneity and immediacy inherent in a conversion experience they were to feel *sensually*. Ideas about the mind associated with the faculty psychology that Shepard fostered through his ministry established the epistemology Shepard's congregants would rely on for interpreting their experience and framing the truth about it. In doing so, it was believed that the saints were simply following the natural intellectual process of the mind when it organizes experience through the invention of arguments.

This theory of knowledge and perception held that the mind "invents," or lays open to view (because they already exist in space) the arguments that make up objective reality, and this process of invention remains completely within the realm of the intellect in that it is responsible for how the discovery of the argument is made. As Perry Miller explains, the operations of the faculty in inventing consists of four "instruments": "first, the senses, which perceive; second, 'observation,' which collects the sense impressions; third, 'induction,' which notes differences and similarities and abstracts generalizations from singulars; and finally, 'experientia,' which, receiving the idea after it has been collected from the perceptions of the senses and confirmed by observation and induction of various examples, pronounces what it is and what it is not."[10] This process allowed for a firm foundation of knowledge about the nature of things, including the nature of the soul, because it offered certainty about the way God's universe works and the relations and patterns exhibited in the perfection and harmony of that universe. This stable foundation was possible because invention "annihilated the distance from the object to the brain, or made possible an epistemological leap across the gap in the twinkling of an eye with an assurance of footing beyond the possibility of a metaphysical slip."[11]

As I demonstrated in the last chapter, the excitation and sensual awakening occurring during conversion was described by Shepard as the perception (sensed as one senses heat from a fire) of the light of the Spirit. But

for Shepard, this heat became "apparent to experience" through a thinking process conceived as a succession of reason's judgments. Through
"thinking," Shepard exhorted, a saint could avoid deception by seeing
"how far [an act] agrees or disagrees with the rule [of the Bible], and judge
of a living act by it." Ironically, though Shepard believed that true saving
knowledge of Christ must be a firsthand experience, not merely understood through report, works, or even doctrinal knowledge, the methodology of technologia and privileging of reason intrinsic to his theology
created an experiential barrier or distance between the sinner and God,
preventing the assurance that accompanies a felt relation needed to close
the most important gap. For Shepard, the burden of proof regarding conversion rested on using an established set of criteria to compare one's
experience to the "rule" in an effort to lend certainty to knowledge
and, therefore, belief about the truth regarding the state of one's soul.
Shepard's epistemology made discerning and disposing the watchdogs of
experience and belief for all stages of the process of conversion.

In contrast, and key to understanding Edwards's rendering of the
conversion experience, is the concept of the affections. They are the
aspect of experience that, as John E. Smith explains, serve as "signposts
indicating the *direction* of the soul" and are rooted in what Edwards calls
"inclination," which brings together two of the mind's faculties, the
understanding and the will, into a motive for action.[12] For Edwards, the
understanding represents the mind's capacity for speculation that is neu-
tral or unattended by any judgment of approval or disapproval. The will,
on the other hand, involves *inclination*, which carries a person beyond
neutrality in the understanding into action. Therefore, the affections, as
Smith states, "stand in a necessary relation to the ideas of the understanding and are also the springs of actions commonly ascribed to the
will."[13]

It is important to keep in mind that Edwards makes a distinction
between affections resulting from the common work of the Spirit and
affections resulting from the saving work of the Spirit. *Religious Affections*, the treatise, is concerned with describing those affections associated
with the saving work of the Spirit. As such, it attempts to describe those
signs that point to the presence of the Spirit dwelling in a saint. In contrast, affections associated with the common work of the Spirit are at
work in the daily lives of unregenerate individuals conducting their actions according to their inclinations. The signs of grace that *Religious
Affections* describes are the kind of affections that are wholly new and
beyond anything that nature can produce. These affections are "religious"
because they allow saints to respond with their entire selves to God's love

and divine glory, implying that the concept of the affections does not divorce the will from the reason. To paraphrase Smith, in the case of religious affections, the Spirit does not operate *"on* the self," as in the case of common grace, the Spirit dwells *"in* the self," having laid a new foundation in the soul.[14] Edwards's concept of the affections marks a significant departure from the faculty psychology of Shepard's time because it offered a description of experience wherein one's judgment of that experience could be suspended and detached from the unrelenting work of conscience. Typical of Edwards's penchant for finding the exact phrase or word to express an idea in its context, his idea of the affections was couched in different terms in different contexts. He would often use the phrase "feeling mind" to express this fusion of the separate faculties of the intellect/head and the will/heart. In addition, there is the more well-known term "sense of the heart," brought to the attention of scholars by Perry Miller in 1948. To reiterate, these phrases do not describe a mode of understanding accessible only to the regenerate, because for Edwards, a "feeling mind" or a "sense of the heart" are forms of perception and knowledge resulting from the *ordinary* work of the Spirit that "puts things in the mind."[15] A "sense of the heart," therefore, is available to any unregenerate who is willing to reject merely "notional" knowledge and experience the meanings of truths encountered more fully, that is, both intellectually and affectively.

Edwards's Miscellany no. 782 describes why a "sense of the heart" is a theory of the mind that, unlike faculty psychology and its emphasis on the role of reason, promotes a consciousness of "things themselves" through a felt and altogether ordinary experience of ideas, what Edwards would term an "actual idea." Miscellany no. 782 captures the essence of Edwards's departure from Shepard's doctrine because it clarifies the limitations of a theology built on an intellectual tradition:

> When in a course of meditations we think of man, angels, nations, conversion, and conviction, if we have anything further in our thoughts to represent those things than only the words, we commonly have only some very confused passing notion of something external, which we don't at all insist on the clearness and distinctness of, nor do we find any need of it, because we make use of that external idea no otherwise than as a sign of the idea, or something to stand in its stead. And the notion need not be distinct in order to that, because we may habitually understand the use of it as a sign without it; whereas it would be of great consequence that it should be clear and distinct if we regarded it as an actual idea and proper representation of the thing itself.[16]

Rather, Edwards continues, in an effort to make our ideas "clear and distinct," in other words, to put them "in our minds," he sets forth the argument that the role of the will/affections is primary: "If we are at a loss concerning a connection or consequence, or have a new inference to draw, or would see the force of some new argument, then commonly we are put to the trouble of *exciting the actual idea*, and making it as lively and clear as we can."[17] Edwards calls this space in consciousness where ideas are excited the "room of the idea," and this "room" acts as the conscious space where not only doctrine, but also all ideas are made "actual" and are therefore "put in the mind." To actualize an idea means to go beyond a notional understanding of the word toward an *experience* of the idea itself through a "sense of the heart."[18] Punching through the façade of words to reach the ideas of God themselves, to collapse the gap between mind and thing was, for Edwards, the fundamental goal of religious experience, though neither he nor Shepard, because of their belief in original sin, could trust that experience. On the other hand, because Emerson eschewed the concept of original sin, he was free to believe, as Miller explains, that there was "no inherent separation between the mind and the thing, that in reality they leap to embrace each other."[19]

Indeed, the cornerstone of Edwards's theology, that of the "sense of the heart," and its relation to the "actual" idea, has its roots in the Puritan doctrine he inherited distinguishing the means of man's salvation by either "purchased deliverance, which is by the blood of Christ," or by "man's *actual* deliverance, which is by the efficacy and power of the Spirit of Christ" (SB, 115; italics added). For Shepard, "actual" deliverance manifests in the process of conversion from the first step of preparation to the final step of sanctification. One's deliverance is actualized by the Spirit of Christ in that at every step the Spirit is present either in its common way during preparation or as a holy principle dwelling in the soul after consummation. In either case, the idea is the same in both Shepard and Edwards: the Spirit of Christ acts as a power that moves the soul. In Edwards's concept of the "actual idea," however, the work of the Spirit acts in consciousness and specifically in the "room of the idea" where ideas are felt, thereby conducting the soul beyond representations of spiritual truths. Therefore, the concept of the "room of the idea" and the "actual idea" powered therein casts reception to the Spirit as a charged moment of potential consciousness generated without the ordered process built into the preparationism favored by the Intellectual Fathers.

Edwards's willingness to eschew the high preparationism of his forbears was cultivated by events both personal and ecclesiastical. After the synod of 1662 (meant to solve divisive issues surrounding church membership) only inflamed dissent, it was, as Philip F. Gura claims, the "arrival in Northampton in 1672 of Solomon Stoddard" that "set the course of the valley's religious history."[20] Even if Stoddard hadn't been Edwards's grandfather, Edwards would have been greatly influenced by this towering figure. Stoddard made his powerful mark on New England by maintaining that the "morass in which the colonists found themselves . . . had originated in his peers' misguided attempts to sustain religious fervor by methods no longer effective, particularly the concept of restricted church membership."[21] Stoddard's boldest claim, however, about the inability of New England's clergy to meet the needs of their congregants in an increasingly complex society provided a legacy of vanguardism for Edwards. As Gura explains, Stoddard held that "New England's problems . . . stemmed from an embarrassing misunderstanding by the colony's founders, who in the eyes of their descendants could do no wrong. . . . who in their zeal to establish a Puritan commonwealth on New England's shores mistook their own notions for timeless truth."[22] Edwards's own conflict with one of these timeless truths, the *ordo salutis*, would become fertile ground for his reconceptualization of conversion. Edwards struggled with the orthodox pattern of the conversion experience, worrying in his diary in 1722 that he had not undergone "regeneration, exactly in those steps, in which divines say it is generally wrought," and writing eight months later, just before he received his degree from New Haven, that the "chief thing, that now makes me in any measure to question my good estate, is my not having experienced conversion in those particular steps, wherein the people of New England and anciently Dissenters in Old England, used to experience it."[23]

Edwards's notion of the "room of the idea" as a highly active conscious space energized by the ordinary work of the Spirit contrasts with Shepard's doctrine directing a saint's attention toward emptying the various "rooms" in the mind of the sins and corruption which block the influx of the Spirit. Saints undergoing the process of preparation, as Shepard and the Intellectual Fathers conceived it, had to make space in the various rooms of the mind for grace to enter. Edwards's "room of the idea" clarifies a significant departure from ideas about the mind and conversion evidenced in *The Parable of the Ten Virgins* and the faculty psychology and theology it represents. Shepard would preach that when a saint underwent the process of preparing for conversion, he or she waited for the Holy Spirit to come into the "room of those things which a man is full of now" (*PTV*, 302). This implies an "emptying" of those six things an individual is full of: sin, darkness, unbelief, Satan, self, and the world. During preparation a saint's conscience worked to empty these rooms so that the Spirit could fill them, respectively, with humiliation, illumination and revelation, faith, the Spirit, sanctification, and glory. This process under-scores the notion that a saint's role in conversion is wholly passive, in that he or she waits, having emptied these rooms, for the Spirit to fill them. True to the tenets of evangelical Calvinism, this process issued the experi-ence of being humbled before God and dependent upon Christ for all. Reception to grace arose, theoretically (or theologically) from "passivity" before Christ resulting from protracted meditation on sin, and though a saint was supposed to feel irresistibly drawn to close with Christ, as many of Shepard's congregants claim they initially feel, the experience of belief was deferred instead, conforming to his ministerial project.

Edwards, of course, also preached the necessity of humbling one's self before God and fighting against those pitfalls of human existence listed above. However, Edwards's belief in the active role consciousness played in piety compelled a new understanding and characterization of that "room" in which reception is created. Instead of creating reception through a clearing or emptying out of the rooms of the six ideas, Edwards recasts reception as a *filling* of the "room" of consciousness with all the actual and suggestive relations and contexts of any idea one wants to actu-alize. This element of desire Edwards privileges in his theory of con-sciousness radically disrupts the prevailing notions of how the mind works according to faculty psychology. Whereas in faculty psychology, an idea enters the mind through reason so it can be judged good or evil and reacted upon appropriately through the will, Edwards put the cart before the horse, as it were. For Edwards, an individual is introduced to an idea and then one's desire can determine the direction the soul takes, constitut-ing a significant break from Shepard's doctrine.

Edwards would deflate the power Shepard had invested in reason to prepare for the conversion experience, finding the epistemology of faculty psychology static and nonconductive. In Edwards's "The Mind" no. 17, he states his position with regard to his departure from the "Old Logick":

> One reason why, at first, before I knew other Logick, I used to be mightily pleased with the study of the Old Logick, was, because it was very pleasant to see my thoughts, that before lay in my mind jumbled without any distinction, ranged into order and distributed into classes and subdivisions, so that I could tell where they all belonged, and run them up to their general heads. For this Logick consisted much in Distribution and Definitions; and their maxims gave occasion to observe new and strange dependencies of ideas, and a seeming agreement of multitudes of them in the same thing, that I never observed before.[24]

Here Edwards recognizes the power Ramist logic had to "order and distribute" his thoughts, to arrange his "jumbled" thoughts into "new and strange dependencies." The pleasure he speaks of stems from the ability of Ramist logic, through its methodology, to categorize and arrange the ideas and things that make up God's universe, allowing saints to detect existent truths and their patterns and, thereby, to comprehend the *"infinitely exact, and precise, and perfectly stable Idea, in God's mind."*[25] Yet, Edwards's departure from this logic consists, as he explains, in the problems associated with this method. Ramist logic was an inherent part of Puritan epistemology, and for the preparationists following in the intellectual tradition, the methodology of logic lent a sense of accuracy to saints' perceptions of the Holy Spirit in their souls. Though Edwards ascribes pleasure associated with intellectual usefulness to the "Old Logick," the passage suggests that he abandoned it for exactly the kind of relationship to God this pleasure established. In light of the development of his epistemology of the affections, Edwards perceived the methodology of Ramist logic as shortsighted in its premise that access to God's ideas occurs when the intellect, through logic, reenacts the divine mind, thereby offering a firm mental grasp of its contents.[26]

Edwards's idealism would mark a significant break from the Puritan intellectual tradition, which built its theories of epistemology, theology, and natural philosophy on logic's method of setting all the particulars of God's universe in their places for transcription of the divine order. The "Old Logick" that Edwards would reject was a powerful tool for understanding. For the previous generation of divines it led to "true perceptions . . . contained in the arts; the arts then are descriptions of reality, enactments of God, and knowledge of them is knowledge of Him."[27] This ordering process led to the abstract ideas constituting the known truths about God's universe. For Edwards, as one can detect from his tone of detachment in "The Mind" no. 17, the pleasure one receives from the ordering process of Ramist logic could not compare to a new kind of logic offering a different experience with his ideas. As he states, it was "very pleasant" for him to watch his thoughts become ordered through "Distribution" and "Definitions" by the "Old "Logick." Yet, he has left unstated why he left the "Old Logick" behind. We can presume that it was for a new "method" offering a different relationship with his ideas. This method would be the idealism he adopted.

Edwards's most revolutionary claim about existence stemmed from his insight recorded in Misc. no. gg:

God did not create the world for nothing. 'Tis most certain that if there were not intelligent beings in the world, all the world would be without any end at all. For senseless matter, in whatever excellent order it is placed, would be useless if there were no intelligent beings at all. . . . Wherefore it necessarily follows that intelligent beings are the end of the creation, that their end must be to behold and admire the doings of God.[28]

As Wallace E. Anderson explains in his introduction to the *Scientific and Philosophical Writings*, it was shortly thereafter in Misc. no. pp, that Edwards, in denying the substantial and independent reality of the physical world, claimed that the "universe could have no existence unless it is known by intelligent beings," and maintained, instead, that it "depends immediately and necessarily for its existence upon God's continual creative activity."[29] Therefore, when Edwards claimed that the world "exists only mentally," he retired Ramist logic's method of transcribing a *substantial* world in favor of a new logic that accommodated the constantly unfolding nature of God's universe existing as an *ideal* world.[30] Edwards's objective idealism dovetailed with Locke's view that secondary qualities in objects, such as color and taste, did not exist in objects themselves, but in the mind. But Edwards also held that even primary qualities attributed to an objective world such as solidity, shape, or motion also exist in the mind of God, which he communicates to us through a train of ideas. Consequently, apprehension of this ideal world was, to quote Anderson again, "direct and immediate, and does not depend upon prior reflection and conscious methodical procedure."[31] Throughout Edwards's work we can see the refinements in his articulations of this experience of immediacy as he defended the basic tenets of Calvinism. In his writings on the will, virtue, original sin, conversion, and God's sovereignty, he continually returns to the project of clarifying the intersection of thought, feeling, and perception in an effort to esteem direct experience without providing fodder for his detractors who claimed he was inciting enthusiasm.

The New Nature of the Soul

The divines of the previous generation, such as Shepard, searched out the hidden divinity within the cosmos in an effort to comprehend God. Their belief in an objective truth to which they had access through technologia reinforced the notion of an abstract relation to God's universe and those truths hidden within it. The method of technologia, though guaranteeing a closure in the gap between subject and object, implicitly underscored the distance, generating a vision of God's divinity as removed and impersonal. However, as evidenced by Misc. no. 87, Edwards's idealism permitted a far more intimate relation between an individual and the divine, constructing a metaphysics whose teleology posited humanity's role in the divine plan: "Intelligent beings are created to be the consciousness of the universe, that they may perceive what God is and does. This can be nothing else but to perceive the excellency of what he is and does."[32]

To this shared end, however, in both Shepard's and Edwards's theology, the common operations of the Holy Spirit aid those who benefit from it by directing an individual's perception to what, in effect, is behind words and the doctrines and concepts they convey. Shepard preached on the distinction between "head" and "heart" knowledge, that a saint can catch glimpses of "things in themselves" in the spaces between words thus:

> Reason can see and discourse about words and propositions, and behold things by report, and to deduct one thing from another; but the Spirit makes a man see the things themselves, really wrapped up in those words. The Spirit brings spiritual things as well as notions before a man's eye; the light of the Spirit is like the light of the sun—it makes all things appear as they are. (*SB*, 127)

Shepard states very clearly here that words cannot represent a spiritual realm that is more "real" than what the words convey. Only the Spirit, as he says, makes "all things appear as they are," offering access to the perfect, stable idea of God's mind. In contrast then, to acquiring a notional understanding of things by report, the Spirit works in the present, generating receptivity to what is behind or "wrapped up" in the words and ideas that constitute scripture and doctrine, referred to by Edwards as "signs" when they are used only speculatively. Though Shepard's theology undertook to delineate and characterize the difference between "head" and "heart" knowledge of Christ, his ministry would ultimately undermine the conversion experience by fueling a more disciplined, rational relationship to God.

In *Religious Affections*, however, Edwards would offer his criticism of the kind of self-interest inherent in the reflective practice of discerning and disposing Shepard esteemed for determining belief. The faculty psychology of Shepard's day compartmentalized the faculties and placed emphasis on reason's responsibility for determining the will and stimulating the affections, one reason why conversion was often thought of by the Intellectual Fathers as "reason elevated." That compartmentalization characterized the affections, to which category Shepard ascribed the character of sin run rampant, as chaotic passions in need of lawful reasoning to bring them under control. Edwards's ideas about conversion, however, grew out of a different picture of the mind which saw the faculties not as distinct entities but as fused, bringing together sensible experience, understanding, and will into the concept of the affections. *Religious Affections* offers, in its twelve signs, the ways by which saints may know that they have undergone conversion by grounding that knowledge solidly within the realm of affections, which are the result of acquiring the spiritual sense. The spiritual sense and the new dispositions that attend it are, as Edwards explains in the first sign,

> no new faculties, but are new principles of nature. I use the word "principles," for want of a word of a more determinate signification. By a principle of nature in this place, I mean that foundation which is laid in nature, either old or new, for any particular manner or kind of exercise of the faculties of the soul; or a natural habit or foundation for action, giving a person ability and disposition to exert the faculties in exercises of such a certain kind; so that to exert the faculties in that kind of exercises, may be said to be his nature. So this new spiritual sense is not a new faculty of understanding, but it is a new foundation laid in the nature of the soul, for a new kind of exercises of the same faculty of understanding. So that new holy disposition of heart that attends this new sense, is not a new faculty of will, but a foundation laid in the nature of the soul, for a new kind of exercises of the same faculty of will. (*RA*, 206)

This definition attempts to describe the role that gracious affections play in a saint's mind, particularly how gracious affections affect certain faculties. The difference Edwards draws, that saints don't receive new faculties but receive a new foundation laid in the nature of the soul, allows him to foreground the central conception of his theology—that conversion and the influx of gracious affections change, not the faculties themselves, but how the faculties operate, and the idea that a saint can know his or her salvation through the "exercises" of a new nature of the soul. The distinction Edwards makes in the excerpt above is especially subtle. It allows him to characterize the new disposition as a holy operation but one that feels as "natural" as a habit. It is so ordinary, in fact, that his description is barely able to make the distinction.

Using analogy to convey this difficult concept, Edwards claims that these new exercises are as the "inward tendency of a stone" as it falls and "shows the way to the center of the earth, more exactly in an instant, than the ablest mathematician . . . could determine, by his most accurate observations, in a whole day" (*RA*, 284). Or, he argues, the new sense is as if a "man's heart be under the influence of an entire friendship, and most endeared affection to another," directing him "far more readily and exactly, to a speech and deportment, or manner of behavior" (*RA*, 283). *Religious Affections* is a treatise about *perception*, making the genuine mark of saint-hood a distinctive new worldview. In a moment that both recalls Shepard's investment in Ramist dialectic as a "mental art" and anticipates William James, Edwards calls a saint's rebirth a new "habit of . . . mind," and though for Edwards these awakenings are the result of a spiritual rebirth through Puritan conversion, the "room of the idea," without which conversion would be impossible, is an act of consciousness possible for all individuals including the unregenerate. In both of the analogies above, which describe a regenerate will, the emphasis is on how the new spiritual sense "shows the way" or directs saints "readily and exactly" in their actions. This cannot be emphasized enough. Edwards articulates here, through the examples of the stone or the friendship, how a new habit, conceived as a "new foundation laid in the nature of the soul" *feels*. In these descriptions, the new nature produces effortless actions, which, because they are new habits, indicate conversion. This means that saints can know they have undergone conversion because they can then detect a difference between old tendencies and new dispositions, and more importantly, saints themselves are the most effective judges of whether the transformation is real because *they* feel the difference. Especially in the example of finding the way to the center of the earth, where the mathematician is being pitted against the "inward tendency of the stone," we can hear Edwards's critique of Shepard's reliance on the sense of control and accuracy lent by his intellectual strategizing. Or, rather, we can hear the tortured calculations of his congregants attempting to establish a new habit of mind through the art of dialectic and to revive their faith in New England.

Sang Hyun Lee argues that Edwards's recognition of habit as the force behind piety and consciousness is the "most innovative element in Edwards' dynamic perspective on reality" because "dispositions and habits . . . can mediate between being and becoming, permanence and process."[33] Lee also points out that "habit functions automatically, in a nondiscursive way. But in this automatic character lies its power and influence" because habits and dispositions "determine the direction of all the intellectual and moral functions of the human self."[34] The automatic power of these new dispositions and habits, however, must be understood in their relation to the kind of power operating in the "room of the idea" that creates the context for their emergence. Because the "sense of the heart" represents the powers of the understanding, will, and sensible experience operating together, it entails an awareness, according to Roger Ward, "that the understanding is oriented toward an object that requires its *full function* to engage and that the will is also constrained by the same object as the proper or satisfying object of the soul's desire."[35] Edwards envisions these new habits and dispositions as a kind of iteration of the soul, even as he claims that it will feel like a new "principle of nature." The new dispositions are like tropings of personal identity—actions, thoughts, feelings, relations, and entire perspectives, may change toward the world even as most of a sense of self remains intact, giving the feeling of transformation an underlying sense of continuity with the past. These kinds of transformations that result in the spiritual sense and new habits are only achieved, however, through the kind of perceptual activity associated with the "room of the idea" where the will and understanding come together in the affections to stimulate the experience of an idea in all its possible contexts. Conversion happens at the moment when, during the height of reception, consciousness reaches its potential for awareness when the "room" fills with an idea and all its contextual radiations. These radiations, in turn, establish new relations with the world that are instatiated through a newly acquired habit or disposition. Indeed, Edwards's notion of the "room of the idea" creates the same kind of potential for perceptual, ideational, and spiritual *migrations* into a new spiritual disposition that Shepard had in mind when he adapted the morphology to accommodate New England as a revived means. In this way, for both Edwards's and Shepard's theologies an original relation to an idea is necessary for conversion. The difference of course is that whereas Edwards's triumph is in describing these relations in affective terms, Shepard is a master at providing the terms for calculating the odds of one's spiritual state.

Religious Affections as a Treatise on Perception

In the first chapter we saw Shepard admonishing his congregants to discern and dispose of the living acts of grace apparent in their experience according to an "exact rule of life" that the Lord provided. This method for evidencing the presence of the Spirit reflects Shepard's investment in the capacity of outward and visible acts to represent signs of grace and reason's capacity to provide certainty about these operations. In *The Parable of the Ten Virgins*, Shepard poses the basic questions that a saint may ask about the conversion experience: "What is this knowledge or seeing of the Lord?"; "How doth the soul see him as he is?"; "Is it possible to know [the Spirit], seeing that a false heart may go so far? especially to know it in itself?" (*PTV*, 120, 124, 221). However, the answers Shepard provides are essentially the template against which his congregants are expected to measure and judge their spiritual states. He admonishes them to "learn to judge of your faith, whether it be of the right make or no," and he provides ample reference and example for his congregants to do so (*PTV*, 129). What cannot be discoursed about (the actual felt relation to God during conversion) does make its way into his sermons, though he cannot describe it beyond stating that a saint will have a saving knowledge of Christ because he or she will know him "as he is." For this reason, Edwards's *Religious Affections* serves as a kind of companion piece to *The Parable of the Ten Virgins* because for as much of an intellectualizing of conversion *The Parable of the Ten Virgins* is, *Religious Affections* is a feat of equal depth in its attempt to describe the *felt* relation to God. Furthermore, in making gracious affections the new relation between a saint and the world and God, *Religious Affections* becomes a meditation on the new perceptive capabilities a saint acquires. The twelve signs are essentially the components and descriptors of not only saints' holy affections, but also their holy perceptions. Edwards's ideas about the mind allowed him to set forth a comprehensive insight into how the Spirit reformulates perception, taking up where Shepard leaves off when he explains in *The Parable of the Ten Virgins* that "there is a light of glory, whereby the elect see things in another manner: *to tell you how, they can not*" (*PTV*, 235; italics added).

In a comparison of Shepard's and Edwards's theories of conversion, this moment wherein Shepard states that the elect cannot tell how they "see things in another manner" foregrounds an epistemological issue at the heart of the ideas about the mind Shepard and Edwards held. The theory of the mind's operations associated with faculty psychology prohibited Shepard from being able to say how saints saw things in a different manner. In the sermons making up *The Parable of the Ten Virgins*, Shepard provides a map of the intellectual process through which saints can judge their behavior and their thoughts during the preparatory stages as well as after conversion. Yet, it is clear that the method of discerning and disposing, indeed a powerful perceptive lens, is applied to the spiritual state of saints whether or not they have undergone regeneration. Therefore, although Shepard proclaims that saints' perception is altered after conversion, that the "manner" in which they see things changes, his description of their relationship to the world and to themselves after conversion remains founded on a dynamic of perception that still consists of the intellectual task of discerning and disposing. Therefore, the exercises of the faculties do not change as they do in Edwards. Shepard's advice to his converted congregants, that a "thinking" Christian, understood as a judging Christian, is never deceived implies that how they interpret or perceive the world isn't impacted by the conversion experience, though they supposedly "see things in another manner." That Shepard does not or cannot describe the new perception could be attributed to the inability of his intellectualized discourse to represent the affective dimension of experience. It could also be attributed to the fact that the highly ordered, mechanistic conception of perception contained in faculty psychology could not accommodate or generate a new theory of perception resulting from a newly conceived dynamic with the world. Therefore, even after regeneration the saints' natural faculty for judgment remains unchanged and unchallenged as the primary way to assess their spiritual state. In addition, it continues to serve as the only reliable means for understanding experience.

Because the exercises of the faculties remain the same after regeneration for Shepard, the sense and experience offering certainty to saints about their conversion are also subject to the same perceptual and epistemological process of discerning and disposing. In fact, the issue of examining one's experience for the signs of grace is brought up for questioning in both *The Parable of the Ten Virgins* and in *Religious Affections*. It was a concern because too much attention paid to one's good estate was the sign of a hypocrite. After Shepard explains how saints should judge their experience against the "rule" the objection is raised: "But I look to Christ, I look to no work. If I have him I have all" (*PTV*, 224). The answer that follows explains that this statement is "true" but instructs saints to "first look to have him, to be comprehended by him, that so you may comprehend him. But because you look for all in him, *will you look for nothing from him?* Will you have Christ sit in heaven, *and not look that he subdue your lusts* by the work of his grace, and so sway in your hearts?" (*PTV*, 224; italics added). In this line of rhetorical questioning Shepard takes a basic tenet of Calvinist theology, that the witness of the Spirit is all the evidence needed for knowledge of regeneration, and drains it of its affective and transcendent power by rerouting the new perception back onto the saints' experience and what can be discerned and disposed toward certainty in intellectual knowledge. "Having" Christ, as it is represented in the ideas framed by Shepard's questions, does not suggest a new relation to the world or a new perception. Rather, the anxiety inherent in this line of questioning reflects a desire to keep Christ close by "comprehending" him, to know him in the only way Shepard is able to express it: by examining one's behavior, thus grounding Christ's presence in the realm of the knowable, the graspable, the certain.

Edwards, in turn, addresses the role that experience plays in examining one's state of regeneration in the second sign of *Religious Affections*, stating that the "first objective ground of gracious affections, is the transcendentally excellent and amiable nature of divine things, as they are in themselves; and not any conceived relation they bear to self, or self-interest" (*RA*, 240). In this sign Edwards discusses the focus or direction that a saint's perception takes after regeneration and problematizes the conception of "experience" in order to define that new direction. For Edwards, finding the workings of grace within experience entices hypocrites to

> rejoice in their admirable experiences: instead of feeding and feasting their souls in the view of what is without them, viz. the innate, sweet, refreshing amiableness of the things exhibited in the gospel, their eyes are off from these things, or at least they view them only as it were sideways; but the object that fixes their contemplation, is their experience; and they are feeding their souls, and feasting a selfish principle with a view of their discoveries: they take more comfort in their discoveries than in Christ discovered, which is the true notion of living upon experiences and frames; and not a using experiences as the signs, on which they rely for evidence of their good estate, which some call living on experiences: though it be very observable, that some of them who do so, are most notorious for living upon experiences, according to the true notion of it. (*RA*, 251–252)

In defining the term "living upon experiences" in this passage, Edwards places the perspective a mind acquires after conversion under scrutiny. Whereas Shepard provides a clear rationale for keeping one's perspective a judging or "thinking" one, to be watchful about whether Christ will "subdue" one's "lusts," Edwards presents the problem of "living upon experiences" in its complexity. He clearly states that a saint who takes more comfort in "Christ discovered" has truly received grace, and the sign of hypocrites is that they feast on "their discoveries." Looking for the benefits of grace in one's experience for evidence of conversion, which are the instructions Shepard gives his congregants, is for Edwards not the perspective a saint acquires after regeneration; in fact, the self-interest inherent in reflecting on one's "discoveries" generates the wrong interpretation of the phrase "living on experiences."

For Edwards, that an individual looks to his or her good works or takes pleasure in obedience to the Bible, both outward signs of grace, does not mean he or she acquired a gracious perspective. Next, he provides yet another layer to this examination of perspective by admitting that the meaning of "living on experiences" is a slippery one in action, that some who examine their experiences for signs of grace can actually be doing it according to the "true notion" of the phrase. Edwards's explanation takes several twists in direction in his questioning of the meaning of the phrase "living on experiences"; by lending a confusing multiplicity to the issue at stake through layering the perspectives on it with the use of the fragments following the colon, the explanation reflects Edwards's belief that judging one's experience for evidence of grace is an endeavor rife with the uncertainty of mere glimpses or guesses at knowing the truth. As we shall see in this chapter, this passage echoes what is implicated throughout his writings, that meaning does not rest in discrete moments of experience served up as certain evidence of grace, but in a pattern of actions and perceptions reflecting a new disposition.

In this second sign, Edwards also begins to build his epistemology of the affections. He states that the second sign establishes the "objective ground of gracious affections" as the "transcendentally excellent and amiable nature of divine things," drawing attention to that new direction a regenerate perspective takes and, therefore, the new approach to the world and self. The new spiritual sense, in laying a new foundation in the soul and changing the exercises of the faculties, establishes gracious affections as the dynamic mediating relations between a saint and the objects of experience. These relations are the result of the affections, or a saint's "feeling mind," a phrase that captures the liveliness of the relation inherent in the new perspective. The power of this perspective seems to reside in its ability to propel an individual outside everyday experiences of time and human concerns:

A true saint, when in the enjoyment of true discoveries of the sweet glory of God and Christ, has his mind too much captivated and engaged by what he views without himself, to stand at that time to view himself, and his own attainments: it would be a diversion and loss which he could not bear, to take his eye off from the ravishing object of his contemplation, to survey his own experience, and to spend time in thinking with himself, what an high attainment this is, and what a good story I now have to tell others. Nor does the pleasure and sweetness of his mind at that time, chiefly arise from the consideration of the safety of his state, or anything he has in view of his own qualifications, experiences, or circumstances; but from the divine and supreme beauty of what is the object of his direct view, without himself; which sweetly entertains, and strongly holds the mind. (RA, 252–253)

In this passage Edwards specifically characterizes the direction of a regenerate perspective and the effect that gracious affective relations have on the mind. This perspective involves a level of engagement that seems to collapse the subject/object boundaries between what a saint "views without himself" and the saint's mind that is simultaneously experiencing the object's "sweetness." The spiritual sense a saint acquires in conversion allows the faculties to respond to the power of Christ's glory in such a way that is rooted in religious affections and that paralyzes or transcends intellectual operations of the mind. The beauty of Christ's glory "holds the mind" in a position of total reception loosened from personal contexts, grounding a saint's understanding of the "ravishing object" in an encounter that makes "certainty" of conversion available only through an aesthetic experience.

Because *Religious Affections* is an effort to describe the new spiritual sense and the perception that results, throughout the text, for every sign, Edwards consistently comes back to the idea that the new spiritual foundation laid in the soul allows the Spirit to dwell there, operating in a way previously unknown to the saint. Among the tactics used to succeed at this seemingly impossible descriptive task are the inclusion of excerpts and examples from the Bible supporting the argument of each sign, Edwards's famous use of carefully chosen words and phrases that surround and penetrate an idea he means to express from different perspectives, and the repetitive use of images and key words, used to elicit the *experience* of the idea he means to communicate. Whereas all of these tactics serve to undergird Edwards's descriptions of the signs, he also consistently returns to examples of what these perceptions and affections are not, and although he quotes heavily from Shepard's doctrine in his footnotes throughout *Religious Affections* to clarify his ideas, his response to Shepard also inhabits the main text through Edwards's continual critique of the "Old Logick."

I would argue that Edwards's description of gracious affections leans on Shepard's doctrine in these contiguously implicit and explicit ways. His tacit conversation with Shepard about the limitations of the "Old Logick" is an integral part of *Religious Affections* in that he continually returns to the idea that the new spiritual sense is unlike any capacity natural man may embody. In the first sign he explains that God may "move" upon man as he "moved upon the face of the waters," and so "he may act upon the minds of men [in] many ways, and not communicate himself any more than when he acts on inanimate things" (*RA*, 202). In addition, this new dwelling of the Spirit differs from any "awakenings and convictions that natural men may have" because "conscience *naturally* gives men an apprehension of right and wrong" and the "Spirit of God . . . helps conscience against the stupefying influence of worldly objects and their lusts" (*RA*, 207; italics added). In the fourth sign, Edwards faces the "Old Logick" head-on when he claims that the new spiritual sense, in acting like a new sight or perception, is even more remarkable than if a man who had been born blind "then at once should have the sense of seeing imparted to him, in the midst of the clear light of the sun, discovering a world of visible objects" (*RA*, 275). This last analogy conveys his point particularly well: having had a new spiritual sense laid in the foundation of the soul, saints see things that they couldn't before.

Of course, Edwards's treatise itself is an embodiment of the immense difficulties of actually describing the new spiritual sense. Though Edwards had the advantage over Shepard in undertaking this descriptive project, Edwards scholars have long recognized his struggles to express his meaning apparent in the treatise. There are, indeed, moments when he conveys the profundity of his idea through all the rhetorical magic of his language, but then there are times when his statements are simple declarations that attempt to capture the heart of the matter, as when he explains that "this spiritual sense" is "infinitely more noble" than "any other *principle of discerning* that a man naturally has" (*RA*, 275; italics added). That Shepard's discourse couldn't accommodate a description of how "the elect see things in another manner" is directly related to his doctrine that intellectualized the conversion experience and the process of looking for signs of grace. Edwards's notion of the "sense of the heart" and, more specifically, of religious affections offered a way to speak about how the elect "see things in another manner" in such a way that made "seeing" more than an act of understanding or comprehending—it made "seeing" an aesthetic response:

> This holy relish is a thing that discerns and distinguishes between good and evil, between holy and unholy, *without being at the trouble of a train of reasoning*. As he who has a true relish of external beauty, knows what is beautiful by looking upon it: he stands in no need of a train of reasoning about the proportion of features, in order to determine whether that which he sees be a beautiful countenance or no: he needs nothing but only the glance of his eye. (*RA*, 281; italics added)

Edwards states in his preface to *Religious Affections* that he will enumerate "what are the distinguishing qualifications of those that are in favor with God, and entitled to his eternal rewards" (*RA*, 84). The main issue surrounding conversion remained for Edwards that of characterizing "saving" knowledge of Christ. Receptivity to that "saving" knowledge also depended on tapping into a spiritual realm that existed beyond the bounds of reason and accessing this realm still involved the work of the Holy Spirit, but Edwards's ideas about the mind's operations meant that consciousness brought into view God's actions and thereby fulfilled God's purposes. In other words, consciousness revealed God's determinations in the course of experience. Shepard's flock would have relied on the power of conscience and the doctrine of preparation to determine which stage of the conversion process they had reached by judging themselves according to the "rule" of scripture and locating their progress within the morphology. A parishioner of Shepard's judged each thought and feeling to determine whether or not the Holy Spirit was at work primarily by detecting a sequential order. By compartmentalizing the dynamics of consciousness and casting the will as "reason elevated," faculty psychology made identifying belief—the movement of the will into new perspectives or relations with the world—difficult to decipher. When they encountered the idea of belief, they attended to it according to the habit of mind advanced by Ramist logic, interrupting the feeling of conviction necessary for conversion. The actual will to believe is halted by this habit. Someone following Edwards, however, would have practiced piety through what he called "attention of the mind in thinking." Both avenues to grace involved a keen observance of one's interior life, and both had discovering God's will and glory as their main objective, but Edwards's "attention of the mind in thinking" removed the burden of tethering one's experience to a recognized doctrinal form. Moreover, because the ordinary work of the Spirit was operating in all souls—or consciousnesses—every man and woman had access to the spiritual realm "wrapped up in words" through the "room of the idea."

Knowledge as Felt Experience

Edwards was, in fact, interested in a sequence of events, but his theories about the mind made consciousness the "ordering" process revealing God's divine and natural operations in the universe. The theory that the material world exists only in the mind made thinking and perception the generator of truth. That is, he believed that the ideas "raised in the mind" in the course of experience corresponded to the laws of God's operations because truth is the *"consistency and agreement of our ideas, with the ideas of God."*[36] Thus, truths emerge when there is the "agreement of our ideas with existence" because they correspond to the natural laws of material reality through God's exciting the ideas in our minds.[37] Rejecting a conception of the world as constituted by individual things and substances existing independent of relations, as well as the Ramist logic used to detect truths among these objects, Edwards's new method of "attention of the mind in thinking" located God's operations within the mind and the detection of truth a profoundly immediate and personal experience. Edwards's idealism permitted him to esteem a kind of self-reflection that was a form of piety rather than a form of self-interest because the attention paid to one's own stream of thought was an act of bringing God's universe into existence and glorifying him. As a result, the moment of conversion, previously broken up into observable units by Shepard, is recast by Edwards as so fluid that all a saint can do is watch it happen in the "room of the idea." The idea that one can or, in fact, *should* observe the workings of God remains consistent between Shepard's and Edwards's theology. However, Edwards's conception of the "room of the idea" allows him to characterize the efforts of thinking, previously associated with preparation, as a kind of spectacle of God's will to be witnessed in consciousness, so even when saints practice "attention of the mind in thinking" they are experiencing the kind of "passivity" associated with merely *watching* God's determinations become manifest.

Edwards had drawn on Locke's theory of epistemology in arguing that truths enter discourse through the use of signs in language that serve their purpose in casual communication. However, he also asserted that the common associations related to a sign used in casual discourse do not, as signs, cultivate receptivity to new associations, arguments, or inferences within thinking and therefore within language. To reiterate, the "room of the idea" becomes the space of reception generating consciousness, and Edwards characterizes this "room" as the mental space given to thought "employed about things themselves." Here, Edwards uses the same theological terms as Shepard to describe a perception that penetrates discursive meaning, but the "room of the idea," which locates that space in consciousness, posits a new relation to the "material" world. Essentially, in Edwards, one views "things themselves" by the actual presence of the idea occurring when an idea is received with all its contextual or suggestive relations. This "actuality" implies that the idea takes on a certain material force when the mind is stretched or overwhelmed in a way that is similar to what Shepard advised when he preached to his flock to undergo the conscious and strenuous task of "comprehending" the idea of God's love in all its infinitude. One finds this emphasis on taxing or stretching the mind's limits in both Shepard and Edwards, but in Edwards, the mind's comprehending work is not distinguished from the felt dimension of that experience. In conflating the understanding and the will, he was able to conceptualize a piety for his parishioners that granted thinking the power to generate a *total* experience of any idea, imbuing that process with the movement or conduction of the soul necessary to faith and belief.

He arrived at the concept through a consideration of Locke's empiricist philosophy, and it led him to ground the workings of grace in the mind's experiences with what Locke called the "idea" of something (defined by Locke as "an object of the understanding").[38] In the course of one's experiences with ideas (and the forms of language and concepts they overwhelm), the process of codification is triggered. But, before that has happened, an individual encounters what is, as Shepard had put it, "wrapped up in words." This receptive moment for Edwards marks a moment of epistemological potential in the "room of the idea." God excites what Edwards calls an "actual idea," which he characterizes as an idea received with all of its relations. When a connection is formed between an idea and its new suggestion or association, one does not perceive the relation between the ideas themselves. Edwards is very specific on this point. Knowledge, he says, is the "perception of the union or disunion of ideas." The distinction is important because according to his logic, the relations between ideas exist before they become discursive, opening to view the mind of God; therefore, they are not technically perceptible, though they may be felt or intuited. Knowledge is not formed through the connections that are *discerned* between ideas, but, as Edwards states in "The Mind," it is formed through the "perceiving whether two or more ideas belong to one another." Wallace E. Anderson clarifies this description thus: "The perception of union or disunion, as Edwards speaks of it, is not the recognition of a relation among the ideas themselves, but a recognition of *the mind's own inability to act otherwise* with regard to them."[39] This is a subtle but important distinction that Edwards makes about the nature of truth, and it rests upon the notion found in his idealism that "all truth is in the mind, and only there. It is ideas, or what is in the mind, alone, that can be the object of the mind; and what we call Truth, is a consistent supposition of relations."[40] Therefore, knowledge occurs according to the stated method of God's acting with respect to the habits of the mind and, because this is the method for how all knowledge happens, it forms the criteria for how *any* belief is generated about God as well as scientific and philosophical truths. Because an individual only perceives the union or disunion of ideas, convictions about anything can emerge *without having arguments to support them*, and these beliefs are "governed by natural dispositions of the mind."[41] Within Edwards's framework, "assurance" is a term that can denote the feeling of having "closed with Christ" during conversion but also of having perceived a new philosophical proposition. Assurance carries each belief forward because the propelling force is the same. Every truth, whether divine or natural, is made apparent in the thinking process itself which accords with God's stated methods of acting. That realm "wrapped up in words," which for Shepard contained the spiritual knowledge behind scripture, exists for Edwards as a space in consciousness where all truths are formed, not only scriptural ones.

The "room of the idea," then, is the space in consciousness where God's determinations structuring the material as well as the spiritual realm are actualized and therefore realized. Through the work of common grace, God allows for actual ideas to be excited in those who haven't undergone conversion, and these ideas are the conduits through which saving grace is introduced. These ideas become, in other words, the "preparatory" stages in the process of conversion, equating an active, lively consciousness with piety. Edwards conflates the work of the Holy Spirit with the processes located in the "room of the idea," thereby situating the conversion experience within consciousness and making the Holy Spirit the conductive force behind knowledge. Consciousness becomes figured as a conductive imaginary in which spiritual and philosophical/scientific truths unfold, bringing God's world into being through thinking and simultaneously leading to the indoctrination of new truths.

Edwards's idealism, therefore, allowed him to characterize faith as a force of the mind. Consciousness revealed all of God's truths, material and spiritual, and the actualizing of these ideas and relations of God's universe in the mind of a saint meant encountering truths in consciousness as sense experience. Edwards adopted Locke's notion that knowledge is gained in the course of sense experience, but whereas Locke held that conscious states subsist in the spiritual or material bodies themselves that are encountered, Edwards believed that one's state of consciousness is immediately produced by God. In other words, sensory experience consists in God's communication of his substance to a mind. The "room of the idea," therefore, is the conscious space where God brings his world into being through his actualization of the world as it is experienced in the mind. The experience of conversion becomes one aspect of the actualizing work of grace—it is the ultimate relation when the idea of God becomes to a saint more than what is represented by a word. The idea of God's love is actualized and, therefore, *felt* in the "room of the idea" during the moment of justifying faith, and as with every other moment of actualization, the space "wrapped up in words" becomes illuminated, and a saint is conducted irresistibly toward a new understanding. In the case of "closing" with ideas about the spiritual and natural world, one perceives the union or disunion of new associations with old ones, thus one can *feel* knowledge happening as a sensory experience before it becomes discursive.

Because of the role that consciousness played in piety, Edwards would spend much intellectual energy describing this space that brought God's universe into being. As the conductive imaginary for truth, its operations, characteristics, and boundaries became the subject of Edwards's scrutiny. This chapter has attempted to show that Edwards's idealism supplied the platform for many of his reconceptualizations of and departures from the theology, natural philosophy, and epistemology of his forefathers, and I have noted the fact that as a part of his idealism Edwards embraced the uncertain nature of knowledge of God. The extent to which uncertainty played a role in the unfolding of God's universe for Edwards, however, is what marks Edwards as a significant transitional figure between Shepard and Emerson.

The Relational Structure of Uncertainty

The testimonies of Shepard's Puritans provide a picture of that process by which an individual interpreted the movement or dynamics of his or her will in the effort to determine whether or not they believed. Because many of the testimonies capture the struggle to recover from the disappointing effects of migrating to the Bay Colony, they provide a picture of the knotty and often painful relations existing between a saint and the environment. These painful relations, of which the migration is a pronounced example, stem from the fact that one's spiritual journey was rife with uncertainty. This was a paradox inherent in Puritan spirituality, that no matter how diligently a saint underwent the process of preparation and then actually converted, his or her ordinary experiences inevitably intruded, throwing up another interpretive hurdle causing doubt to flare up again. For Shepard, conversion was a matter of distilling as much uncertainty from the process as possible, to the extent that he shunned a preaching style that would bolster the affective qualities of the experience belonging to the humbling, preparatory stages in order to promote the intellectual stability provided by a ministry focused on spiritual discipline. The picture of the mind that faculty psychology provided and the epistemological certainty offered by Ramist logic laid out clear rules of reasoning that attempted to shut out or deflect the role that uncertainty played in discovering truth. The confessions of Shepard's saints illustrate that very battle to regain a sense of certainty or expectation for New England's place in their regeneration. The axiomatic response that re-invents New England's role as a means to grace serves to cement it within

Shepard's doctrine of preparation. *The Parable of the Ten Virgins*, there-fore, is a collection of sermons providing a template for reasoning, guiding saints in a journey to find stable, clear, unalterable truths about the condi-tion of the universe and their souls.

Edwards's idealism, on the other hand, in making consciousness the realm of God's universe, allowed him to recognize a kind of horizon or fringe to the mind beyond which existed truths that would become known through daily living and experience. His idealism created a horizon in the mind toward which the understanding should always be straining in search of the truth. What lies within the fringe may be beyond one's ability to see or understand distinctly, but Edwards is very clear that this fringe in consciousness is valuable because it is the space where potential truths reside. Edwards's idealism would generate new "rules of reasoning" marking yet another significant departure from Shepard: whereas Shepard built a template for reasoning that attempted to distill uncer-tainty from the process, only recognizing it as a threat to the spiritual discipline he worked to maintain in his parishioners' lives, Edwards the-orized that one should look directly into the horizons of consciousness in the search for truth. He would argue that the reasoning process requires a healthy respect for both the horizon and the need (when the situation calls for it) to make our ideas clear:

> It is no matter how abstracted our notions are—the further we pene-trate and come to the prime reality of the thing, the better; provided we can go to such a degree of abstraction, and carry it out clear. We may go so far in abstraction, that, although we may thereby, in part, see Truth and Reality, and farther than ever was seen before, yet we may not be able more than just to touch it, and to have a few obscure glances. We may not have strength of mind to conceive clearly of the Manner of it. We see farther indeed, but it is very obscurely and indistinctly. We had better stop a degree or two short of this, and abstract no farther than we can conceive of the thing distinctly, and explain it clearly: otherwise we shall be apt to run into error, and confound our minds. (*Mind*, 50)

Because consciousness reveals God's hidden will through the vicissi-tudes of daily experience, Edwards's "room of the idea" is a vital recogni-tion of the *contextual* nature of perception and knowledge and the power this context has to move the mind. This relationship between perception, knowledge, and context is best articulated in Edwards's *Freedom of the Will*, written eight years after *Religious Affections* in response to the threat of Arminianism and its adherents' revolt against the doctrine of irresistible grace. The issue was a serious one for Calvinists because the Arminian belief in self-determination shut God out of the world. The *Freedom of the Will* is Edwards's defense against the Arminian accusation that Calvinism's tenet of predestination denied man his liberty. The entire inquiry rests on a couple of short, concise sections at the beginning of the work spelling out a theory of perception and defining the will's relation to that perception. Edwards begins by defining the will as "that by which the mind chooses anything. The faculty of the will is that faculty or power or principle of mind by which it is capable of choosing: an act of the will is the same as an act of choosing or choice."[42] These acts of "choosing" are at the heart of his argument for the will's freedom, and he is careful to enumerate the contextual factors that "determine" our choices and will. He makes the argument that the "motive" standing the strongest "in the view of the mind" determines the will, and that by motive he means "that which moves, excites or invites the mind to volition, whether that be one thing singly, or many things conjunctly."[43] To stress this point he clarifies that whatever the motive is it must be "extant in the view . . . or perceiving faculty. Nothing can induce or invite the mind to will or act anything, *any further than it is perceived*," and these motives, or that which moves the mind to act, is termed by Edwards as "good" or the "greatest apparent good."[44]

These formulations underscore the characterization of the mind he began as early as 1719 with the ideas he began to jot down during his education at the Collegiate School entitled "Notes on the Mind." They build a picture of a "feeling mind" that seeks out harmonious relations to the environment. Whatever draws "the inclination" or moves the will must be that which "suits the mind" and is ultimately "good." Interestingly, by the end of these introductory sections, Edwards has dropped the use of the term "determine" to express the relationship between an individual and the environment and has replaced it with the verb "is." His final definition, that the "will always *is* as the greatest apparent good *is*," binds an individual inextricably to the environment, characterizing human experience as harmonious with the environment and annihilating, through an *act* of perception, the distance between subject and object in an intimate way.[45]

Edwards's purpose in these opening sections of *Freedom of the Will* tends to focus on linking the will's inclination to the apparentness of objects in view. This notion captures the contextual nature of perception and knowledge, and his definition of the will (that it is "as the greatest apparent good is") makes experience the grounds for epistemology because all knowledge is revealed through the degrees of an individual's felt relation to God. Experience, for Edwards, offers the possibility of "finding out Truth" because an individual can only have "very few in view at once," unlike God who has "all in one view" and "perfect ideas of all things at once" (*Mind*, 52). The will, as the felt inclination toward one's environment, whether it is a prairie, a city, or an idea, moves an individual *by degrees* into relations with the mind of God, and this movement constitutes a harmony with God's world manifesting as the "pleasures of the senses" and not as, Edwards states, the "object of judgment" (*Mind*, 44). Consequently, this pleasure emerges from an unseen aspect of experience to which we respond on a felt or aesthetic level—there exists a "proportion of motion" occurring, for example, as a result of the pleasing vibrations received from a piece of music. The inclination of the will bends in accordance to this proportion of motion because the "organs are so contrived that, upon the touch of such and such particles, there shall be a regular and harmonious motion of the animal spirits" (*Mind*, 44).

Edwards's phrase for this harmonious relation to God is an individual's "consent to Being," a phrase that captures his departure from Shepard because it explicitly grants an individual an active role in both reasoning and his or her spiritual journey. This active role manifests as a kind of seeking out of harmony:

> How exceedingly apt are we, when we are sitting still, and accidentally casting our eye upon some marks or spots in the floor or wall, to be ranging of them into regular parcels and figures: and, if we see a mark out of its place, to be placing of it right, by our imagination; and this, even while we are meditating on something else. So we may catch ourselves at observing the rules of harmony and regularity, in the careless motions of our heads or feet, and when playing with our hands, or walking about the room. (*Mind*, 45)

Once again, Edwards returns to the central role that *observation* plays in one's harmonious relation to God's will. In the above example, Edwards reflects on how automatic and natural it is for the feeling mind to seek harmony. Though in this example Edwards uses a wonderfully mundane image to express how powerless one is to resist this urge to seek harmony, the real insight he provides is yet again about the piety practiced in "attention of the mind in thinking." In the above example he writes about how the mind enjoys arranging marks on the wall into "regular parcels" so that "we may catch ourselves at observing the rules of harmony." There is in this excerpt, however, not only a statement *that* the mind seeks regularity, or a description about *how* the mind seeks regularity, but an argument that this seeking of harmony is itself a form of observing God's rules or laws of regularity. For Edwards, when one attends to the mind's process of seeking these relations it is a form of following or *observing* God's laws. It is the same pious attentiveness he ascribes to the metacognitive practice that occurs in the "room of the idea" where one observes one's relations to God unfolding through the "sense of the heart."

The method of thought imagined by Edwards in his theory of the "attention of the mind in thinking" and the central role that observation plays in discovering God's will in consciousness outlined above support the claims David Jacobson develops that characterize Edwards as a proto-pragmatist figure. Jacobson clarifies Edwards's theory of knowledge as a "logic of relations" by refuting previous attempts by Edwards scholars to claim him as either an empiricist or an idealist and placing him, rather, in a philosophical tradition leading to Charles Sanders Peirce, William James, and John Dewey who embraced the pragmatic method. He claims that Edwards's concept of the "sense of the heart" does not represent some "vague emotionalism," but consists of a "method of judgement that conflates understanding and will in a new *propositional capacity*."[46] Jacobson argues that in rejecting the assumption that reason can provide sure grounds of knowledge found in both empiricism and idealism Edwards was able to develop this "logic of relations" by refuting the category of substance necessary to the methodology and claims of certainty inherent in Ramist logic.

According to Jacobson, Edwards wanted to establish a method of thought that understood proposition as relational, underscoring what is "implicated throughout his writings, that meaning rests, if not in a substantial ground, then in the effective relations—or the effects of relations—that can be observed."[47] Because Edwards identifies truth as a "consistent supposition of relations between what is the object of the mind," he places meaning and truth, Jacobson explains, "in the problematic mode," rendering assertions of truth as hypothetical or provisional. Furthermore, because the "sense of the heart" involves inclinations, or has a directional effect, affections characterize the new propositional judgment as one that "has meaning only to the extent that one is willing to act upon it: a proposition, therefore, that bears within it the *conviction* of the individual."[48] It is, finally, "derived from the circumstances in which it emerges, and it directly responds to them, with an assertion of what might be, or more exactly, of what the individual is *willing* to suppose is the case."[49] The propositional capacity that Jacobson describes consists of the exercises of the mind occurring in the "room of the idea," and, more specifically, in the power that the "room" derives from its dynamics of contextualization. The "room" offers hypothetical truths, but a truth only gains meaning if one is, as Jacobson points out, willing to act on it. Propositional judgments that may be generated in the "room" have no bearing, pragmatically speaking, if they do not result in conviction and become, as William James would say, what "*happens* to an idea."[50]

The Relational Power of Evangelical Humiliation

In the sixth sign of *Religious Affections* Edwards addresses this moment of conviction or willingness that, he argues, arises out of the experience of evangelical humiliation. The idea of evangelical humiliation is central to both Shepard's and Edwards's descriptions of the conveyance of grace and resulting conversion in *The Parable of the Ten Virgins* and *Religious Affections* because, as Shepard explained in *The Parable of the Ten Virgins*, "for though Christ will convey rich grace to his people, yet it shall be by love" (*PTV*, 62). The feeling of being overwhelmed by God's love was, for Shepard, the moment when a saint couldn't resist the influx of grace, but, as we saw in the previous chapter, in describing that moment, Shepard held fast to an intellectual tradition, casting that moment in terms of "comprehending" God's love, an act of volition that undercut the feeling of passivity Shepard's saints were supposed to feel. However, Edwards states in the sixth sign of *Religious Affections* that it is only out of a *heart* overcome with gracious humility that "all truly holy affections do flow" (*RA*, 339). Because Edwards's theories of the mind and religious experience inhere within the idea of evangelical humiliation, the experience and the view of the self resulting from it are the most important indicators of a change in the nature of the soul.

Restricted to the experience of spiritual conversion, evangelical humiliation indicates a change in the nature of the soul for Edwards because the idea of God's love becomes more than just a sign in the room of the idea—it becomes an experience allowing saints to observe their relations with God resulting from the actualization of the idea of God's love, triggering the conviction necessary to act on the experience.[51] In order to convey the extent to which the description of evangelical humiliation demonstrates Edwards's "logic of relations" it is necessary to quote at length. In the passage below I have placed emphasis on those terms and phrases that cohere into a description of conversion capturing Edwards's ideas about the mind and the "sense of the heart," and ultimately, that dynamism occurring only in the liminal space of relation:

But that is the nature of true grace and spiritual light, that it opens to a person's view the infinite *reason* there is that he should be *holy* in a high degree. And the more grace he has, the more this is opened to view, the greater *sense* he has of the infinite excellency and glory of the divine Being, and of the infinite dignity of the person of Christ, and the boundless *length* and *breadth*, and *depth* and *height*, of the love of Christ to sinners. And as grace increases, the *field opens* more and more to a *distant view*, till the *soul is swallowed up* with the *vastness of the object*, and the person is astonished to think how much it becomes him to love this God, and this glorious Redeemer, that has so loved man, and how little he does love. And so the more he apprehends, the more the smallness of his grace and love appears strange and wonderful: and therefore is more ready to think that others are beyond him. For wondering at the littleness of his own grace, he can scarcely believe that so strange a thing happens to other saints: 'tis amazing to him, that one that is really a child of God, and that has actually received the saving benefits of that unspeakable love of Christ, should love no more: and he is apt to look upon it as a thing peculiar to himself, a strange and exempt instance; for he sees only the outside of other Christians, but he sees his own inside.

Here the readers may possibly object, that love to God is really increased, in proportion as the knowledge of God is increased; and therefore how should an increase of knowledge in a saint, make his love appear less, in comparison of what is known? To which I answer, that although grace and the love of God in the saints, be answerable to the degree of knowledge or sight of God; yet it is not in proportion to the object seen and known. The soul of a saint, by having something of God opened to sight, is *convinced of much more than is seen*. There is something that is seen, that is wonderful; and that sight brings with it a strong *conviction* of something vastly beyond, that is *not immediately seen*. So that the *soul* at the same time, is astonished at its *ignorance*, and that it *knows so little*, as well as that it loves so little. And as the soul, in a spiritual view, is *convinced* of infinitely more in the object, *yet beyond sight*; so it is convinced of the *capacity* of the soul, of knowing vastly more, if the clouds and darkness were but removed. Which causes the soul, in the enjoyment of a spiritual view, to complain greatly of spiritual ignorance, and want of love, and *long and reach after more knowledge*, and more love. (*RA*, 324–25; italics added)

The passage is a description of the "room of the idea" in which the idea of God's love is actualized, thereby opening up a space where belief, or conviction, in "something vastly beyond" is generated. During conversion, grace opens to a saint a view of the "reason there is that he should be holy in a high degree." In fact, this passage demonstrates what James Hoopes has argued, that in Edwards, an individual experiences conversion when grace conveys the new idea or "reason" why a saint should be holy. Though saints may have a doctrinal notion of holiness, they have yet to *experience* the reason why they should be holy. It is a subtle but important distinction that a saint receives a new idea through grace. This view happens by the simultaneous experience of the intellect and the heart in conversion, for as Edwards shows, with the increase of a saint's "reason" for being holy, the "sense" of divine glory coordinately grows. That simultaneity leads the saint to experience the "boundless length and breadth, and depth and height" of Christ's love, an important descriptor of the magnitude of the love, figured in terms of being overwhelmed sensorially. The infinitude of Christ's love represented in the passage above was also the central image for Shepard used to prompt the conversion experience. Its use and unique placement within the three sermons thus far examined points to its role as a conductive image or idea, stimulating a sensory experience in the case of Edwards and the earlier Shepard and an intellectual experience in the case of the later Shepard, whose particular presentation of the idea bespoke his emphasis on spiritual discipline.

The role a saint's perception plays in conversion is central to this passage in that the *view* increases as grace increases—a field of vision "opens more and more," emphasizing the highly active state of perception that conversion entails for Edwards. It is an experience when the entire self, through heightened reason, sense, and perception, is propelled by grace beyond the normal bounds until the "soul is swallowed up with the vastness of the object." In fact, it is a saint's active perception, resulting from grace of course, that seems to trigger the transcendent moment. Yet, the collapse of the boundary between subject and object, the transcendence itself, does not signal the end of the conversion experience. Instead, it prompts a new view that turns back on the self, establishing a new understanding of a saint's relationship to God through humiliation. Edwards explains that grace operates to affect a perspective offering the experience of transcendence which leaves in its wake a fresh view of one's "inside" because "the more he apprehends, the more the smallness of his grace and love appears strange and wonderful." It is easy to underestimate the role that humility plays in the conversion process described here, but the idea that transcendence necessarily involves a view of one's own "spiritual ignorance, and want of love" and generates a longing to "reach after more knowledge" of the state of one's soul is a figuring of conversion that places self-reckoning at central stage in this imagining of the mind. The idea that conversion leaves old worldviews, knowledge, and selves in its wake will become an important factor in Emerson's literary style and James's pragmatism.

That moment of transcendence described above includes yet another aspect bringing to bear the feeling of conviction attending a "sense of the heart" that David Jacobson discusses. As Edwards states, having "something of God opened to sight" convinces a saint of something "vastly beyond," or "much more" than is seen. A saint is convinced of "infinitely more in the object, yet beyond sight" and convinced of the "capacity of the soul of knowing much more." In Edwards's rendering of this aspect of conversion, a saint becomes convinced, or, in other words, *willing to believe* in the "capacity of the soul" to move beyond the boundaries of ignorance or old knowledge. The term "convince" derives from the Latin *convincere* and means to refute, convict, or prove, and if what is "proved" in this passage is the "capacity of the soul," then Edwards articulates what Shepard could not, that a will to believe can happen under circumstances, or in certain contexts, wherein the proposition is hypothetical, and one can, through a feeling of potential, and not necessarily with a clear truth in sight, feel convinced of one's regeneration.[52] Because of his idealism, Edwards ventured a legitimate place for uncertainty in the formation of knowledge by permitting a space within consciousness inhabited by obscure and indistinct truths. This picture of the mind casts conversion as a continual process of searching for those truths, only clear and distinct by degree, yet representative of the next horizon of a saint's potential and therefore the direction the soul must aim for. Ironically, Edwards's idealism actualized Shepard's injunction to his parishioners through an instatement of the "vague," to use James's term for the "necessary condition for the exploratory search for new truths."[53] Yet, that Edwards recognized the quality of the "vague" in consciousness as a kind of saving disorientation does not mean that he believed events were random and meaningless. In fact, his *instatement* of the "vague" may have led to his *reinstatement* of the testimony of conversion as the test of church membership. As a Calvinist, he remained committed to the idea that a saint could still testify to the cause of his or her conversion, and the ability to say how one knew he was saved indicated whether that cause was divine. Of course, that knowledge was dependent on the perceived changes in one's habits and disposition, an issue that William James would directly address in *The Varieties of Religious Experience* through his investigation of the role that perceptions play in the structuring of belief.

Edwards's figuring of these epistemological and spiritual breakthroughs as sensory experiences that "swallow up" a person allow him to develop a theory of consciousness that characterizes the mind as spiritually alive when a saint feels, immediately, those old categories, signs, and relations being overwhelmed and subsumed by regenerate ones. Assurance, that all-important feeling, happens in the course of the mind's operations when a saint is compelled by new truths. Piety has been reconceptualized by Edwards as a saint's attention to the limitations of language, doctrines, definitions, concepts, and other frameworks for understanding, and a godly person becomes one who is committed to the overwhelming but constantly unfolding experience of God's glory. Yet, what is so interesting about the description of evangelical humiliation excerpted above is that at the heart of this depiction of the "room of the idea" where true grace and God's love are actualized is a great deal of anxiety felt by a saint regarding his or her relationship to a *community* of saints. The excerpt is carefully developed to characterize what happens to the idea of grace in consciousness when a saint experiences the "sense of the heart," and I would offer that its structure problematizes one result of evangelical humiliation: an isolation reminiscent of the experiences Shepard's saints relate of the migration's power to dissolve communal expression. This isolation occurs in Edwards's passage after the "soul is swallowed up," when the saint is overwhelmed by God's love. Ironically, in terms of their describing a familiarity with the *ordo salutis*, both Shepard's saints and Edwards relate these moments of being "swallowed up" with the "vastness" of an "object." They describe the effect of having everything they know or believe subsumed by an overwhelming sensory experience. And they indicate the exigent movement, or *migration*, into new relations with the God, world, and self.

One of these relations is a saint's to other Christians. At the moment when old relations are subsumed by regenerate ones, a saint, according to Edwards, "sees only the outside of other Christians" and "looks upon" his or her experience as a "strange and exempt instance." In Edwards's theory of the effects of the "room of the idea," this temporary isolation suffered is an essential consequence, for in a theory of consciousness which posits the spiritual sense as a new foundation laid in the soul, then the self-reckoning which results involves migrating into original relations with all social and cultural frameworks, and, according to Edwards, this especially means reestablishing relations to one's most vital discursive community, a fellowship of Christians. The difference, of course, between Shepard's saints and the experience Edwards describes is that Shepard's saints are testifying to not having converted, and Edwards is illustrating what happens to the idea of grace leading up to spiritual conviction. Nevertheless, Edwards and Shepard's saints are all demonstrating a similar phenomenon—the profound ability that an "actual" experience of an idea has to compel original relations to God, world, and self. In the case of Shepard's Puritans it took the form of the disappointing reality of New England, of experiencing the migration through a "sense of the heart," but it provoked the same kind of consequence, a reestablishing of relations to the church.

Indeterminacy as a Conductive Force

Edwards's own recounting of his conversion in his "Personal Narrative" captures the process of having been "convinced" of his salvation in ways that he could not understand, but that nevertheless provided assurance:

> I remember the time very well, when I seemed to be convinced, and fully satisfied, as to this sovereignty of God, and his justice in thus eternally disposing of men, according to his sovereign pleasure. But never could give an account, how, or by what means, I was thus convinced; not in the least imagining, in the time of it, nor a long time after, that there was any extraordinary influence of God's Spirit in it: but only that now I saw further, and my reason apprehended the justice and reasonableness of it. However, my mind rested in it; and it put an end to all those cavils and objections, that I had till then abode with me, all the preceding part of my life.[54]

Hence, the "Personal Narrative" does not describe a conversion experience demonstrating any orthodox notions of preparation or means; it is instead a testimony of "disposition," providing a reckoning of the new spiritual sense's operation in his soul. Edwards's own personal narrative reflects what Gura explains were the expectations Edwards would have had for the testimonies of his congregants when he reinstituted the test of membership: "There had to be reason to think that the candidate did not make such a profession by merely complying with a prescribed form. Rather, he had to signify honestly what he was conscious of in his own heart. In other words he had to speak to the transformation of his will that eventuated in godly actions."[55]

Shepard's saints bore the spiritual burden of having inherited a relationship to the material world overshadowed by a conversion process placing them at odds with nature in an interpretive struggle to discover certain truth about the universe and the state of their souls. Edwards's saints heard a different message. His message placed them in a relationship with nature conceived as what Lee calls "mutuality grounded in the common God-given destiny that nature and humanity share."[56] Lee claims that this mutuality is fully expressed when the regenerate mind, through the power of "imaginative perception," understands and loves material entities as images and shadows of divine things.[57] In turn, Lee explains, the "book of nature" has certain advantages over scripture because these "physical images . . . facilitate God's communication to perceiving beings."[58] Edwards states in number 70 of *Images and Shadows of Divine Things*:

> If we look on these shadows of divine things as the voice of God purposely by them teaching us these and those spiritual and divine things, to show of what excellent advantage it will be, how agreeably and clearly it will tend to convey instruction to our minds, and to impress things on the mind and to affect the mind, by that we may, as it were, have God speaking to us. Wherever we are, and whatever we are about, we may see divine things excellently represented and held forth. And it will abundantly tend to confirm the Scriptures, for there is an excellent agreement between these things and the holy Scripture.[59]

"Excellently," "agreeably," "abundantly"—these are not the terms Shepard's saints used to describe the unfolding glory of their relationship to God's universe. Edwards, however, found in nature infinite ways to relate to God. Human experience, and the variety and vicissitude inherent in it, was conceived as a valuable, indeed central, aspect to the glorification of God, and one's reception of grace remained an extraordinary experience, though figured by Edwards as altogether ordinary. Grace and the conversion experience become reinterpreted through Edwards's reading of Locke as "simple" sensory impressions, but instilled with a new principle in the perceptual realm that Edwards called a "sense of the heart." His "sense of the heart," therefore, allowed him to maintain a mysticism that prevented him from sinking into philosophical materialism: with it, the mind retained an unaccountable element that prevented the reduction of experience into a synthesis of data and systems of thought as Locke, and Ramus before him, had configured. Edwards's inchoate ideas about the relation between uncertainty and conviction, which share a space in the "room of the idea," are pertinent to Emerson's interest in the changing notion of causality and what nature's creative force meant in the nineteenth century. The "room of the idea" emerges as a precursor to Emerson's and James's conceptions about consciousness as an ever-evolving, originating process whose continual production of perceptual truths patterns the operation of grace.

William James would say much later that faith is a "believing attitude," and as we saw with Shepard's Puritans, the morphology of conversion provided a way to interpret the movement of their wills and maintain a believing attitude. As faith happens in the course of experience, it leads an individual to new truths or paths, epistemological and theological, creating new radiations in consciousness. Charting and making sense of these new radiations poses the interpretive problem because they create new spaces in between or outside recognizable modes of understanding, in the movement from one conceptual resting place or paradigm, to the next. Ontologically, faith and conversion could be understood as a troping of the self, wherein conversion constitutes a turning toward new radiations in consciousness, leaving old selves in its wake. Yet, conversion is a continuance, a development of a former self, signifying the constant work of self-reckoning and scrutiny needed to fuel the search for new horizons. Edwards identified a new spiritual perception as the distinguishing feature in regeneration, and *Religious Affections* is a spectacular feat of description and of searching to find the language for that description. The new language he found to convey what the new spiritual sense and perception were guided his congregants, as Shepard's ministry guided his, on their paths to sainthood. Edwards's investigations into the nature of our relationship to language made explicit the idea that language is the material of experience and the potential of experience, that it is both the means and the end of perception. Words, as the conveyers of ideas, simultaneously hold truths and carry saints toward them, allowing a web of consciousness to be spun, revealing both the connecting threads and the points of convergence, very much like the recorded testimonies of Barbary Cutter and Sir Starr.

Despite Shepard's attempts in his sermons to distill as much uncertainty from the process of conversion, the testimonies of his congregants prove, ironically, that though the Puritans lived within the framework of a deterministic universe, uncertainty was the defining experiential force in that process. Their testimonies demonstrate the impossibility of knowing anything with certainty, especially their own salvation, *because* language shaped perception. Therefore, their struggle to fit grace into the limitations of syntax and grammar can be seen as a tacit affirmation of the experience of discord, instability, and an uncertain universe. Edwards, in contrast, would identify the experience of indeterminacy as the necessary condition for conversion because the process of conduction between stored up truths and potential new truths creates a mental space wherein the optimal conditions for new perception exist. It is this investigation of the experience of indeterminacy that leads to the characterizations of the perceptual realms found in the testimonies of Shepard's saints, in *Religious Affections*, in Emerson's essays and *Nature*, and in *The Varieties of Religious Experience*. It is the realm that makes it possible to conceive of oneself as a part of a whole, to feel both the harmony and the discord that accompanies the ongoing process of establishing belief and truth during conversion.

CHAPTER **3**

Ralph Waldo Emerson and the "Universal Impulse to Believe"

For Emerson people were no longer categorized as elect or unregenerate, but they remained souls/consciousnesses interpreting the universe, and their purpose in this world remained aligning their axis of perception with those unbounded "invisible infusories" and "ethereal currents" in an attempt to profit and grow from an uncertain and chaotic universe. Emerson's essays present a world that "tilts" and "rocks," in which all things "swim" and "glitter," and in which all relations are "oblique" and "fleeting." It remains a world in which one struggles to make meaning and secure the truth about those relations. Even so, Emerson would prophesy in the Divinity School Address that eventually our ability to cope with our earthly existence would arrive: "The time is coming when all men will see, that the gift of God to the soul is not a vaunting, over-powering, excluding sanctity, but a sweet, natural goodness, a goodness like thine and mine, and that so invites thine and mine to be and to grow."[1] This chapter examines what brought Emerson to this decep-tively simple characterization of (and call for) faith and how his essays and *Nature* demonstrate the energy and purpose of a figure intending to direct an individual's attention to his "constitution" because "in propor-tion to the energy of his thought and will, he takes up the world into himself."[2] This conception of conversion echoes the preparatory steps of the Puritans, yet it places the individual, and not the Holy Spirit, at the center of this ecstatic process in a position of self-reckoning that affirms the world as a nurturing, sustaining resource for an ever-expanding con-sciousness.

Creating Meaning at the Edge of the World

In Emerson's aestheticizing of scripture, so abundantly evident through-out his essays, the idea of conversion in its theological sense is almost non-existent. However, its absence as a theological concept and a term returns as a force of language that, in the Augustinian sense, is everywhere and nowhere in his essays. Both Stanley Cavell's and Richard Poirier's schol-arship have illuminated the coordinately repellent and attractive aspects of Emerson's style which challenge the reader's experience with his language. In Emerson's essays, as Poirier points out, circles represent the fluidity of his sentences because within their structures there is always a movement from the text and a movement toward the text enacted in the reader, an experience that ties a reader's conversions overtly to language. These "turnings-toward" and "turnings-from," as William James would later call them, mirror the process that the Puritans conceptualized as searching for signs of grace: the "conversions" we experience with Emerson's language are a consequence of searching for meaning within or between the words, sentences, and paragraphs of his essays. When we read Emerson's sentences we are engaged in a search for truths that feel, as James would describe it, "hot" or "vital" to us which, in turn, allow us to recognize which ideas are "cold" to us. In this way we embark on a pilgrimage for meaning within his essays, immersed in the experience of continual epistemological regeneration characterized by Emerson as spir-itual growth but explicitly tied to the growth of consciousness into new and discursive "spheres of thought."[3] This polar dynamic establishes a pattern of perspectival transitions that Emerson symbolizes in his image of the staircase in "Experience." His question for the reader standing on the staircase, "Where do we find ourselves?" is no longer an obstacle, as it was for the Puritans, but a moment of receptivity and meditation. Edwards's "room of the idea" now includes Emerson's staircase, as it were, and the "steps" mediating the experience of grace find representa-tion in a solidly "ordinary" figure.

Like Shepard and Edwards, Emerson hoped not only to enlighten his audiences to what James would call the "sick" state of their souls—to minister to his audience's spiritual health—but also to provide the means to access "the gift of God to the soul." Situated within this historical con-text, Emerson becomes an avatar of the Puritan Reformed practice of ministering the conversion experience to a congregation. Stanley Cavell has argued that the concept of conversion has been "reborn," so to speak, in Emerson's use of the word "aversion" and that this incarnation is inflected with the "discontinuous" aspect of the concept of conversion.

Cavell stresses that for Emerson the aversive aspect of conversion creates space in which anything new can be experienced or said, but that this rebirth also creates the problem of "unapproachability" regarding words, objects, and, of course, America, in Emerson's theorizing on the nature of experience and knowledge. Cavell argues that for Emerson, "if the world is to be new, then what creates what we call the world—our experience and our categories ('notions' Emerson says sometimes; let us say our every word)—must be new, that is to say, *repronounced, renounced*. In 'The American Scholar' this is something called *thinking*."[4] Cavell's analysis seeks to show why Emerson deserves the title of "philosopher" so long denied him, to show "in what way, or to what extent, or at what angle, Emerson stands for philosophy."[5] Indeed, Cavell's assertion that for Emerson creating the world anew demands that every word be repronounced and renounced situates Emerson's textuality within a particular intellectual lineage harking back to Thomas Shepard's imperative presented in the first chapter, that is, his recognition that to revive his saints' faith in America as a means to Christ demanded the re-bracketing of New England as a new means and the ability of his saints to "repronounce" the new idea and "renounce" the failed one. This is the central recognition that reverberates throughout these thinkers' ministrations— that the spiritual and, therefore, intellectual vitality of a community, in fact the actual formation of community, depends upon the very repronouncing and renouncing Cavell speaks of.

Though Cavell does not historicize Emerson's concept of conversion, he provides a discussion of our experience with an Emersonian essay, showing the ways that Emerson's textuality draws forth a reading experience comparable to the one that the Puritans sought in using the Word of the Bible as a means to grace. He characterizes an Emersonian essay as "a finite object that yields an infinite response," a concept echoing the Puritan Reformed experience of gaining access to the "saving" knowledge of Christ "wrapped up in words."[6] Moreover, the intellectual/spiritual inheritance is embodied even more concisely in Emerson's essays when we remember that it was the Puritans who first went beyond Luther in claiming one could access the power of scripture through the reading process as well as through hearing the Word.

Defining an Emersonian morphology of conversion entails articulating what Emerson might have understood as the "stages" of the process. Lee Rust Brown locates these "stages" at the boundary, or relation, between what William James would call "abstract ideas" and "concrete realities," what Brown calls the "edge of experience" that "cuts its way through the world at a point beyond the direct grasp of knowledge."[7] In this sense Emerson translates the Puritans' experience of God's "hidden will" into what Brown calls "secret" experience, which is transcendent because it has not yet been codified. Our sense of the "edge," therefore, in his essays (and in our lives, he argues) relies on our alternating intelligible and affective perception of the meanings each conversional—and conversational—circle generates by creating and blurring the boundary between what has been grounded in discourse and what remains to be perceived. We still see, as Shepard claimed, "but as in a glass," and Emerson's power as a theorist and writer lies in his ability to represent the conversional space as a liminal realm where every aspect of human experience is characterized so that the "divine" and "ordinary" become interchangeable conceptual terms. For Emerson, revelation is never distinct from the instrumental; the ecstatic becomes inextricable from common language, perception, and environment, a difference Edwards made because of his Calvinism. Of course, as we saw in Chapter 2, Edwards's own language in *Religious Affections* betrays the difficulty he had in describing the difference between ordinary and saving operations of grace, and I would argue that in the process of his attempts to make language represent the difference, he often succeeds more at blurring it. Emerson's textuality, on the other hand, allows him to fully realize the interchangeability of the ordinary and the divine within the movements of his sentences, provoking an intimacy with that quality of perception taking part in the "edge of experience," what William James would later call the "darker, blinder strata of character," where we "catch real fact in the making."[8]

Emerson's Ecstatic Mode

Charles Lloyd Cohen calculated the odds of a Puritan being one of the elect at "1000 to 1 against," showing that although "God elects but few . . . salvation [was] not a gamble."[9] To beat the odds, saints underwent the preparatory process, demanding that they negotiate a liminal ontological space: despite preparation's required focused introspection and heightened awareness of their experience in the world, doctrine dictated that they were helpless to do anything to achieve grace, that the Holy Spirit directed all aspects of their coming to Christ in conviction, compunction, and justification. In effect, they were charged with coordinating and maintaining a dual perceptual mode of active passivity—experiencing their own subjectivity through an active examination of themselves as the passive objects of God's power. Despite the odds, Puritans were instructed to be obedient to the revealed will of God in the Bible because it was the standard by which they discovered if they were elect. The only thing to do, therefore, was to use all the means possible to become receptive to grace and the faith that accompanied it, the role of reading and hearing the Word being the most powerful conduit of the Holy Spirit's saving work. Perry Miller asserts in *Errand into the Wilderness* that this "ecstatic" mode can be traced through New England religious thought from Puritanism through Jonathan Edwards to Emerson. However, this claim has proven to be controversial because no direct intellectual line can be established between the strict Calvinism of the first-generation Puritans and Emerson. After the Great Awakening, New England's Puritan tradition began to suffer division as Edwards and his followers in the Connecticut Valley defended "affections" as the central role in religious experience and liberals in Boston and Harvard College argued for a more rational faith. Emerson was Boston-born, and though he rebelled against the reasonableness of his father and college, he seems, according to Phyllis Cole, "to stand on the other side of a cultural and geographical divide from the theologically orthodox Edwards tradition."[10] However, as Cole points out, if we look beyond the influences of pulpit and geography, the continuity of an ecstatic mode may be found closer to home.

Cole has traced Emerson's family lineage back to his eighteenth-century forebears, who were active in the fervent evangelical movement of the time to determine the continuity of an ecstatic mode from the orthodox Puritanism of the seventeenth century to Emerson's transcendentalism of the nineteenth century. Cole explains that the "eighteenth-century Emersons and their in-laws . . . stood in the significant minority of their region, supporting the Awakening even as Harvard turned against it. They publicly endorsed Edwards's major theological works, hosted George Whitefield's divisive preaching, and offered fervent sermons for the conversion of their respective towns."[11] This spiritual strain continued in the family and thrived in the life of Emerson's Aunt Mary Moody Emerson, who fostered an intellectual and spiritual knowledge of the ecstatic tradition in Emerson and his brothers. Cole claims that Mary Emerson's reverence for the saints of the Emerson family came with "a piety of heart that through life called [Emerson] to solitude amidst the crowd of his modern friends" and sparked an "institutionally unaffiliated search for inspiration."[12] Mary Emerson's influence on Ralph Waldo is well documented, and in Cole's attempt to draw a line tracing the ecstatic mode from the original Puritans to Emerson she looks directly at Mary Emerson, showing how she straddled both traditions of orthodox Calvinism and Romantic intuitionism. Cole claims that Mary Emerson's lifelong enthusiasm for "seeking God in moments of joyful consciousness" and finding revelation "in the mind's intuitions and nature's phenomena as well as in the Bible," led to Emerson's "opting for a philosophy based on sentiment rather than 'bare reason.'"[13] In the end, however, and to Mary Emerson's dismay, the "sentiment" Emerson was looking for could not be found in the Unitarianism he initially embraced but eventually believed had become lifeless in its intellectualism.

Perry Miller's own articulation of how the Puritan ecstatic mode remained a powerful influence on New England religious thought would support Cole's focus on Mary Emerson as a cultural conduit. She would seem, in fact, to embody a cultural moment in which the division between Calvinism and Unitarianism was more blurry than distinct:

> The emergence of Unitarianism out of Calvinism was a very gradual, almost an imperceptible, process. One can hardly say at what point rationalists in eastern Massachusetts ceased to be Calvinists, for they were forced to organize into a separate church only after the development of their thought was completed. Consequently, although young men and women in Boston might be . . . the children of rationalists, all about them the society still bore the impress of Calvinism: the theological break had come, but not the cultural. . . . We do not need to posit some magical transmission of Puritanism from the seventeenth to the nineteenth century in order to account for the fact that these children of Unitarians felt emotionally starved and spiritually undernourished.[14]

Even beyond the persistence of a Calvinist notion of passionate piety, of which Mary Emerson is a good example, Miller shows that the continuities between Edwards and Emerson can be found in an Edwards who retained the element of mysticism that lay beneath the dogma of orthodoxy. Though Edwards "forced into his system every safeguard against identifying the inward experience of the saint with the Deity Himself, or of God with nature," Miller explains that the imagery dominating the descriptions of his perception of divinity in the world betrays a sense of things more aligned with the mystical element of Puritanism.[15] Miller is careful to note that the mysticism he sees in Edwards cannot be supported by Edwards's doctrine, only that it can be found in the "texture" of Edwards's thought, in the images and descriptions of God in his works expressing a wonder and awe at the beauty and life God communicates to everything in the cosmos, emanating divinity to each particle.

Miller argues that within Edwards's concept of God's divine effulgence lies the conclusion that "if God is diffused through nature, and the substance of man is the substance of God, then it may follow that man is divine, that nature is the garment of the Over-Soul, that man must be self-reliant, and that when he goes into the woods the currents of Being will indeed circulate through him."[16] Preventing Edwards from formulating these concepts, however, was orthodox theology, set down in the Word of God teaching that "God and nature are not one, that man is corrupt and his self-reliance is reliance on evil."[17] Nevertheless, the drive existed for Edwards and the Puritans before him, as it did for Emerson, to seek out a communion with the divine in the contexts available—in the howling wilderness, or a clearing in the forest, or walking through a bare common. The ecstatic mode persists, Miller concludes, in this drive, or what he calls "effort," to "confront, face to face, the image of a blinding divinity in the physical universe, and to look upon that universe without the intermediacy of ritual, of ceremony, of the Mass and the confessional."[18]

The "effort" Miller speaks of, which is in fact the effort culminating in the conversion experience, was for the Puritans highly ordered and institutionalized. Every nuance of the emotional, psychological, and spiritual experience was codified within the discourse of each ministry. Saints had only to interpret their experience according to preexisting descriptions and rules for interpretation in order to make sense of their spiritual path. Their efforts to convert, systematized as the *ordo salutis*, framed an affective cycle that saints experienced throughout their lives to reaffirm and continually reorient themselves toward religious life. Yet, as we saw in the conversion narratives of Chapter 1, experiencing conversion wasn't as straightforward as the *ordo salutis* made it seem because the saints' lived manifestations of faith did not necessarily correspond to the encoded process of faith. Their *discursive* knowledge of the workings of grace often did not facilitate the *saving* experience of it, the most glaring example being the testimonies of Shepard's saints whose expectations that New England would be a successful means were met with disappointment. In general, however, the problem of detecting faith was rooted in their "defective" human perception, a problem exacerbated by the doctrine of preparation, which stated that saints could predispose themselves to grace. Therefore, understanding how and when faith was implanted and their experience of it were often misaligned. Saints were told that they could have undergone the transformation and been unaware of it, or it could come suddenly and they may not recognize it. They were charged with the interpretive feat of attempting to discern which events, thoughts, and feelings were the result of saving grace and which were the result of ordinary human frailty. It was this difference that Edwards would take up in *Religious Affections*, not only in that the entire treatise is structured around the purpose of describing what are signs of true grace, but also through his treatment of the difference between "ordinary" grace and "saving" grace, a subtle classification within his broader category of religious affections. These distinctions are attempts to offer a kind of compass for the epistemological and ontological maze Emerson would capture with the question, "Where do we find ourselves?" at the start of "Experience." His answer, "In a series of which we do not know the extremes," figures an epistemological/ontological framework anathema to the highly systematized stages of the *ordo salutis* by which Puritans codified the "extremes" of the process and provided a template for assuring that the cause of the process was divine. Despite the inherent impossibility of the task, they were to stay obedient and use all the means available to perceive grace at the moment it was granted.

If we consider the experiential piety of the Puritans, as Miller does, by removing the conceptual frameworks maintained by orthodox theology, we may find that Emerson's notion in "Spiritual Laws" that "man is a method, a progressive arrangement; a selecting principle, gathering his like to him," describes the complex role of an individual in the universe whether in seventeenth-, eighteenth-, or nineteenth-century New England.[19] Essentially, the concept of man *as a method* takes as a starting point the idea that humans inhabit a difficult and uncertain space on earth. This idea was obviously written into the theological worldview of the Puritans, which condemned them to a life of depravity and sin and bound them to discovering knowledge—through a methodological investigation—of their fate as one of the elect. For Emerson, though the doctrines of original sin and innate depravity no longer applied, the world is dizzying in its amusement park qualities of tilting and rocking. In addition, things "swim" and "glitter" and, as noted before, our relations with people are "oblique" and "casual." Emerson continually poses the question of where we find stability. His answer, in "a perpetual inchoation," provides little comfort. Yet, finding our footing in the universe becomes critical to our well-being and happiness, though these moments are always described by Shepard, Edwards, and Emerson as temporary and only part of a larger affective cycle.

That these moments of well-being are only temporary does not diminish their importance. In fact, these are the moments for which the *ordo salutis* was designed and about which Emerson develops his ideas about the human imperative to access the power available through the spiritual correspondence between humans and nature. This correspondence could be realized through our perception of the "higher laws" of Being. In "Self-Reliance" he urges his audience to "obey no law less than the eternal law" and to have "no covenants but proximities."[20] And, in his 1838 address to the senior class of Harvard's Divinity College, he exhorted the students to "behold these infinite relations," to "behold these outrunning laws, which our *imperfect apprehension* can see tend this way and that," and thereby, to become "newborn bard[s] of the Holy Ghost."[21] Emerson recognized that our perception of these "outrunning laws" is at best fleeting and that this perceptual fragmentariness characterizes our relation to the world and God, claiming in "The Method of Nature" that a "man's wisdom is to know that all ends are momentary, that the best end must be superseded by a better."[22] These moments are where Emerson believes we find power and life, and for Shepard, Edwards, and Emerson, an individual practices, or, in Emerson's case, embodies a method for arriving at what is essentially the experience of truth and beauty, the moment of transcendence beyond earthly contexts and their symptomatic fragmentariness. This is Miller's "ecstatic mode," which he traces from New England Puritanism to Emerson—the experiential/perceptive imperative necessary to realize the "social world" that Andrew Delbanco argues is hardly possible for us to imagine anymore.

Divine Methods of Thinking and Perception

To understand the development of the ecstatic mode, however, we cannot sever it from the problem of perception that these writers wrestled with in theorizing it for themselves as well as in describing it for their audiences. What were the effects of sin for the Puritans and Edwards (the rebellious will or the unruly affections that clouded their vision) appears in Emerson's thought as "imperfect apprehension," but the means by which the effects of sin are overcome, articulated in all of their works, entail what was best expressed by Edwards as an "actual idea" arrived at through a disciplined intellectual process, a mode of thinking theorized by each. Moreover, that mode of thinking is framed by an overarching affective pursuit. In the case of Shepard's saints, the preparatory process, which led up to belief and therefore conversion, evolved in the New World as a form of persistent spiritual discipline enforced by Shepard's newly American rational figurations of faith. In this way, Shepard does not foster the kind of ecstatic mode we would associate with Edwards and Emerson, but he nevertheless constructs and ministers a kind of "actual idea" when he revives New England in the morphology as a new means. This move on the part of Shepard is essentially related to the act of troping that both Edwards and Emerson are engaged in when they demand a re-meaning, asserted through their compositional acts, of fragments from the past. Shepard's reconstruction of New England, in effect, takes the fragment of the morphology left over from the effects of the migration and tropes it for a new life in New England. New England had to become an "actual idea" in order for it to be of any use to the saints. The fact that Shepard transcribed these testimonies of a will to believe in New England as a means can be considered an early example of a compositional act engendering and enforcing a discursive community, an attempt to capture, in language, the life force of an "actual idea."

These tropings by Shepard, Edwards, and Emerson, and the necessary "actual ideas" that generate them, are undertaken in the hopes of fostering the spiritual and intellectual health of the community and a society free of the ills associated with what William James calls a "sick soul." What Shepard achieves, however, in his efforts to prevent the new colony from deteriorating into the sick spiritual and intellectual state that old England represented, is a thoroughly un-ecstatic method of interpretation. His method enforced the kind of empirical mode necessary to analyze both the material and ideal contents of experience for signs of grace, but his emphasis on spiritual discipline, and on sin as entity, grounded the ecstatic-affective dimension of the process of conversion in that intellectual pursuit as well. Shepard is important to understanding the legacy of the ecstatic mode in America, however, because his ministry and the testimonies of his saints inform, through their un-ecstatic expressions, the central role that discipline and a method of thinking have played in Edwards's and Emerson's philosophy. We tend to focus on the cultural inheritance of the concept of transcendence and ecstasy, but this cannot be divorced from what has been an intertwined legacy in American literature—the evolving theories of a method of thinking necessary to achieve that state. I would offer that it would be equally as productive to think of these writers in terms of how they represent an "actual idea" or the "sense of the heart," which is where they focus most of their energies in their attempts to describe the intellectual and imaginative habits responsible not only for the "ecstatic" moment, which transcends discourse, but for establishing a community of believers.

As I have discussed, Edwards infused the Puritan method bequeathed to him by the Intellectual Fathers with a "sense of the heart," a method of perception making the affections the central conductive force for the soul, yet allowing the affections their full potential for that force because his idealism set forth a theory of the mind that made piety the product of an active consciousness. In doing so he equated the strength of that piety with the strength of a "feeling mind" as it practices "attention of the mind in thinking"—an angle of vision turning the powers of observation back onto one's thought process in an effort to bear witness to the generative power of consciousness, the "actual idea," in bringing God's world into being.

What is important about Edwards's call for "attention of the mind in thinking" is its ability to capture the essence of the liminal experience a Puritan inhabits when called upon to see oneself as both the object of God's grace and the observer of its workings, a space that posits those moments in consciousness as the prime moments of reception of grace. It is a picture of the mind equating piety with what James calls the "strenuous mood," the exertions necessary for acting according to the full extent of one's own consciousness. It is in line with a Puritan epistemological tradition, and in Emerson it becomes the best way to ensure that an individual is not thinking or acting according to the authoritative forces of tradition, history, or rhetoric. When Edwards conceptualized man as the "consciousness of the universe," he prefigured Emerson's notion of man as a creative force within it. Edwards's concept of "attention of the mind in thinking" theorized an epistemology that, like Emerson, placed an "ongoing process of interpretation and recomposition, an ecstatic method of knowing," at the heart of experience rather than an arrival at any one specific idea or truth.[23]

In this way, a method of thinking has served to characterize a certain practice of piety for Edwards, Emerson, and even Shepard, the difference being that in Shepard's New World ministrations the ecstatic moment was drained from the experience. Ramist logic set forth the method of "discerning" and "disposing" as a template for saints to gain certain knowledge about the state of their souls, and as shown in Shepard's sermon series on the parable of the ten virgins, he characterized a pious Christian as a "thinking" (conceived as a judging) Christian. Edwards's concept of "attention of the mind in thinking," however, equates piety with the immediate reception and translation of emergent truths, and, as Cavell argues, Emerson casts thinking as the continual work of "renouncing" and "repronouncing" our experience and categories to make the world "new." Importantly, the central role that thinking plays in the theologies/philosophies of Shepard, Edwards, and Emerson is in how this kind of pious thinking increases the odds that an individual will not be deceived, that the truths encountered will contribute to redemption because, as William James argues, "previous human thinking" has not yet "peptonized and cooked" them for "consumption."[24] This is the imperative fueling the theologies and philosophies of these writers—to create the necessary means for having a "saving" experience propelling us beyond the confines of the words and categories structuring our worldview. But, it is also a pious method of thinking that holds converting individuals together through a communal intellectual/spiritual discipline and habit that generates personal and cultural renewal.

Emerson scholars attribute his adoption of a theory of mind and written style reflecting this "ecstatic method of knowing" to his visit to the

Jardin des Plantes in 1833. But it is important to keep in mind that this method was intuited and articulated by Edwards via idealism much earlier. What Emerson found at the Jardin des Plantes was a new language for understanding and reflecting the method of nature and of natural historians within his own written work and investigations into the nature and confluence of consciousness and spirit. Emerson did not simply recognize that "ecstasy is the law and cause of nature": he adopted science as the method of knowing, stating in "The Method of Nature" that "because all knowledge is assimilation to the object of knowledge, as the power or genius of nature is ecstatic, so must its science or the description of it be."[25] The ecstatical "state," Emerson continues, is a *divine method*," for it "seems to direct a regard to the whole and not to the parts; to the cause and not to the ends; to the tendency, and not to the act."[26] Moreover, the method of nature, which is the method of thought and perception, cannot be explained or analyzed: "That rushing stream will not stop to be observed," because "its permanence is a perpetual inchoation," and it is "by piety alone, by conversing with the cause of nature, [that man is] safe and commands it."[27] These descriptions of the indescribable dynamics of "the divine method" contain the energy behind Emerson's departure from Christian tradition when we consider the central role that observation and explanation played in Shepard's saints' lives and even in Edwards's idealism. When Emerson states that man *is* a method, he locates divinity *within* man, whereas Edwards's theory of "attention of the mind in thinking" is a brilliant blend of Calvinism and the science of his day: he was able to combine the felt experience of spontaneity and immediacy with the divine from the observational remove of the sinful self.

Emerson claims divinity for humans, but this does not imply that the method for "confront[ing], face to face, the image of a blinding divinity" is any less necessary for remaining in productive touch with experience. According to Robert Milder, Emerson's "call to the soul" took on a revolutionary edge answering the "groveling materialism" of society: "The future, as Emerson imagined it, rested on a full-scale reorganization of consciousness even more transformational than Christian conversion because it led individuals beyond the orthodoxies of Scripture and the example of Jesus to a terra incognita of spiritual being that promised to remold traditions and social institutions."[28] Cast as an ethical imperative in the Divinity School Address, the mind's reception to those higher laws Emerson claims "refuse to be adequately stated" becomes the agent of social change.[29] In a particularly apt description of the altogether ordinary and quotidian presence of the divine laws in our lives, he observes that they "will not be written out on paper, or spoken by the tongue. They elude our persevering thought; yet we read them hourly in each other's faces, in each other's actions, in our own remorse."[30] Jesus is no longer the mediator for the power of the Spirit, as this quote demonstrates; instead, access to it is as abundant a resource and is as easily tapped as finding it in a friend's smile. As Albert J. Von Frank explains, Emerson believed we have choices to make in this world about where we go for the resources that enable us to realize our potential as spiritual beings: "if we are not content to be colonized by the external requirements of family, church, social position, occupation, and political party—if we are dismayed at the thought of having constantly to negotiate the emergent conflicts of a multitude of incoherent affiliations" we must turn to the "access that we all have to things timeless and unaccidental, from the original source of life, or the regime of spirit, where, if anywhere, native coherence is, and the home of truth and beauty."[31]

This life-giving force is as pervasive and dynamic in the world for Shepard's Puritans and Edwards as it is for Emerson—one need only have the perceptive abilities, or "angle of vision," to gain access. Shepard's Puritans were instructed that they would see the beauty and truth of God's holiness after they had experienced conversion, though, as Shepard pointed out, "to tell you how, they can not." Edwards, on the other hand, attempted to do what Shepard could not, that is, describe what these holy perceptions are after the "spiritual sense" has been laid in the foundation of the soul. Edwards attempted to describe how the world appeared to one who had received grace, and his descriptions of the delightful emanations of God's holiness present a world not unlike Emerson's in the entirely diffuse presence of the divine. However, though this power is available to all, only those with the right perception can access this power. Even Shepard's and Edwards's Puritans, who believed the world consisted of "sheep" and "goats," and had to discover which one they were, had to pursue the path that may or may not have led to the conversion experience. They chose whether or not to embark on a journey of perceptual alignment with the Spirit through preparation. And so it remained with Emerson: one has access to the "regime of the spirit," but that access requires an axis of perception that can only be achieved through a practice of piety or method that creates a saving reception.

Satisfying the Desire for Meaning

Tracing Miller's "ecstatic mode," then, from Edwards and the Puritans to Emerson might take a more direct route through an intellectual tradition that fostered a disciplined practice of method in thinking demanded as the work whose reward was the ecstasy of conversion. The method that

Emerson adopted is the subject of Laura Dassow Walls's book *Emerson's Life in Science: The Culture of Truth*, and in it Walls addresses Emerson's turn to the method of science as a way to combat the chaos of materialism. Through the method of science "the intellect seized the fragmented and unmeaning phenomena of the world and forged them into meaningful, productive wholes."[32] Walls points out that his revelation in 1833 at the Paris Muséum d'Histoire Naturelle, prompting the claim that he would "be a naturalist," proved influential for his early science lectures. Yet what is unclear, she observes, is the effect of this revelation for the years following 1836, noting that in a journal entry of this year Emerson claims that he in fact "cannot be a naturalist, until he satisfies all the demands of the spirit. Love is as much its demand, as perception."[33] That love and perception is the necessary combination to meet the Spirit's demands reminds us of the twin elements of the conversion experience articulated by Shepard and Edwards in which the "discerning and disposing" of nature, though integral to aligning the axis of perception, could not instigate the conversion experience alone. Affections, or the reception of God's love, consummated the process by making the reception of the Spirit "actual" through a felt experience of God's love. Just as Shepard's Puritans knew (though they didn't actually experience), and Edwards felt, Emerson recognized that he occupied "the midpoint where love and perception perfect each other, attuning mind and nature to each other, detaching objects from personal relation to see them in the light of thought, and kindling science 'with the fire of the holiest affections' to send God forth anew into his Creation."[34]

Walls notes that Emerson inherited the Protestant theology imported by the Puritans to the New World, which held that science was a part of faith, but that he was specifically Baconian in his views. The scientific revolution carried out by Bacon, Galileo, Kepler, and Newton held that man can know the mind of God and posited that the "creative mind, whether human or divine, was one and the same," allowing man an "original" relation to the universe because the study of nature revealed God's divine will and Logos.[35] Francis Bacon's contribution, in pointing out that man is the author of the book of Revelation and God is the author of nature, articulated scripture's relationship to nature as one of lock and key. Walls explains that Emerson took from Bacon this idea that the book of nature was a "key" unlocking the mind of God and argues that he "took the next logical step, reading in nature the key to the self."[36] Moreover, she shows that Emerson's American Scholar was above all an "interpreter of nature" in the Baconian sense because he adopted science as a "quality of mental action" that "read[s] order into a universe that persistently threatened to fly apart."[37] Walls specifically ties Emerson's adoption of the method of science to a Baconian tradition because Bacon insisted on a self-disciplinary program promoting an active seeking of knowledge as opposed to the passive reception of others' views. Bacon insisted on a method that would generate new knowledge through the turn to nature and away from books. Being able to read order into the world meant penetrating the facts constituting its turbulence for the laws and principles of life itself, the stable idea and the truths behind the flux, and this demanded, in the Baconian tradition, that man invent knowledge through the continual exercise of his creative and intellectual faculties. Though Walls aligns the method of thought Emerson adopted specifically to the Baconian tradition, that method was a more central component of the Puritan tradition than she recognizes, and it is ironic that after he does adopt the method of science and finds it lacking, he looks to his Protestant heritage to complete his vision of the kind of approach to experience his spirit demanded.

Emerson's turn to science introduced him to natural philosophers such as the Swedenborgian Sampson Reed and the astronomer John Herschel, who were articulating an epistemology celebrating the imagination's role in penetrating spaces of consciousness wherein the "perpetual inchoation of ideas" took place. Emerson would recognize, as did Edwards, the importance of this liminal realm of consciousness, in which as Emerson states in "The American Scholar," the "preamble of thought, the transition through which it passes from the unconscious to the conscious" takes place.[38] This conscious space where "a perpetual inchoation of ideas" occurs provides the feeling of tendency in experience, the feeling of perpetual arrival at truthful descriptions of self and world. In *The Principles of Psychology*, William James would conceptualize this feeling of tendency as the "vague," as the "rapid premonitory perspective views of schemes of thought not yet articulate."[39]

Natural philosophers were arguing for the legitimate role of imagination in penetrating the recesses of consciousness in scientific discovery, and Emerson would argue for the central role the "vague" plays in what David C. Lamberth calls "gaining purchase on life."[40] Indeed, Emerson would have found the natural philosopher's attempt to gain "purchase on life" as powerful a personal pilgrimage as the Christian process of conversion. Lamberth examines how Emerson's treatment of the idea of experience in his essay of the same name argues for a definition of experience that does not limit it to "something we have now and again," but as "something we stand, think, and move both in and with."[41] He looks to the opening segment of "Experience" in which Emerson asks "Where do we find ourselves?" for an image of experience conveying a sense of it being an active process:

We wake and find ourselves on a stair; there are stairs below us, which
we seem to have ascended; there are stairs above us, many a one, which
go upward and out of sight. But the Genius which, according to the old
belief, stands at the door by which we enter, and gives us lethe to drink,
that we may tell no tales, mixed the cup too strongly, and we cannot
shake off the lethargy now at noonday.[42]

Lamberth asserts that this figure of experience harkens back to the ante-
cedent Latin *experiri*, "an active verb meaning to try or to test, a usage
bringing to mind both the benign . . . notion of experimentation, but
also . . . the more tense trials and tests of faith . . . so closely attended to
by Jonathan Edwards's *Treatise on Religious Affections*."[43] Of particular
interest to how this understanding of experience ties into both religious
experience and natural philosophy, however, is how experience, as Emerson describes it, becomes a metaphor for perception, how the trials and
tests that experience imposes upon us cannot be dissociated from the fil-
ter we call perception because "gaining purchase on life" is a process in
which our perception determines the contours of experience: "Experience flows and interfuses always changing, making difficult our quests
for vision and insight, groggy as we are due to our heavy droughts of
lethe. . . . Experience is, for Emerson, the substance of our lives, but it is
never radiant. We see through a glass darkly."[44] Our experience, once
again, flows through a "glass darkly," identifying perception as the central problem for aligning our axis of vision with the higher laws of existence. What proves most valuable over and over in these journeys of
discovery is a penetrating imagination that is always on the "edge of experience." The natural philosophers Emerson read were exploring the
ways in which one could account for and best utilize the limited faculties
available; it is the project Edwards undertook, incorporating the scientific knowledge of his own time but containing it within Calvinist
doctrine.

Emerson was particularly attracted to Sampson Reed's emphasis on the
active powers of the mind. In Reed's *Observations on the Growth of the
Mind*, Emerson would have encountered Reed's definition of reason,
which he carefully distinguishes from "what it was a few centuries past."
Referring to the Ramist logic of Shepard and the Intellectual Fathers, he
attempts to facilitate the extinction of that brand of reasoning:

Syllogistic reasoning is passing away. It has left no permanent demonstration but that of its own worthlessness. It amounts to nothing but the
discernment and expression of the particulars which go to comprise

something more general; and, as the human mind permits things to assume a proper arrangement from their own inherent power of attraction, it is no longer necessary to bind them with syllogisms.[45]

Reason's job, according to Reed, was simply "tracing the relations which exist between created things, and of not even touching what it examines lest it disturb the arrangement in the cabinet of creation," which is an apt metaphor for the attempt on the part of those who practiced Ramist logic to get ahold of those divine ideas to secure their knowledge of them.[46] Reed's distinction is important here because he is using new concepts for terminology that had hitherto provided a mechanistic theory of mind. Reason is no longer the intellectual capacity esteemed by ministers like Shepard who grounded conversion in the attempt to secure knowledge. Instead, reason "traces" relations: it "measures the distance of objects, compares their magnitudes, discerns their colors, and selects and arranges them according to the relation they bear to each other."[47] This "hands off" approach clarifies that reason alone cannot provide the means to grace; instead, the work of reason is accompanied by the imagination, the "creative power of man," which "shall coincide with the actively creative will of God."[48] The pairing of reason with imagination endowed man with a creative power so potent that with "every approach to Him, by bringing us nearer the origin of things, enables us to discover analogies in what was before chaotic."[49]

These new conceptions of reason and imagination remind us of the epistemological and ontological frameworks of the Puritan experience of conversion, of the coordinate work of the understanding and the will, or, as Edwards would have it, the understanding and "inclination." Edwards, rather than Shepard, would recognize and describe the life-giving intersection and dynamics of the understanding and will to a point that stretched the limits of his orthodox views. Sampson Reed, in turn, articulates a theory of the mind and conversion that Edwards could not because of the constraints of Calvinist doctrine. Whereas Edwards tacitly incorporated elements of desire, choice, and the creative power of human consciousness to bring God's world into being, Reed claims these aspects outright, situating man's mind at the creative center of the universe, granting consciousness the capacity to recognize and direct the tendency of the soul. In a particularly beautiful passage, Reed describes the full aspect of consciousness as a conductive imaginary, echoing the moment in Edwards when his insight into the importance of making our ideas clear incorporates the idea of a horizon or fringe in consciousness in which truths reside, yet lie beyond our powers of articulation:

As our desires become more and more concentrated to those objects which correspond to the peculiar organization of our minds, we shall have a foretaste of that which is coming, in those internal tendencies of which we are conscious. As we perform with alacrity whatever duty presents itself before us, we shall perceive in our own hearts a kind of preparation for every external event or occurrence of our lives, even the most trivial, springing from the all-pervading tendency of the Providence of God.[50]

In this passage, Reed recognizes the power that objects of nature have when in correspondence to the organization of our minds, but he also speaks of a kind of "preparation" occurring in the "internal tendencies" that crystallize in those correspondences, a "perpetual inchoation," as Emerson would put it, in the "orderly development of the mind." Reed's organic metaphor of the growth of the mind illustrates a perpetual cycle of correspondence, tendency, preparation, development, and correspondence, grounded in the shared work of reason and imagination.

Because for Reed all growth is from within, there is almost no distinguishing a difference between the truths occurring in the course of the mind's "ordinary operations of nature" and the truths occurring in the course of one's engagement with the Word of God. As Reed explains, the Word of God simply supplies yet another resource for the growth of the mind in its union with the "Divine Will" through "Divine Truth." In the process of regeneration,

revelation so mingles with everything which meets us, that it is not easy for us to *measure* the degree to which our condition is affected by it. Its effects appear miraculous at first, but after they have become established, the mind, as in the ordinary operations of nature, is apt to become *unconscious* of the power by which they are produced.[51]

Walls's term for this is an "extraordinary technology of self- and world-making" which is "available everywhere, not only in 'the sublime and beautiful' but in 'the near, the low, the common.' Every object, even the most mundane, is printed with the seal of God, and from any object truth may be unfolded."[52] For Emerson, nature is no longer divorced from self; it "*is* mind in its growth and lawful unfolding; and mind *is* nature, mind bodied forth in matter," and the vision of the world that this theory of the mind generates infuses the low with sublimity, and when an individual is committed to the growth of the mind, perception becomes habituated to regard the low as sublime.[53] John Herschel claimed that man "walks in the midst of wonders: every object which falls in his way elucidates some principle, affords some instruction, and impresses him with a sense of harmony and order."[54] Reed, in turn, describes the sublime relation we encounter in the course of our "ordinary" lives, emphasizing what Emerson would call the "ecstatic" nature of man's method:

> As we behold the external face of the world, our souls will hold communion with its spirit; and we shall seem to extend our consciousness beyond the narrow limits of our own bodies, to the living objects that surround us. The mind will enter into nature by the secret path of him who forms her; and can be no longer ignorant of her laws, when it is witness of her creation.[55]

Emerson was drawn to the theory of mind Reed set forth for its articulation of the active role that consciousness played in its relations with the divine will, but Reed was only one writer Emerson looked to for theories about the mind that helped him articulate his idea of "man as method." Samuel Taylor Coleridge, John Herschel, and Immanuel Kant among others all emphasized the active power, or "reason," that the mind exerts in approaching truth. Coleridge emphasized reason as "an active power in the self that is capable of self-determination," and argued that it provided more trustworthy knowledge than the senses because it was rooted in moments of direct intuitive perception. The astronomer Herschel considered the "nature of human creativity in science" and valued the "power to make new discoveries" more than the discoveries themselves. Kant, like Coleridge, rejected Locke and Hume, looking for "primary truth in the fundamental nature—we would now say the deep structure—of the human mind," insisting that "we have more in our minds than can be accounted for by the simple accumulation of sensory experience."[56] Reason, as Laura Dassow Walls explains, looks "straight through the material world to the preexisting causal 'idea' of God," and to "comprehend this one generative idea was to comprehend how all the scattered pieces are actually united parts of the whole."[57] To understand the generative idea was to piece together sequences, properties, and relations to comprehend the higher laws determining all aspects of the material world.

Yet, reason had to be accompanied by imagination in order for the full creative potential of man to be realized. Walls defines imagination as "reason's projection into the material world *beyond* mind, the necessary mediator between 'ME' and the 'NOT ME' without which reason would be, literally, unrealized."[58] As the faculty allowing man to transcend his observational, intellectual, and visual frameworks, the concept of the imagination provided a way to account for that realm in consciousness where what Herschel calls "the frontier of knowledge" provides an inexhaustible resource of power. Edwards, who was stretching the limits of orthodoxy with his theories about consciousness, conceptualized this realm as a horizon beyond the limits of explanation and logic where undiscovered, indistinct truths and the bodies of knowledge they form reside. For the natural philosophers influencing Emerson, this horizon constitutes the liminal space where belief is negotiated and realized or, I would argue, chosen. Figuring this space was a cardinal project for writers such as Herschel, Reed, and Coleridge because they were addressing a cultural anxiety surrounding experimental constructions of truth.

Their works, like Edwards's and Emerson's, set forth theories of the mind specifically addressing how our convictions emerge from discoveries about the world as well as our own "vital and intellectual faculties." They demonstrate that while the universe was no longer a Calvinist one, the work of consciousness in the process of discovery remained focused on creating reception to natural and spiritual truths through a process of combined intellection and intuition. In other words, it is easy to see the aspect of scientific discovery calling for fact and verification, but what these natural philosophers demonstrate is that science is no less an affective pursuit given to the same moments of aesthetic transcendence as religious conversion, figured in Emerson's beautiful image of the "private observatory, cataloguing obscure and nebulous stars of the human mind" in "The American Scholar."[59]

Emerson read John Herschel's *Preliminary Discourse on the Study of Natural Philosophy* in 1831. It discusses the power that humans discover through the exercise of their consciousness and provides a template for gaining access to that power. Herschel's text is divided into three parts addressing the "general nature and advantages of the study of the physical sciences," and in the first part Herschel seeks to characterize the nature of the relation between man's consciousness and nature by articulating the relationship as one of "use." Moreover, he describes nature as an inexhaustible resource of use to humans, not simply for the discoveries made but for the *joy* of the process itself. Herschel claims that access to power resides in what I would call an *axis of gratification*, in that to the extent that consciousness expands to penetrate the mysteries of nature, its desires are met, and its needs and wants for further knowledge and power expand. The following passage of Herschel's describes a process of ever-expanding consciousness, of ever-seeking the inchoate conscious state, wherein views can "enlarge" in a continual process—Edwards's "room of the idea" to make room *for* the idea as it were—to satisfy the always already desire for more knowledge and power. This passage echoes that same aspect of conversion described by Edwards as evangelical humiliation in which acts of self-reckoning register a pattern of *differences* detectable to the extent that one is growing spiritually in God through an "enlargement" of views. These "enlargements" carry the soul into a collapse between subject and object, or in Puritan conversion, into closure with Christ, which he casts in the sermon "A Divine and Supernatural Light" as an experience whose power is felt as a "satisfying" experience. In order to capture what is truly the religious fervor behind Herschel's feelings about the act of discovery, it is necessary to quote at length:

> But so constituted is the mind of man, that his views enlarge, and his desires and wants increase, in the full proportion of the facilities afforded to their gratification, and, indeed, with augmented rapidity, so that no sooner has the successful exercise of his powers accomplished any considerable simplification or improvement of processes subservient to his use or comfort, than his faculties are again on the stretch to extend the limits of his newly acquired power; and having once experienced the advantages which are to be gathered by availing himself of some of the powers of nature to accomplish his ends, he is led thenceforward to regard them all as a treasure placed at his disposal, if he have only the art, the industry, or the good fortune, to penetrate those recesses which conceal them from immediate view. Having once learned to look on knowledge as power, and to avail himself of it as such, he is no longer content to limit his enterprises to the beaten track of his former usage, but is constantly led onwards to contemplate objects which, in a previous stage of his progress, he would have regarded as unattainable and visionary, had he even thought of them at all. It is here that the investigation of the hidden powers of nature becomes a mine, every vein of which is pregnant with inexhaustible wealth, and whose ramifications appear to extend in all directions wherever human wants or curiosity may lead us to explore.[60]

The axis of gratification acts as the engendering correspondence between nature and man's consciousness that permits access to the "hidden powers of nature." These investigations are products of each consciousness desiring to penetrate all mysteries in search of knowledge generating conviction. However, not all investigations satisfy man's curiosity. Herschel recognizes that there are places where these investigations are thwarted by limited powers of consciousness. He addresses such impenetrable phenomena as "*how* [man's] will acts on his limbs," and "by what means [man] becomes conscious" of himself as a "thinking, feeling, reasoning being."[61] These phenomena address what Edwards would call "inclinations": those moments of consciousness constituting "the immediate communication between that inward sentient being, and that machinery, his outward man" that move man through experience but remain a mystery because the connection between body and mind/soul cannot be known through a train of reasoning.[62]

In contrast, Shepard's Puritans were asked to *reason* the connection between what they believed or felt and the "molecular action in the brain"—that state being the influx of grace, which was conceptually a *spiritual* change, but was also supposed to affect a saint *physically* through a change in perceptual acuity. Shepard's Puritans wanted a bridge of reasoning in order to determine a correspondence between their thought and feeling to a certain state of their souls, which was understood as a spiritual metamorphosis, but had no less of a physical effect. The "power" Shepard's Puritans were trying to access could not have been attained, Herschel would have concluded, because they were trying to do the impossible, that is, reason a connection between their feeling, believing selves and the "molecular action" of grace on their perception.

Edwards, on the other hand, granted consciousness a place in his theology through the concept of the "feeling mind," which conveyed a more complex understanding of consciousness as the seat of the soul. As a result, the influx of grace, and the power a saint gained access to, was realized through feeling and not reasoning. Hence, Edwards's notion of the "new spiritual sense" laid in the "foundation of the soul" gave grace's influx a truly physical aspect by corresponding the feeling of the experience to a new "sense." Because Edwards was able to describe in *Religious Affections* the permanent changes a saint's perception undergoes after conversion, he came close to making an argument for a correspondence between the affections and a "physics of the brain." The "foundation" or "physics" in the soul is a new one, and wholly spiritual, but he articulates the new perception in *sensual* terms, rendering the spiritual in terms of new physical acuities in vision, and hearing, and the brain. In this way the experience of conversion, the influx of grace, becomes a metaphor for the generation/regeneration of consciousness. As we shall see in the upcoming discussion on Emerson's written style, his dizzying sentences render the connection between what we are thinking (and being led to believe) and the physical experience inextricable and immediate, conflating thinking and physical experience in each moment.

Lost Amid Abstraction

In their efforts to theorize and describe the experience of conversion, what these writers continually return to is the idea of consciousness as an "inner sense," a view Antonio Damasio argues has been held by as diverse a group of thinkers as Locke, Kant, Freud, and William James, as well as himself. Much like Edwards's relation of thinking to feeling in his formulation of the "sense of the heart," the "inner sense" is "selective; it is continuous; it pertains to objects other than itself; it is personal."[63] Interestingly, the definition of "core consciousness" Damasio provides relates to many of the questions and formulations regarding ideas about the mind addressed by the Puritans, Edwards, and Emerson in addressing the problem of conversion. We hear in Damasio's descriptions of core consciousness, echoes of Shepard's Puritans' problems with "closing with Christ," Edwards's concept of the "actual idea," and Emerson's emphasis on "genius's" relation to action:

> Core consciousness is generated in pulselike fashion, for each content of which we are to be conscious. It is the knowledge that materializes when you confront an object, construct a neural pattern for it, and discover automatically that the now-salient image of the object is formed in your perspective, belongs to you, and that you can even act on it. You come by this knowledge, this discovery as I prefer to call it, instantly: there is no noticeable process of inference, no out-in-the-daylight logical process that leads you there, and no words at all—there is the image of the thing and, right next to it, is the sensing of its possession by you.[64]

The same problem admitted by Herschel regarding the impossibility of locating the part of the brain that makes the discovery seems to remain a mystery for neurologists such as Damasio: "What you do not ever come to know directly is the mechanism behind the discovery, the steps that need to take place behind the seemingly open stage of your mind in order for core consciousness of an object's image to arise and make the image yours."[65] Emerson calls this phenomenon the "universal impulse to believe," a term that manages to contain the physiological potential and ability, because "man is a method," to body forth ecstatic knowing.

However, Herschel considers more what man *can* know regarding his "sentient self" through reasoning, articulating an act of consciousness echoing Edwards's "attention of the mind in thinking." For Edwards one can become aware, through conscious reflection and examination, of the "ordering" process consisting of a train of causes that constitute the path of our experience. Much like Edwards in *Freedom of the Will*, Herschel claims that the will is determined by causes, and the two men would agree that the will responds to an axis of gratification because, as Edwards explained, the will "is as the greatest apparent good is." Yet Herschel is able to articulate what Edwards's Calvinism would not permit him to say explicitly: despite the seeming determination of the will by causes, our knowledge of those causes actually generates *choices* and allows us "to act or not to act":

> When he contemplates still more attentively the thoughts, acts, and passions of this his sentient intelligent self, he finds, indeed, that he can remember, and by the aid of memory can compare and discriminate, can judge and resolve, and, above all, that he is irresistibly impelled, from the perception of any phenomenon without or within him, to infer the existence of something prior which stands to it in the relation of a *cause*, without which it would not be, and that this knowledge of causes and their consequences is what . . . determines his choice and will, in cases where he is nevertheless conscious of perfect freedom to act or not to act.[66]

Herschel, like Edwards, recognized the contextual nature of the freedom of the will, grounding its "inclinations" in the "perception of any phenomenon without or within him," maintaining that it was within the act of *attention* that the "world within him is thus opened to his intellectual view, abounding with phenomena and relations, and of the highest immediate interest," and by these views one is made to continually realize that "this *internal sphere of thought and feeling* is in reality the source of all his power."[67]

Also within these conceptions of the space of consciousness there is always the fringe and horizon beyond which investigation can reach because ideas are as yet too "abstracted," as Edwards would say. Herschel calls it the "frontier of knowledge," affording a "distant glimpse of boundless realms beyond, where no human thought has penetrated, but which yet he is sure must be no less familiarly known to that Intelligence which he traces throughout creation than the most obvious truths which he himself daily applies to his most trifling purposes."[68] Within this outer space of consciousness, beyond the horizon of what can be distinguished or tested as a truth lie those indiscernible or *vague* truths because they are as yet unformed. Emerson would take up this project of the *instatement* of the vague in theories of the mind, drawing connections between the role it plays in perception and, therefore, epistemology. It is why, as Robert D. Richardson shows, Emerson held that "it is always the instructed eye, not the object seen, that gives the highest delight, that connects us with the world," and that it is for this reason "his favorite symbol for inquiry and knowledge and wisdom was the image of the active eye."[69] For Shepard and Edwards as well, the trope and the goal are the same: to "see" things

"as they are," to see what is "really wrapped up in those words" and penetrate beyond the limitations of signs and static concepts. And in order to
align the axis of their congregations' views correctly, it was their role as
ministers to "instruct" them and inculcate a habit of mind equating piety
with an active, lively consciousness. Laura Dassow Walls claims that
Emerson read in Reed's *Observations on the Growth of the Mind* that the
"mind's essential characteristic lay in its 'power of acquiring and retaining
truth,' which was achieved only by active and continual exertion."[70]
Indeed, Emerson came upon this idea in Reed, but this notion had already
been articulated in Reformed theology and had been a defining experience in New England culture since the Puritans transplanted the doctrine
of preparation and exhorted their flocks to "comprehend" the infinitude
of God's love and wisdom.

William James would say much later, "the sustaining of a thought
when I choose to—this is a legitimate exercise of the 'will to believe.'"
Because of the spiritual discipline he enforced, Shepard's Puritans were
not afforded the freedom to sustain the thoughts/feelings they had that
might have led them to experience the power available through a feeling
of grace. Edwards could, on the other hand, begin to conceive consciousness as containing the dynamics that made sustaining a thought possible.
His notions of the "room of the idea," the "sense of the heart," an "actual
idea," and "attention of the mind in thinking" were all ways for him to
conceptualize consciousness as a conductive imaginary whose role in conversion was to sustain the activity of a "feeling mind" in forming affective
conviction. As in the works of Edwards, Reed, and Herschel, the sustaining of a thought when one chooses creates not only the axis of gratification
but generates the inclination of the will to fulfill that desire.

The freedom and ability to sustain a thought, to allow the combination
of intellect and imagination access to see things "as they are," has relied,
in Shepard and Edwards, and remains so in Emerson, on an individual's
commitment, described earlier, to the constant "exertion" of consciousness in exceeding frameworks of understanding encoded by language to
penetrate the abstractions "wrapped up in words." As such, those indistinct truths lying at the edge of consciousness constitute the place of the
vague in which one is encouraged to establish the feeling of relations to
those emergent truths through creative reasoning. Consciousness
remained for Emerson a discursive medium, a collection of known truths
and bodies of knowledge holding the potential for growth beyond those
frames to become closer to God. As the interpretations of nature by which
man "takes the world into himself," Emerson's idea of conversion translates what the Puritans called "using" all the "means" to perceive grace

into another incarnation of the idea of "use" in that man, not God, becomes the creative center by "using" nature's resources to fully realize man's divinity in the process of rendering truth self-evident.

One of these "means" was the very language Shepard, Edwards, and Emerson employed to help their audiences see what was "wrapped up" in the words they were using. I have discussed to what extent Shepard's ministry was unsuccessful at effecting and affecting conversion through a disciplined search for certainty of spiritual knowledge, whereas Edwards incorporated a liminal space in consciousness—a place of the vague—in his theory of consciousness, rendering glimpses of truth the engine of spiritual discovery and the "sense of the heart" the entry point of those glimpses. Walls claims that Emerson's turn to science was in itself a deliberate move to get "beyond the perishable language of men and things, and enter directly the mind of God."[71] He attempted to do this, Walls notes, through "endless metaphorical play," sifting the universe "through bits of itself, until the point was clearly to arrive at no one triumphant solvent metaphor but at the metaphorical relationship itself."[72] This kind of thinking renders truth "not an essence but a relationship between bodied beings" or "a way of living in a universe in which every relationship is a dynamic balance of mutually destabilizing opposites."[73] Metaphor for Emerson is a vehicle for sustaining thought in that imaginative space suspending truth in formation, propelling an investigator beyond static notions into a conscious space requiring the same ontological state of active passivity the Puritans embodied in their receptivity to grace. The original relations established through what Donald Pease calls the "metaphorizing power" are nothing less than moments of conviction in the process of discovery when new truths are experienced relationally through the inclination of the will.[74]

Anyone who "reads" Emerson understands how his sentences force his audience into a certain mode of experiencing his ideas that disrupt familiar reading habits. One needs, in the spirit of the "metaphorizing power," to *figure* them out, as it were. One cannot read them in the standard linear fashion. Instead, his audience must become habituated to a thinking process enacting the process of discovery described by Reed and Herschel—becoming readers/natural philosophers who turn to their powers of reasoning and imagination to make meaning out of what often feels like the chaos of his sentences. Emerson writes so that his readers will need to discern the truths of what he says through the same process that a scientist undertakes—by becoming comfortable with the nature of investigation and the constant feeling of being lost in the place of abstraction, or the "vague."

For Edwards, conversion hinged on the blurry views afforded by "something that is seen, that is wonderful" because they indicated the direction of the soul. Shepard's Puritans, however, were uncomfortable with blurry views of anything because they desired certitude. They desired accuracy in perception, to know that the phantasms generated in their minds mirrored the thing in nature. The logic of invention was an attempt to overcome their human fallibility, to overcome inaccuracy in the interpretation of sensory input. Perry Miller asserts that "sinful man tries all his life to see things as they are, to apprehend truth and to act by it, but at every endeavor his senses blur, his imagination deceives, his reason fails, his will rebels, his passions run riot."[75] These views of what Edwards called "something" result from actual ideas stimulated in the thinking process precisely because they generate the relations establishing new horizons in scientific, philosophical, and spiritual worldviews. In Edwards's formulation, the soul is constantly moving into these views, feeling its way in the relations that channel the will to believe in the "something" emerging from the vague. As shown in the previous chapter, Edwards held that conviction about both scientific and spiritual truths often crystallize in consciousness without evidence or proof to support the feelings of conviction. In fact, Edwards's discussions of "actual ideas" and the "sense of the heart" set forth the anti-intellectualist theory that an aesthetic response to the beauty of an idea and the "satisfaction" of that experience are enough "proof" of its validity to carry the soul into new relations with God and the world.

Cultural Tropings

Emerson scholars, in turn, have explored the central role these blurry views of emergent meaning play in what Eduardo Cadava notes is Emerson's concern with the "unknown effects produced by politics, history, rhetoric, or nature."[76] Cadava takes a look at how Emerson's use of language engages "changing historical and political relations" to "alter and set in motion" those "shifting domains of history and politics" through a "mobilization of terms from one shifting context to another."[77] Cadava argues that Emerson's use of the shifting contexts raises awareness of how language "conditions the possibility of what we call history and politics," urging readers to "begin to account for how language works historically to establish reference and meaning."[78] Therefore, reading Emerson is a lesson in the relations between the transitory and the permanent. Cadava shows that Emerson's pervasive referencing of the weather reflects his desire to inscribe within the movement of his language the very unpredictability of nature and "to trace the permanency of the infinite variability that makes nature nature."[79] As such, the transitoriness of Emerson's language, reflecting the method of nature, registers not only the movements of the thinking process, but also the limits of that process. Cadava takes as his point of departure the fact that the word "climate" is derived from the ancient Greek word *klima*, which refers not only to a latitudinal zone but also an "inclination" or "slope." Climate, he argues, "refers to both what falls from the sky and what falls away from the understanding."[80] Cadava's insight brings us back to what appears to be the joint imperative of Edwards and Emerson—to lead us toward the "something" that is incalculable or uncontrollable. Although Cadava does not know whether Emerson knew that the ancient Greek root for "climate" was *klima*, denoting an inclination, he argues that Emerson uses the word "inclination" to describe the movement of the will away from the understanding and toward abstraction and theorizes that the movement is grounded in the soul's context, suggesting Emerson's willingness to conceptualize the terms of thinking as atmospheric or in the grandest context of all—of charting stars in the "private observatory" of one's mind.

In addition, Cadava shows how Emerson's use of language as the movement of nature enacts a process of transformation meant to encourage a rethinking of our relations to politics, history, rhetoric, or nature. These transformations that mobilize terms "from one shifting context to another" draw our attention to the way these terms mean in their differing contexts and realign our relations to those terms whose previous context had heretofore determined their meanings. Extricating certain terms from history and putting them back into play undermines the power history and its contexts hold to determine how we think. At this point in drawing connections between Shepard, Edwards, and Emerson regarding the role that conversion has played in American intellectual history, it becomes clear that the role of the "actual idea" is primary. Though Shepard fostered spiritual discipline, he was aware of the contextual nature of the will and that a will to believe depended on meaningful terms—working terms that were alive in their specific context. The faith of his saints depended on his ability to mobilize "New England" as a new term, as an "actual idea," in the morphology precisely because the context had shifted. Indeed, the sermon series on the parable of the ten virgins is an expression of Calvinist doctrine in response to the New World context. It is a remarkable way to imagine the kind of work that Edwards and Emerson do with their own compositional acts—mobilizing an entire culture and society in a new direction, an imagined migration to new spiritual and intellectual shores.[81] It is also a remarkable way to understand Shepard's own transcriptions of the testimonies. His notebook is a kind of material representation of Emerson's "bare common," a compositional space containing individual expressions of attitudinal alignment with the Holy Spirit, a collection of the efforts of lone voices finding a renewed "common" faith. Cadava presents Emerson's imperative:

> If we are to lessen the chances that we will simply repeat the structures of authority we seek to change, we must try to understand the genealogy of the language we use—we must try to understand the history that is sealed within this language and which, if not taken into account, may align us without our knowing it with positions we oppose.[82]

The centrality of Edwards's "actual idea" has been lurking in American literary criticism in significant ways. Having divined the need to re-circulate terms and ideas in order to "give a new direction and purpose to fragments of the past," his *Religious Affections* is an explicit demonstration of this effort.[83] Whereas Emerson's sentences provide the shifting contexts needed to rethink an idea, Edwards's extensive quoting of Shepard combined with his efforts to articulate conversion according to the new concepts of idealism allowed Edwards to "trope" Calvinist doctrine and terminology in the way that Richard Poirier attributes to the Emersonian pragmatists he discusses in *Poetry and Pragmatism*. Edwards's quotes from Shepard are literally textual "fragments" from seventeenth-century New England that he takes up to put back into circulation. Moreover, as with all troping, Cadava notes, "the new can only be new, really new, if it is produced through memory and repetition—but a memory and repetition which at the same time introduce a new element."[84] The quotes from Shepard not only serve as points of departure for Edwards, but they also ground his idealism in the Calvinist doctrine he remained devoted to. In other words, they provided a stable doctrinal platform in which he could root and justify his new terms and concepts. An "actual idea," the "sense of the heart," and a "feeling mind" all became the tropings and inflections of the idea of conversion that Edwards would use to make the doctrine of grace *his* own: "Every age must write their own books," Emerson would say, and Edwards was the embodiment of this ideal, writing *the* philosophical and theological treatises for his age.

Yet, Edwards did not only write the books of his age, delivering the concept of conversion back to saints anew with terms informed by his idealism; the new concepts of an "actual idea," the "sense of the heart," and a "feeling mind" transformed the act of conversion into the conscious experience of rethinking and realigning (or repronouncing and renouncing) one's relation to the "politics, history, rhetoric, and nature" that Cadava claims Emerson's sentences would enact. Granted, Edwards would not have conceived of religious conversion as a rethinking of one's relation to any one of these earthly contexts because conversion was still safely anchored to the doctrine of grace, but in situating the reception of grace and the will to believe within an act of consciousness that felt like the paradigm shifts resulting from scientific and philosophical acts of imagination and discovery, he located the power for personal and cultural renewal within consciousness, understood as a pious receptor of the higher laws of God. Conversion for Edwards denoted the rebirth of the soul into Christ, but the same act of consciousness also stimulated saints into rethinking their relations to both nature and history, thereby conducting the soul into new worldviews and new identities based on the projection of the self into these new worldviews.

Emerson's Ministrations

Edwards's sensitivity to the nexus of language, perception, and truth places him in a direct line with his predecessor Shepard—it was a minister's calling to calculate the effects of the intermingling of these and other nuances of Calvinist theology. Shepard enforced spiritual discipline through his ministry, but he also revived his saints' faith by reviving New England as a means to grace, and Edwards sparked the Great Awakening. In turn, Emerson's own work as an essayist and lecturer takes up this ministerial calling in tending to the health of America's souls. Emerson's articulation of the intersection of language, perception, and truth, that intersection being the *soul*, can be found in the essay "Circles." Richard Poirier sums up the dynamic as a "discursive formation," what a good minister would be a master at controlling:

> "Circles" in Emerson are equivalent to what are now sometimes referred to as "discursive formations." Neither of these is to be confused with pacified versions that go by the name of "shared" or "communal" assumptions. A "circle" or discursive formation does far more than passively reflect or represent some form of truth or knowledge presumed to be external to it. Rather, an Emersonian "circle," like a Foucauldian "discursive formation," actively creates truths and knowledge and then subtly enforces their distribution. It follows that truths and systems of knowledge are to be viewed as in themselves contingent, like other convenient fictions, and scarcely the worse, if you are an Emersonian

pragmatist, for being so. It is fictions that give us hope. Among those forms of knowledge or truth created by an Emersonian "circle" is knowledge by any individual of its sense of identity and selfhood, along with the language by which that self is codified or becomes articulate. More significant still, a "circle" also determines the vocabulary by which the self learns to *resist* its own sense of identity, especially since that identity should be recognized as, in part, an imposed one.[85]

Of course, the idea that truths are contingent holds that those truths are subject to unseen effects, that they are conditioned by "something" that is as yet not seen, as Edwards would have it. Even in a Calvinist universe, one makes discoveries of God's truths that, though they are preexistent in the mind of God, are as yet unseen to the human eye—they exist as God's hidden will. Truth in this sense is not exactly contingent upon unforeseen effects, because they are, in fact, known to God, but they are contingent upon what the human eye cannot see. Therefore, even in a Calvinist universe, the soul is always moving in the direction of those truths formed in the discursive formations Emerson calls "circles." In addition, the living faith Puritans sought to embody called upon them to continually renew their knowledge of their election, to continually renew their "sense of identity and selfhood" through the affective cycle of their experiential faith. The soul, even in Calvinist theology, is "more nearly a function," as Poirier claims it is in Emerson, "and yet no determination is made as to when the function occurs or from where it emanates. The soul has no determinable there or then, no here or now."[86] Rather, as in Emerson's thinking, it only *"becomes"* because it "appears or occurs only as something we feel compelled to live into or to move toward *as if* it were there."[87]

Therefore, because the doctrine of grace does not limit the movement of the soul in Emerson (because the concept does not limit the view), we see a full realization of the essential and saving quality of the vague. We live in the direction of the soul, in the indistinct "something that is seen, that is wonderful," and this "something" is wonderful because, as Poirier notes, it is in these "premonitory gestures or transitions"—and I would add views—that the soul "reveals itself" by "abandon[ing] one form or an incipient form for the always beckoning promise of another, though this 'other' will also prove a limitation."[88] These places of the *"as if"* serve the same purpose as the work of imagination does for the natural philosophers discussed earlier. By opening up a conscious space for potential truths through the process of discovery, one elicits the feeling of conviction or will to believe in "something"—until that something has been tested through experience or experiments. Poirier calls the presence of these "premonitory gestures or transitions" of the soul within Emerson's writing his "superfluity." Emerson is able, Poirier explains, to "refloat the world, to make it less stationary and more transitional, to make descriptions of it correspondingly looser, less technical, more uncertain."[89] Indeed, this is clearly the opposite goal of Ramist logic, whose reliance on the syllogism, Miller explains, was the Puritans' way of lending "constancy to animate their judgments."[90] In Emerson's time, natural philosophers such as Herschel and Reed were generating acceptance of a science manifesting these same "looser, less technical, more uncertain" descriptions of the world: the convictions that resulted (that feeling accompanying *seeing beyond*) can be thought of as the soul's inclination toward rebirth into new relations existing as theoretical constructions of the self and world through belief. And the soul "knows," Poirier claims, that when it constructs new worldviews "it is creating only a new orbit or limit as it surges past and sweeps up the boundaries of an old one," so that the soul "knows" that "its progress is forever threatened by textuality, by contraction of work into a text. Thus the creative impulse which is the soul discovers in the very first stages of composition that it wants to reach out beyond any legible form, that it wants to seek the margins, to move beyond limits or fate."[91]

Considering Poirier's description of the dilations of the soul as contingent orbits, continually threatened by contractions into composition, it is ironic that Shepard's Puritans faced this very problem in being required for church membership to compose a story of their conversion and even more so that Shepard transcribed them into a permanent form of that contraction. Their conversion narratives, therefore, become an awful symbol of the soul's "legibility" manifesting the "contracting" work of conscience so present in the saints' lives. Emerson's essays, on the other hand, "ask to be read as an allegory," Poirier explains, "in which the movements of the soul in its circles represent the movements of creative energy in his sentences and paragraphs."[92] The purpose of this creative energy, of Emerson's "superfluity," is to thrust us into a place of uncertainty, where we are confronted with the disorienting space of the "actuality," to use Edwards's term, or transitoriness of the experience of his sentences. Placed in this position, we must find our own way through a thoroughly undisciplined examination of our response to the context in which we find ourselves, looking inward rather than to any authority for that response. In this way Emerson compels us to "minister" to ourselves. Our responses realign our axis of view, constituting the saving act of new perception and offering renewed access to the power of Spirit. In the Puritan saints' experience, knowledge of their election could only be achieved if they chose to embark on the perceptive pilgrimage. Though their souls had been predestined as either elected or damned, they could only realize this fact through perceptual alignment with the Holy Spirit. They could not choose their election, but they could choose to discover their election, becoming, in a sense, natural philosophers of the soul.

Without the concept of the Fall or the doctrine of election to frame his theory of the mind, Emerson could fully endow consciousness with the power to know through experience, and experience in knowing, the higher laws of Spirit. In Emerson, it is not about whether one is "elect" or "unregenerate," but how one sees the world and self, or, more specifically, how one chooses to see the world and self. That we can choose our "election," as it were, because we can choose to realign and rethink our relationship to the world, underlies the purpose of the "superfluity" present in *Nature*. As Philip Gura notes, *Nature* and its "superfluity" were not readily accepted by the likes of conservative Unitarian ministers such as Francis Bowen who found *Nature* "painful" and "frequently bewildering" to read, complaining that the reader was too busy "hunting after meaning, and investigating the significance of terms."[93] These complaints would emerge, Gura demonstrates, from controversies over the philological premises held by the Unitarians who "championed an empirical, rational reading of the Bible."[94] Transcendentalists such as Emerson, whose religious beliefs were originally aligned with Unitarianism, came to question and finally reject this theology framed by the empiricist philosophy of John Locke. The philosophical stronghold of empiricism was a major hurdle for those who wished to challenge its theories of the nature of man, which maintained that one could understand God better through "logical language" and that nature was absorbed through "multiple nerve endings." Influences on Emerson such as Reed and Coleridge, however, proved to Emerson that nature could move man to a higher spiritual plane through the interpretive acts of the reason. Gura argues that with the publication of *Nature*, "America's bondage to Lockean epistemology was symbolically broken": what Bowen thought was Emerson's overuse of nouns and adjectives in *Nature* was Emerson's attempt to "free his contemporaries from the constrictions of a vocabulary inadequate to describe their profound religious experience."[95] *Nature* was Emerson's declaration that the "mediation between God and Man—Nature and Spirit—was not something experienced only by the historical Christ" but that the "machinery of transcendence . . . was available to all men, if only they could accept a vocabulary, as well as a theology, based on their intuitive insight into the natural world."[96]

Acceptance of a new vocabulary and theology depended on the reader's willingness to learn the perceptual habits, and appreciate the perceptual qualities, inherent in transcendence to that higher spiritual plane. *Nature* provides the steps for doing so. In a phrase that provides concision to Edwards's theory of perception at the beginning of *Freedom of the Will*, Emerson claims in the first chapter called "Nature" that when we approach nature with a "poetical sense in the mind" we mean the "*integrity of impression* made by manifold natural objects."[97] The term "integrity" used here captures the sense, discussed earlier, of the complex intermingling of language, perception, and truth, and of the desire and choice to engage one's environment or context in such a way that increases one's chances of "tak[ing] up the world" into oneself. That choice alone cast the world as an inexhaustible means to one's happiness. One's "integrity of impression," for Emerson, leads one not down the path to knowledge of election, but into a perceptual realm allowing an individual to distinguish between a "stick of timber of the wood-cutter" and the "tree of the poet." One is not born "saved": one adopts a saving perception.

Both Laura Dassow Walls and Lee Rust Brown discuss how Emerson's insight at the Jardin des Plantes solidified his transition from an empiricist mode of reading nature to one employed in the study of natural history, resulting in the conceptualizing and writing of *Nature*. Brown explains that what happened in the midst of the cabinets was Emerson's realization that the "Muséum's classifications were not only vehicles for communicating nature's meanings; in a surprisingly literal sense, they made up the form and content of meaning itself" because "opaque images were conceptually broken and dissolved."[98] For a spectator in the Muséum, "classification belonged to the contemporary realm of intellectual activity," recovering a divine plan that "was immanent in nature rather than . . . dictated at the beginning of history" and interpreted by a "retrospective reference to the dicta of scripture or sacred history."[99] These natural facts, rather, "introduced the eye into an *otherwise invisible world of referential and compositional practice*."[100] Brown recognizes the connection between the hermeneutic tradition of the Puritans and Emerson's response to the "hieroglyphic aspect of nature" embodied by the Muséum, but he does not provide a discussion of the complexity imbedded within that hermeneutic tradition and the issues of mind, perception, nature, and the reception of Spirit that preoccupied Shepard and Edwards and which Emerson inherited.[101] To attribute Emerson's introduction to the mind's role in aligning the axis of perception to the Spirit solely to his revelation at the Muséum elides his longstanding and familiar knowledge of Calvinist theology and experience.

Walls, too, provides an impressive examination of Emerson's adoption of the principles of natural history, but she too does not tie Emerson's interpretive imperative to a Reformed tradition that defines the conversion process as the experiential nexus of mind, perception, nature, and Spirit. Like Brown, she recognizes *Nature* as a text whose purpose is to represent the various stages of perceptual approaches to nature as the route to transcend fact. Importantly, her reading of *Nature* includes the recognition of the human tie to the materiality we want to transcend, echoing the unfortunate situation that the Puritans saw as the Fall. In addition, Walls's reading of *Nature* discusses how Emerson's theory that "nature is animated by man" relies on the "self-evidencing interplay of mind and matrix, whereby the external world is necessary for the mind's realization, and mind or concepts are equally necessary to assemble a world of dead atoms into living meaning."[102] *Nature* enacts the transition from an empirical realism to transcendental idealism because the "ascending chapters or 'cantos' in *Nature* describe the necessary steps or stages in this marriage [of mind and matrix] and prophesy its ultimate fruit, man, with his divinity fully recovered."[103] Therefore, *Nature* teaches us to read the landscape not only of nature, but of our minds as well. Each chapter, as an ascension to a new perceptual stage, teaches us how to use nature as a means to realize our divinity and to reflect on our own thinking process in the interpretive act.

Nature incorporates the tools with which to experience what Leon Chai calls "transparent seeing," a form of perception in which "perception . . . becomes conscious of itself as an act of pure seeing and assimilates the thing seen to the act of seeing."[104] In this way,

> mind experiences the transparency of things (their capacity for assimilation) and hence the unbounded nature of perception itself, the absence of any opaque objects obstructing its field of vision. This *unboundedness* of perception constitutes the *Infinite*. . . . As such, it is no longer something external to us (a God outside us) but rather within ourselves.[105]

Here, Chai stumbles upon the idea of *feeling* (what he refers to as seeing) the "Infinite," what Emerson calls the "unbounded substance," achieved through acts of perception penetrating the externalizing forces of ordinary vision and discursive understanding. It is an act of seeing equivalent to Edwards's "sense of the heart," and it constitutes a transcendentalist's version of the Puritan experience of conversion when the saints might, as the early Shepard exhorted, "not take in a little" but "comprehend the height, depth, length, breadth of Christ's love." In fact, in characterizing the Infinite as "no longer something external to us (a God outside us) but rather within ourselves," Chai's argument informs my connections between the Puritan dilemma over how grace's workings were conceptualized and theories about the nature of perception. Chai's formulation of "transparent seeing," offering the assimilation of the Infinite, echoes the conceptual and descriptive dilemmas Puritans faced in theorizing conversion, because, as Chai shows, the Infinite is experienced both as an external force in man's life and is felt internally through assimilation. As such, in Puritan doctrine the experience of unbounded perception of God's love could be represented as man's voluntary return to God or as God's turning of man to him because, as Chai notes, the act of "transparent seeing" marked the intersection of the two, thereby blurring the boundaries and character of its effects.

Both Walls and Brown call what happened to Emerson in the Muséum a "revelation," with Brown noting that Emerson was getting tired of his experience in Paris as a flâneur, that it "came as a kind of relief or release from pressures that had been building throughout his stay."[106] That Emerson had a "revelation" leading to his insight into God's divine plan is an ironic moment in the history of America conversion narratives. What so many saints longed to experience—the moment of irresistible insight into God's divine plan and the attendant realization of one's own calling—came to Emerson in an immediate, *affective* moment of transcending an earthly context to see the divine idea beyond it. He recorded in his journal a sort of testimony of the experience—a conversion narrative—of this newly acquired "sense." He felt "an occult relation between the very scorpions and man," declaring, "I feel the centipede in me,— cayman, carp, eagle, and fox. I am moved by strange sympathies." Indeed, he had the experience of seeing what was "really wrapped up in" the Latin words designating the plants and natural objects within the cabinets. He experienced what Brown calls the "dynamics of transparency" the Muséum embodied with its classifications, referring "events to the activities of reading and interpretation, in which the mind manages to see 'through' (both by means of and in spite of) figured surfaces in order to clarify initially invisible meanings."[107]

What Emerson presented to the public with the publication of *Nature* was not unlike the *ordo salutis* the saints used to advance along the perspectival stages one needed to prepare for the reception of the Spirit. Tacitly understood by the saints, but explicitly presented to readers of *Nature*, was the choice to embark on a perspectival pilgrimage aligning the axis of one's vision with the realm of the ideal/spirit, significantly improving the odds of one's salvation presented at the beginning of this chapter. Whereas the morphology of conversion was conceived as a path for realizing one's predestined place in God's plan, removing the possibility that a saint could do anything to effect grace, *Nature* presents a series of options for perceiving and reading nature, specifically for deciding whether one wants to be a person who, with a transcendental idealist perception, sees a "tree" (like a poet) or one who remains locked in an empirical worldview and sees a "stick of timber" (like a wood-cutter). Each chapter addresses a kind of perception, which is captured in the chapter's title. The first chapter invites readers to consider whether they have the perspective of a wood-cutter or of a poet, setting up the following chapters of *Nature* in much the same way as Edwards envisioned *Religious Affections* and how Shepard's morphology is organized—as a series of signs against which an individual can interpret experience to mark the progression of the soul. In *Nature*, as Brown, Gura, and Walls remark, the kind of perspective each chapter addresses is more transcendent by degrees, weaning the reader from an empiricist mode of perception in "Commodity" to a transcendental one in "Spirit." In addition, within each classification of perspective by chapter, Emerson provides classifications of each classification within each chapter to further habituate us to the "invisible steps of thought" *Nature* provides.

These classifications within classifications introduce the variety of "undiscovered regions of thought" man has at his disposal, what Emerson asserts is available through the "doctrine of Use." For example, in the chapter called "Beauty" he breaks down this rubric into three aspects, the first being the "delight" we feel from the "simple perception of natural forms." For those of us who suffer from being "cramped by noxious work or company," we can find pleasure as long as we "can see far enough," as long as we can see the "sky and woods." The second aspect he broaches is the "spiritual element," the "high and divine beauty which can be loved without effeminacy" and is that "which is found in combination with the human will." This type of perception Emerson challenges can only be attained "in proportion to the energy of [one's] thought and will" because an individual is "entitled to the world by his constitution." Finally, the third aspect of beauty through which the world may be viewed manifests "as it becomes an object of the intellect." "The intellect," Emerson explains, "searches out the absolute order of things as they stand in the mind of God, and without the colors of affection." And in this searching, the "beauty of nature reforms itself in the mind, and not for barren contemplation, but for new creation." His conclusion to this chapter sums up his argument by stating, "the world thus exists to the soul to satisfy the desire of beauty." These classifications within classifications demonstrate his central argument that "Nature always wears the colors of the spirit," that it is through our own *willingness* that we delimit our perception of nature. In a deceptively simple sentence in the first chapter of *Nature*, Emerson sums up the moment in *Religious Affections* where Edwards describes the experience of evangelical humiliation during conversion, in which a view of "something" opens to expose the horizon of belief and of one's own potential: "In the tranquil landscape, and especially in the distant line of the horizon, man beholds somewhat as beautiful as his own nature."[108]

By presenting classifications of perception in the chapter headings and then comparing in each chapter the various kinds of perception producing a stick of timber or a tree, Emerson not only provides the stages necessary for ascending from lower facts to higher ideas, he presents the experience of transcendence as a choice the reader makes. *Nature* makes us conscious of the perceptual role in experience and clarifies the variety of ways open to us, through perception, that nature can be used to realize God's divine plan. In this way, *Nature* constitutes an actual idea, in the Edwardsean sense, of perception, offering not a rigid scheme for gaining knowledge (of one's election), as in the case of Shepard's morphology, but conceptualizing a sort of mechanism within consciousness that generates the process of knowing. *Nature* provides, for anyone who wishes, what Brown calls the "transcendental element" that the Muséum exposed Emerson to, that element being the "technique itself, the a priori 'device' through which nature was identified as both patent fact and latent power."[109] Whereas the *ordo salutis* presented stages of spiritual progress that referred to established models of experience found in scripture and doctrine, *Nature* locates the "transcendental element" or device within perception and consciousness stimulating the ongoing process of growth. It is the "universal impulse to believe," and because it functions as a fact of human consciousness, it assures Emerson that every American has the constitutional potential to become a "newborn bard of the Holy Ghost" and embody the moral law that will perfect democracy.

Though conversion was a cyclic event in the course of a saint's life, the *ordo salutis* defined the affective and epistemological experience in terms of a one-time event defined by historic precedence. The stages themselves do not have imbedded within them a dynamic reflecting the lived experience of the cyclic imperative. This is because conscience was the force structuring the steps, reinforcing them as separate, distinctive elements defined by clear experiential and perceptual prerogatives. *Nature*, on the other hand, is structured so as to take into consideration the ongoing process of conversion realized through the "universal impulse to believe," the transcendental "device" found in consciousness. Walls explains that the first half of *Nature*, constituted by the chapters "Commodity,"

"Beauty," "Language," and "Discipline," argue that nature's purpose is to educate us, that it is "made to serve" because "human reason gradually converts all the kingdoms of nature to the single kingdom of his will."[110] At this point in *Nature*, Walls argues, Emerson must "take up the problem the first half has created," that man has dissolved nature and subjected it to his will: "If nature's final end is to educate, or discipline, humanity through the agency of law, does physical nature actually exist?"[111] The answer, which he arrives at in the chapter "Spirit," objects to the idealism his theory proposes by claiming that his theory must be "progressive" (the missing crucial element in the *ordo salutis*) and therefore must hold that "there must then be something left outside the all-dissolving power of culture to act as a guide. . . . Just as consciousness cannot exist without objects, objects must exist outside consciousness."[112] The transcendental idealism Emerson presents in *Nature* structures our relation to objects as one in which, "one moment we are rebuilding nature in our own image [and] the next, nature is inviolable."[113]

Unlike the rigidly linear representation of conversion of the morphology, the representation of the "marriage" of mind and matrix in *Nature* captures the recursive dynamic of man's transcendent uses of nature. Yet, like the morphology, *Nature* provides the reader with a template for a way of seeing, which is always a form of reading, articulating an individual's use of the "means" for penetrating the facts of existence to see beyond them into the ideas of God. Therefore, *Nature* becomes, in effect, an *ordo salutis* with the means built into it for overcoming its own structure, an aspect of the process one would expect from Emerson who asks us to continually "look at the world with new eyes." It provides a practical account and habituates a practice of looking at the world "with new eyes," in effect creating practitioners of transcendentalism.

For Emerson, as Brown explains, this penetration to the ideas beyond the visible objects of our earthly context finds its expression in the metaphor of transparency by which the "eye converts opaque boundaries into transparent media."[114] This transparency function, opening the door to the idea behind objects—and hence revelation—cannot be divorced, Brown explains, from the actual biology of a human eyeball. As such, ordinary perception and revelation become indistinguishable and Emerson endorses this marriage by presenting the various classifications within each chapter of *Nature* side by side, thereby equalizing, or showing the varieties of perception, both ordinary and transcendent, working together to produce the correct perceptual axis necessary for "transparent seeing." Brown makes an important contribution to understanding Emerson's transparent eyeball passage in *Nature* when he explains that "transparency manifests itself only as an attribute of the medium lying between two discontinuous realms: the opaque eyeball that beholds [the retina] and the opaque surface that appears 'behind' or 'on the other side of' the transparent medium."[115] The transparent medium becomes active when we acquire new objects, and our desire for them, Brown claims, is "purely constitutional," because the eye "needs the new opacity, the new figure, in order to focus beyond, or through, the figure that more immediately blocks its observation."[116] In other words, with each activation of the transparency function between the subject and object, a new distance opens between the next object of focus and the subject. Brown argues that we move through experience in this way, by "tricking" or "troping" our way "through the suffocating solidity of the natural sphere."[117]

Transparency occurs in "adjustments of attention," in the transitions between intellectual focus, appearing or disappearing "only in the context of the shifting relations created by the intellect in its transit from old to new objects of focus," hence the "progressive" element included in Emerson's theory of transcendental idealism articulated in the chapter in *Nature* called "Prospects."[118] New prospects exist in both the new objects of focus and their expected conversion into transparency, appearing only "when the eye converts opaque boundaries into transparent media and thus sees through one defining, restricting form . . . to the image of more attractive things on the far side."[119] Brown's work goes a long way to explain the significance of the transparency metaphor for Emerson's work, describing its ethical and practical implications for American culture, and I would add to his discussion by noting that the efforts at focus Brown describes, the "attention" given to objects demanded by the constitution of the eye, make transparency the conductive force priming the space of the *vague*. Although Brown makes clear that transparency can only occur between two opacities, the idea of transparency foregrounds the need or impulse behind acts of attention. It is this physical impulse Brown describes so well that compels the search for new objects on the fringe of consciousness where the ordinary and divine are translated on equal terms. Edwards hailed this transitional moment by describing the conversions of opaqueness to transparency and back again as "*something* that is seen, that is wonderful," and it is felt as "a mode of awareness of the necessary distance between the self and its provisional objects."[120] The figure of Emerson's transparent eyeball, therefore, is a celebration of the receptive mode of active passivity so necessary to the conversion process of his forebears. The transparent eyeball is a mode of active searching after objects and their opaque secrets, which, in turn, primes the space of the vague for reception to the meaning-making project of the subject. Because, as Brown shows, "the essence of the transparent medium is to be between two things," Emerson's eyeball represents that place on the stairs "of which we do not know the extremes." It is a homely figure similar to Edwards's "room of the idea," but no less powerful for expressing the ongoing process of knowing, of converting the world into truth.

Emerson's aestheticizing of scripture allowed him to fully realize through his literary style the dynamics between an individual and the forces of history, society, rhetoric, and nature. The "universal impulse to believe" propels each of us beyond the discursive formations structuring what we know, or think we know, about ourselves and the material universe. It guides us beyond what we can explain or calculate into a sacred, vague space in consciousness where inchoate truths emerge and we are, hence, reborn into new relations. Though in Shepard's and Edwards's theology a saint's spiritual rebirth marked a new life in Christ, the saint's ties to Christian historical tradition and doctrine remained intact. Emerson, however, conceptualized conversion as liberation from *all* forms impeding the expansions of our "mental horizons." It is, therefore, not surprising that the historical concept of conversion, determining so many facets of his Puritan forebears' lives, is absent from his work. It is itself reborn in Emerson as a process of knowing rather than resting in the known, of constructing belief by turning away, as well as toward, history and what we consider to be the facts of our context to determine our own futures.

CHAPTER 4

William James's Uncertain Universe

Theory as Theology in The Varieties of
Religious Experience

Thus far we have seen how Thomas Shepard, Jonathan Edwards, and
Ralph Waldo Emerson undertook to minister a saving experience to
their congregations/audiences. We have seen an evolution, however, in
how each theologian/philosopher conceived a method of thinking aimed
at fostering a pious attitude. Shepard used the *ordo salutis* as a disciplinary
tool, having adapted it to fit the circumstances of the New World context.
Edwards, without sacrificing the integrity of the doctrines central to Calvinism, theorized conversion and a new "Logick" by adopting the idea of
consciousness as an active, creative force bringing God's world into being.
His concept of the "sense of the heart" as the feeling of conviction structuring not only spiritual but also scientific and philosophical beliefs about
the world foregrounded spontaneity and immediacy in the perception of
truth. By conceptualizing conversion as a process occurring in no particular preparatory order, Edwards freed his congregation from a preexisting, generic pattern of experience and made piety a matter of "attention
of the mind in thinking"—a form of spiritual experience turning a saint
away from external forms and toward the constantly unfolding glory of
God's universe occurring in consciousness. Emerson would then, through
his literary style as a whole, and especially through the structure of *Nature*,
attempt to habituate his audience to a type of thinking in which individuals minister to themselves through the continual process of converting
the world into truth. This idea of the conversion process placed the
responsibility for personal and cultural renewal squarely on the shoulders
of individuals and their ability to determine how history, rhetoric, nature,
and language structured reality and what their relationship to this reality
was. *Nature* acts as a kind of *ordo salutis* but with an important difference.

134

It habituates its readers to a transcendental idealism enlivening the process of knowing, rather than adherence to a rigid scheme for gaining certain knowledge.

A Method of Thinking after Darwin

With the breakdown of stable religious and scientific conceptual systems in the nineteenth century precipitated by Darwin, the roles that belief and uncertainty played in people's lives had to be reckoned. This chapter examines the central role the conversion dynamic plays in William James's work, focusing on his development of a psychology of religious experience in *The Varieties of Religious Experience* and of pragmatism as a philosophy whose premise that "truth is what happens to an idea" affirms the process of belief as conversional. Conversion finds a conceptual home in modern philosophy as James's pragmatic hermeneutic, a habit of mind tying conversion overtly to the process that drives consciousness. James characterizes conversion as the experience of the gap between a fact and its interpretation, a space in consciousness at the intersection of an individual's encounters with the unknown or indeterminate and his or her own thinking process informed by a "vital" collection of ideas. It is responsible for the ongoing work of establishing belief in the face of uncertainty, and in the spirit of Edwards, *The Varieties of Religious Experience*, as a sustained rendering of this process, embodies a "room of the idea" of the concept of conversion. Through the gathering and arranging of countless testimonies in *The Varieties of Religious Experience*, James anchors the process of conversion and the constituting and reconstituting of beliefs and bodies of knowledge in discourse and various discursive communities. In doing so he emphasizes an individual's continual efforts at reaching these "stages" of personal and cultural renewal, specifically through the adoption of the empirical method, which he advocates should direct all scientific and religious enquiries and is, because of the nature of the pragmatic hermeneutic, "founded in feeling."

Writing to his brother Henry in 1868, William James noted, "the more I think of Darwin's ideas the more weighty do they appear to me, though of course my opinion is worth very little."[1] This simple remark belies the complexity of this long, fervent decade. Not only was it the decade that followed the publication of Charles Darwin's *The Origin of Species*, but it was an especially tumultuous decade for James personally and professionally. His need to form his own opinions about scientific, religious, and philosophical questions was inextricably tied to his personal crisis that marked the 1860s. In his book *Science and Religion in the Era of William James*, Paul Jerome Croce distinguishes the various influences on James during this decade, stressing the defining convergence of James's process of individuation as a young adult at the Lawrence Scientific School at Harvard and the massive ideological upset brought on by the publication of *The Origin of Species*. Croce's examination of the cultural shift of the period 1820–1880 leads him to the conclusion that what he calls the "eclipse of certainty" triggered by Darwin would be the defining issue for this period and for William James's work.[2]

Defining "certainty" as a "cultural category indicating confidence or assurance in any particular idea or belief," Croce argues that although the nineteenth century began with pervasive certainty about scientific and religious outlooks, certainty in these areas began to slip as a result of several forces of change stemming from market competition, religious debates, scientific discoveries, and geographic expansion and shifts in social roles, among other things.[3] Croce identifies James as an apt figure to study because James's family background, shaped by his father's belief in the teachings of the theologian Emanuel Swedenborg, forged a lasting curiosity about religious experience, and his father's unconventional beliefs about raising children allowed James to explore many different interests before he felt self-imposed pressure to choose a career. Setting him on his career path and finally throwing him into the midst of the Darwinian debates at Harvard was his decision to become a scientist. James entered the Lawrence Scientific School in 1861 and, as was noted earlier, James was a young adult only beginning to identify and understand his own interests and their meaning in his life when he was faced with the religious, scientific, and philosophical revolutions that were beginning to be assimilated by America's intellectual elite.

Ultimately, Croce argues, James would accept the centrality of uncertainty in scientific and religious ideas, but it would take years for him to formulate "philosophies that cope with uncertainty."[4] Indeed, James would be a forerunner in the cultural struggle to conceive belief in the face of uncertainty, and as David Hollinger points out, *Pragmatism* would eventually offer the most sustained rendering of the cultural and individual process through which bodies of truth evolve. Hollinger calls this rendering a "natural history of belief" because James describes "how human beings, as a behavioral fact, form their ideas and change them in the course of experience, both individually and collectively. . . . He points to how scientific ideas change, how ideas we take to be true in one generation are so often replaced by other ideas later."[5] Hollinger explains that this is for James an empiricist's approach to life, and he places it within a historical context that recognizes the kind of originative work performed by Shepard's own collection of testimonies:

> Life as actually lived . . . suggests that we reside in an uncertain universe with real conflicts and real victories and real defeats. In such a world we cannot take anything for granted, including the salvation of those who are justified by faith. James is saying to members of his own religious tribe that in order to vindicate even the most rudimentary aspects of the old faith, they have got to come to grips with the radical contingency of the human process by which culture is created, reproduced, and critically revised.[6]

Indeed, the testimonies of Shepard's congregants reflect the cultural work his ministry needed to foster in order to ensure the success of the covenantal mission of the new colony. The saints' disappointment in New England as a means to grace called for Shepard to address and respond to the radical contingency of his saints' experiences of the morphology of conversion. Having thrown the lived process of faith into a new context, the migration's effects demanded that New England's place in the *ordo salutis* be "critically revised." The process through which the new Puritan community was established involved collecting the testimonies of religious experiences, thereby lending foundational power to the new discursive, and therefore, cultural weight of that shared worldview made public by their application to church membership. In a voice echoing the ministerial directive of Shepard's sermon series on the parable of the ten virgins, Emerson begins "The Transcendentalist" by arguing that "the first thing we have to say respecting what are called *new views* here in New England, at the present time, is, that they are not new, but the very oldest thoughts cast into the mould of these new times."[7] Ironically, the radical contingency associated with the process of personal and cultural renewal brings us full circle, as it were, to yet another collection of religious testimonies: James's series of Gifford Lectures, published as *The Varieties of Religious Experience* in 1902, is an assemblage of spiritual confessions reflecting yet another effort to synthesize a response not only to an "uncertain universe" but to mobilize a "critical revision" of cultural categories.

Though Charles Darwin is mentioned only a few times in the *Varieties*, the work nonetheless demonstrates James's keen understanding of the full import of Darwin's argument and an urgency conveying James's profound shift to a new worldview that was a result of Darwin. As Croce explains, Darwin's disruption of the stable conceptual systems of his time was not necessarily attributable to the idea that humans had evolved from lower primate forms, but simply from his mode of argument:

> Although Darwin tried to adhere to contemporary inductive standards in his analysis of the emergence of species, his data was too remote, his causal agent too chance filled and his theory too conjectural to provide proof. . . . His theory of species development was the first major scientific theory to rely centrally on probabilistic thinking.[8]

Because the processes of evolution were unobservable, Darwin could not provide proof for his theory. Instead, he relied on the gathering of innumerable facts that could point toward an interpretation. He could then build a hypothesis explaining the patterns he had discerned, but he would have to convince his audience of the new interpretation based on his ability to integrate the masses of facts into his theory. These "probabilistic laws," as Croce calls them, could explain the patterns perceived in the facts, but a potential believer in these laws would have to accept the argument without any proof. That conceptual systems could be built on the yawning gap of uncertainty would hand down a Darwinian legacy steering scientific understanding of the world down the path of explanation rather than proof ever since.

The Origin of Species and the era of uncertainty it began generated important questions for all: What is its significance to philosophy? To religion? To culture? James deliberately begins the *Varieties* by prompting his audience to enter into this mode of inquiry by drawing it into an examination of the gap that exists between a thing and what it means to each individual. The answers to these questions would, for James, establish what he calls a "spiritual judgment" which determines a work's usefulness to people on an individual and a cultural level. James, however, modifies this term to a very potent one. Hence, his audience is asked to consider "revelation-value" as a way of thinking about how to estimate a work's worth, which is a suggestive term that does not get defined explicitly by James in the *Varieties*. James proposes the Bible as a test for establishing revelation-value in the first lecture of the *Varieties* to make such a determination. One way is to question a thing's origins, or how it came about; and the problem of determining a thing's origins presents James with the opportunity to draw an issue into the light and make a distinction by establishing "a general theory as to what the peculiarities in a thing should be which give it value for purposes of revelation."[9] The distinction he makes has to do with the terms on which we receive a work: we either accept a work despite human error and composition, or we fool ourselves by thinking we can determine the conditions under which a work was produced. This distinction is very important because it can determine how James's own lectures will be received, and it is also an inherent aspect of the kind of methodology he uses to build his argument in the *Varieties* because once a work becomes unmoored from what James calls the "historical facts" of its emergence, he is free to employ probabilistic thinking and interpretive hypothesis. Moreover, the distinction allows James to reinvent the concepts of "origin" and of "fact." I would argue that these two words are put into play in such a way that launches the *Varieties* into its task of characterizing and energizing the gap that exists between a work/thing and its "revelation-value" (or what it means to us). James needs to explode this gap, and he begins by destabilizing the ideas of "origin" and "fact," two realms of knowledge that would otherwise ward off the intervention of the interpretive mode in the search for meaning.

Using the Bible to represent any religious phenomenon, James argues that established modes of inquiry into such phenomenon ask certain questions: "Under just what biographic conditions did the sacred writers bring forth their various contributions to the holy volume? And what had they exactly in their several individual minds, when they delivered their utterances?" (*VRE*, 4). His response to these popular questions is to dismiss them and to redefine how such facts should be received: "These are manifestly questions of historical fact, and one does not see how the answer to them can decide offhand the still further question: of what use should such a volume, with its manner of coming into existence so defined, be to us as a guide to life and a revelation?" (*VRE*, 4–5). As James argues, even the Bible wouldn't fare well if historical facts were the only criteria for determining revelation-value because, as he asserts a little later on, "existential facts by themselves are insufficient for determining the value [of a book]" (*VRE*, 5). His argument will rely, instead, on his re-figuring the notion of fact. The new definition emerges in a theory that serves as the foundation for his hermeneutics, a methodology presupposing the interpretive act as the primary act determining the revelation-value of a work to its interpreter: "A book may well be a revelation in spite of errors and passions and deliberate human composition, if only it be a true record of the inner experiences of great-souled persons wrestling with the crises of their fate" (*VRE*, 5). Indeed, this new definition of existential fact grounding knowledge in the act of recording and composition, which implies human error, would leave any determination of revelation-value impossible simply because of the new fact's historical "unreliability." For James, existential facts that are historically based are insufficient to determine the revelation-value of a book, whereas existential facts conceived as a "true record," while also insufficient, at least imply the impossibility of determining such features of fact that a historical inquiry claims to be able to produce. That neither type can solely determine the "revelation-value" of a book places the burden of making that value judgment on the interpreter of those facts and hence the meaning that can be constructed.

The dismissal of the "origins" of a work conceived as the biographic conditions of the writer or what was going on in his or her mind at the time of writing as a basis for making a value judgment allows James to assert a new understanding of "origin" that is more amenable to a pragmatist. Within the context of an interpretive imperative, an origin occurs any time new meaning is made or a new hypothesis is proposed—as Emerson would phrase it, "an original relation to the universe" is created. This disconnection of a work's revelation-value from historical fact allows James to use the empirical method to gather religious experiences into a collection reflecting the "true record" he advocates. The empirical method ultimately serves James because, as he argues, it prevents him from imposing any of his own "over-beliefs" or the equivalent thereof—expressing a bias toward any one of the organized religions such as Buddhism or Christianity. Moreover, the empirical method affords the best conditions under which *variety* of religious experience can be illustrated and individual consciousness revered. From this variety, the experiences that were "pattern-setters" for all the "imitated conduct" that James says one finds in mass religions are presented for reconsideration in a newly interpreted way. James slyly calls these pattern-setting experiences "original," not simply because they represent un-imitated conduct but because, I would argue, he has presented them in that "revelatory" way, as newly interpreted. This is part of the originative work going on in works that James argues have revelation-value. These works allow an individual to become acquainted with the kinds of particulars that James finds so valuable: the works are revelatory because they present particulars arranged by an interpreter who perceived underlying patterns, and the fracturing and rebuilding of meaning involved in the interpretive process constitute the ongoing production of new or "original" worldviews. In this way, the empirical method suits James's hermeneutics, because it reflects a pragmatist's need to adjust and readjust knowledge and belief about the world.

Belief as Perceptual Adaptation

James must address his audience's anxiety surrounding his treatment of the collected religious experiences as "facts" because this new framework places them in the public arena doing a specific kind of "original" cultural work challenging cultural norms. Therefore, he calls upon his audience to have patience with him because he is sure he can prove, by the end of his lectures, not to have diminished the profundity of the religious experiences he has collected by treating them as "facts." I would argue, however, that it is precisely because he treats the testimonies as though they were facts that he grants them vital cultural power. Scholars have noted that the portions of the testimonies that James excerpts *carry the force* of having been understood by the testifiers as being caused by a higher power, while those portions including the claims of the cause are left out. By excising those parts of the testimonies that discuss the cause of the religious experience, James has in fact underscored the centrality of an individual's personal belief that the source of his or her religious experience was the result of a higher power. Although James has contained those beliefs within his own interpretive project, a rhetorical move that also subsumes those beliefs within his own compositional practice, he has not diminished their profundity in the least, but granted cultural power to those personally held beliefs about the origins of the experiences.

Although Wayne Proudfoot has called James's excerpting of testimonies of religious experience "apologetic," he has drawn attention to the cultural power associated with determining the "origins" of a belief.[10] He has compared Jonathan Edwards's and William James's analyses of religious experience from the standpoint of their respective regard for the causes (the origins) of the experience (in other words, whether or not the experience was a result of God's intervention or the subconscious or even a stomach-ache). The comparison is interesting because it recognizes the very issue at the heart of James's response to uncertainty. Proudfoot argues that although both Edwards and James understood that an assessment of a religious experience must be based on the pragmatist notion that subjects show signs of that experience in their practice, they diverge in their opinion about the role that should be played by a subject's *belief* about what *caused* the conversion to take place. Proudfoot argues that Edwards's interest in the fruits of a subject's religious experience stems chiefly from what the fruits infer about the cause of the experience. Edwards must determine that the conversion experience had supernatural origins, whereas James believes that the cause or origin of a belief or experience is "irrelevant to our assessment of it."[11]

Proudfoot concludes that James arrives at this notion because he has misread Peirce's "The Fixation of Belief," which proposes a scientific determination of truth that emerges *distinct* from an observer's perception of that truth and, therefore, the separation of a belief from its origin seems to Proudfoot to be made by James in that Peirce's confidence in the certainty of science prompted James to believe that when scientists go out into the world, they test hypotheses and are therefore immune to their own perceptual mediumship. However, James doesn't state anywhere that the cause of a belief is "irrelevant." He simply complicates the issue by examining how sturdy the "origins" of a truth are and by arguing for the discursive framing of all knowledge, including scientific "fact-finding," which is not immune to the effects of a perceptual medium. On the contrary, James would be the first to admit that all belief stems from our perceptions, and his decontextualizing of the excerpts in one way allows him to contextualize them in a new way. In addition, the fact that he excerpts seems to me to be a way to recognize implicitly that a subject's belief about the causes of a religious experience is in itself the result of an interpretive process.

For James, all "facts" are mediated by perception. Whether a hypothesis is a scientist's or a theologian's or a philosopher's, it "originates" from a subject's consciousness, or even from the unconscious—this is the thread running through James's hermeneutics that he calls a "science of religions." The *Varieties*, in fact, doesn't eschew the perceptual origins of the religious experiences it contains, but rather vigorously sustains a characterization of the perceptual realm (the space between a fact and its interpretation), which James presents as thoroughly deceptive, unpredictable, spontaneous, and ultimately *uncertain*. In James's struggle with uncertainty, he found that it was at the roots of human inquiry into both natural science and the ideal world of religion; he argued for an epistemology that would ultimately embrace this uncertainty and provide a methodology for interpreting experience and converting it into truth. The methodology rests on the understanding that our hypotheses about the world are at best guides emerging from information, events, hunches, and previous hypotheses. From there, one tests the hypothesis and, if it proves to be useful, it becomes a part of a new worldview paradigm and, if not, it is discarded. So, a more accurate conclusion about James's position with regard to the origins of beliefs about the natural, or any other world, is that they are never irrelevant—just indeterminate.

The epistemological space opened up by the impact of evolutionary theory prompts James to complicate the problem of confidence in causes of belief by consciously and controversially adopting the discourse of psychology to build an argument claiming that *as a matter of perception*, religious experience encompasses a much wider realm of concrete experience whose causes cannot necessarily be ascertained. As Gerald Bruns argues, James would have understood that a subject's belief about the origins of a religious experience *was* a part of that experience because for James knowledge and belief are social and linguistic. James doesn't mistakenly omit a subject's belief about an experience; he engages the interpretive gap that exists, even for the subjects whose testimony he uses. Responding to James's explanation about his "treatment" of the religious experiences, Bruns supports the idea that origins exist in the slippery, shadowy, unpredictable region of interpretation and discursiveness:

> At the outset of "Mysticism" . . . James says "Whether my treatment of mystical states will shed more light or darkness I do not know, for my own constitution shuts me out from their enjoyment almost entirely, and I can speak of them only at second hand." . . . What is it, however, to speak of them at first hand? Keep in mind that what James studies in the *Varieties* are not religious experiences given as empirical phenomena but, rather, firsthand accounts of such phenomena. The point to mark is that these accounts are given almost entirely in the traditional language of theological discourse. These experiences come down to us, in other words, not as "pure" experiences that we may construe as we will in any language that is authoritative for us but as already interpreted experiences, that is, experiences which are already theological in their self-understanding.[12]

Bruns recognizes the testimonies as having been already understood in a particular way and as being taken up by James as already discursive. Although James employs different discourses such as those of psychology and biology to re-construe the testimonies, the excerpts are ultimately taken as interpreted theologically by their subjects. And yet, the first thing James does in the *Varieties* is call the excerpted experiences he has collected "original," thereby shifting the conceptual framework for what can be considered "factual" evidence for a claim and what role that claim plays in belief. For example, Jonathan Edwards, who needed to establish that God was the cause of a subject's religious experience, relied on the evidence provided by a subject's outward behavior or on the testimony provided by the subject that there was real change in his or her emotional or intellectual behavior. The evidence, however, always needed to point toward the cause. James, on the other hand, is not looking to pin belief to a specific cause because it must remain open to interpretation and testing. James's evidence always points toward the next belief about the world or the next hypothesis that will open up more spaces for interpretation and adjustments in worldview. It is this space between the thing and its interpretation that allows the imagination to construct a "world" of knowledge and belief.

The *Varieties* promotes the role that perception and imagination play in belief by working to resolve the opposites James faced in the 1860s: those of absolutist science and dogmatic religion. He is able to do this by characterizing an internal reality whose interaction with a physical world cannot produce a defining boundary. James's non-dualistic approach to experience, therefore, places the shadowy region of consciousness at that boundary. A full rejection of certainty in religious experience and in science would entail a dismissal of the claim that one can have access to "things in themselves," and, for James, God is included as a "thing in itself." Charlene Haddock Seigfried has contributed to our understanding of why James grants a subject's affective response to experience a central role in the work of cultural revision by examining James's "pragmatic hermeneutic circle": the idea that "truths emerge from facts; but they dip forward into facts again and add to them; which facts again create or reveal new truth."[13] She stresses the notion that it provided an alternative to the debate (that had hardened as a result of Darwin) in the 1860s between realism and idealism, and that the alternative places uncertainty at the heart of experience:

> Since all appropriations [of the world] are interested, we cannot erase the trail of the human contribution, try as we may. In James's criticism of science, he argues that we should not even want to eliminate the subjective contribution of feeling in our appropriation of objects because then we would be forced to accept the positivist claim that we are determined by objects.[14]

And, taking into consideration the determining nature God's role had in a "certain" universe, the "subjective contribution of feeling" Seigfried speaks of coordinately frames James's philosophy with regard to religious experience. The pragmatic hermeneutic circle is inherently unstable; everything we believe about the world and ourselves originates in the flux of this non-dualistic dynamic. The *Varieties* is such a massive work because James takes on the challenge of characterizing the human condition in an uncertain world and is wholly committed to fleshing out a subject's pragmatic relation to it—with a major twist. James would like to offer the suggestion that to experience this non-dualistic world is in effect to "be religious," and when he explains why he has subordinated the intellectual part of religion to the feeling element in the *Varieties*, the answer mocks all stable conceptual systems:

> Individuality is founded in feeling; and the recesses of feeling, the darker, blinder strata of character, are the only places in the world in

which we catch real fact in the making, and directly perceive how events happen, and how work is actually done. Compared with this world of living individualized feelings, the world of generalized objects which the intellect contemplates is without solidity or life. (*VRE*, 501–2)

That these darker "strata of character" enliven the world provides the central concern of the *Varieties*, and the multitude of aspects of the human condition, therefore, necessarily generates this "uncertain" universe.[15] However, each chapter, whether explicitly or not, addresses the issue of approaching this uncertainty in that the adaptations an individual makes to experience, understood generically as "beliefs," prove to have an ameliorative function in an uncertain world. Believing has an adaptive power—the capacity to forge relational ties to new circumstances and contexts also built into these darker strata. In this way, the pragmatic hermeneutic "circle" might be better understood as a *spiral* in order to emphasize the open-ended nature of experience or of scientific and philosophical inquiry favored by pragmatists; belief remains tenuous until it has proven itself to work and only then does it "dip forward into facts" again, indicating an ever-increasing depth of meaning coordinate with an ever-widening expanse. The *Varieties* embraces uncertainty as a fact of experience in that it illuminates these darker strata, but more so in that it celebrates the human potential for growth.

The Varieties of Religious Experience as an "Actual Idea" of Conversion

As an explication of consciousness as the space where experience plays itself out in individual lives, the *Varieties* is carefully structured in how it presents the process of a pragmatic hermeneutics. The beginning chapters recalibrate how we understand certain feelings, and James depends heavily in the early chapters on throwing religious experience into new perspectives and introducing a vocabulary that sheds new light on certain concepts. Terms such as "sentiment of reality," "instrumentality of pure ideas," and "moods of contraction" and "expansion" need to break apart old understandings of experience as well as provide stable new conceptual ground for his audience. Granted the whole of the *Varieties* introduces new terms for consideration, yet the first few chapters are interesting in the persuasive power they demonstrate. One particular moment in "Circumscription of the Topic" reaches such a rhetorical momentum in James's definition of religion that although one may not be able to grasp his idea intellectually, the force of the words evokes the sense that we know what he means:

Religion, whatever it is, is a man's total reaction upon life, so why not say that any total reaction upon life is a religion? Total reactions are different from casual reactions, and total attitudes are different from usual or professional attitudes. To get at them you must go behind the foreground of existence and reach down to that curious sense of the whole residual cosmos as an everlasting presence, intimate or alien, terrible or amusing, lovable or odious, which in some degree every one possesses. (*VRE*, 35)

That we are asked to "get at" this "total reaction," which means to "go behind the foreground of existence" and reach a "sense of the whole residual cosmos," is one of the more amazing moments where James relies on our inner life of feeling and potential for a wide variety of feeling to help guide us to a better acquaintance with these "darker strata."

What does it mean to "get at" these places, especially places where a sense of the "whole residual cosmos" exists? James's entire argument assumes our familiarity with what we understand as our own "total reaction." He does not, as he says in the end, depend on the intellectual grasp his audience may have on religion. In fact, as Gerald Bruns argues, much of the *Varieties* creates the sense that an intellectual grasp is inherently impossible when it comes to religious experience: "This sensation of being haunted by alien or inaccessible meanings—this experience of the hermeneutical strangeness of religion, where sense is not abolished but, one might say, withheld or forbidden—is present everywhere in the *Varieties*."[16] His audience, therefore, must be won over solely through his ability to touch deep reservoirs of feeling and to provide a resonance with those feelings because at every turn it must accept the validity of what it "knows" nonintellectually or feels haunted by. From knowing what it means to feel "polarized" and "magnetized" by ideas, to experiencing "equilibrium succeeding a period of storm," his audience must accept that his work doesn't "prove" anything: it simply provides a guide for realizing how vast and mysterious and powerful the experience of consciousness is. Yet, at the same time, he builds into this rather unwieldy characterization of consciousness the conceptual and highly imagistic means to advocate a method of thinking to approach an uncertain universe. The notion of conversion is maybe not the cornerstone of the *Varieties* (for I would argue the foregrounding of feeling plays that role), but it is most definitely the hinge on which swings the varieties of religious experience he discusses. The experience of conversion becomes in the *Varieties* a trope that carries the weight of not only capturing James's idea of the adaptive nature of religious experience but also expressing the underlying structure of the pragmatic hermeneutic spiral.

The idea of conversion, for James, is the figure for the dynamic structure of consciousness as a mental universe of chance and indeterminacy, an acknowledgment that was possible not only because evolutionary theory argued for a physical universe based on these same uncertain principles, but also because religious experience in and of itself proved to have aspects of the indeterminate itself, particularly related to what he calls the "transmarginal" field. In his chapters on conversion, James employs more rigorously than in the rest of the *Varieties* naturalistic terms in order to convey the congruence he perceived between the worldview offered by evolutionary biology and the philosophical framework that grew out of the patterns and tendencies he detected in religious experience. Within the scope of the *Varieties*, the chapters on conversion allow James to make a transition from his more general discussion of the aspects of religion in the previous chapters to a more naturalistic or biological rendering of religious experience. In fact, James is not so delicate in the transition that he makes: when the first chapter on conversion barrages the reader with testimonies of subjects having undergone the transformative experience of conversion, James flatly states, "it is natural that those who personally have traversed such an experience should carry away a feeling of its being a miracle rather than a natural process" (*VRE*, 228). The argument for consciousness as a natural process builds throughout the chapters on conversion as images of flowers and fruits and crystals begin to appear. Though critics of the *Varieties* seem to agree that its purpose is to render a rationalistic account of religious experience through James's use of the field of psychology as an interpretive device, his use of metaphors borrowed from the natural world, including waves, fertility, energy, and growth, serves a descriptive purpose that has a more poetic function because the interpretive imperative is built into it. Instead of rendering religious experience solely as brain activity, James compliments his psychological account with poetic elements that present to a *viewer* a picture of that mental space providing the atmosphere for the dynamic between a fact and its interpretation—the pragmatic hermeneutic spiral.

These descriptive elements speak to the larger task that James undertakes with the *Varieties* of "converting" his audience to the dynamics of a philosophy built on uncertainty. James argues in the chapters on conversion that the "re-crystallization" of the feelings, ideas, and beliefs in a person's consciousness around a new "habitual centre" of energy occurs through a process involving the projection of one's self onto a new set of ideals. John E. Smith has offered an explanation for why James's image of

the stream was so apt a descriptor for this sense of tendency or directionality experienced in consciousness. He states that James departed from the
classical empiricism of Locke and Hume which held that experience was
a "veil somehow standing between the one who experiences and the
so-called 'external world' " when he adopted the pragmatists' emphasis
on the "activity and engagement of the subject in experience and especially on the close connection between experience and the formation of
habits or patterns of behavior in response to the challenge of a situation."[17]
James would focus his analysis on the directionality of experience, and in
doing so he would conceptualize the central role that the feeling of tendency has in it. The *Varieties* provides the best description of the feeling of
tendency in its rendering of the "transmarginal field" as the place of
emergent truth. Smith explains that

> one of the reasons for the stress on the atomic in classical empiricism
> was the difficulty of not being able to find an acceptable "impression"
> answering to the directionality we encounter in processes of both the
> physical and organic worlds, to say nothing of the experience of change
> and growth of ourselves. James was aware of the problem as is evi-
> denced by his use of the figure of the "stream" in his description of
> thought and consciousness. If the field of awareness is basically a flow
> or succession in which states interpenetrate each other and those which
> have passed leave traces on those yet to come so that at each point there
> are indications of what might or could come next, any analysis of these
> states into clear-cut and atomic units must result in the banishment of
> tendency from experience.[18]

The *ordo salutis*, and especially Shepard's version of the morphology of
conversion, is a good example of the organization of experience into
atomic units, demonstrating the very banishment of the feeling of tendency from experience that James esteems. As enforced as the early
"units" of conversion were by Shepard, those feelings of tendency sig-
naling Shepard's Puritans' faith would be suppressed in the effort to
maintain a "clear-cut" foundation for knowledge made "certain" through
efforts at rational apprehension.

In the *Varieties* conversion experiences can result from slow incubation within a subject's consciousness or from the influences of an outside
force. As James says, "new information, however acquired, plays an
accelerating part in the changes" (*VRE*, 197). The new information that
James presents provides the means for his audience to project itself onto
a wider field of imaginative and interpretative possibilities. The

following passage illustrates the beauty with which he is able to describe consciousness almost as though one were looking through a telescope at one's own mindscape. It presents a survey of the mind's processes in conversion:

> As our mental fields succeed one another, each has its centre of interest, around which the objects of which we are less and less attentively conscious fade to a margin so faint that its limits are unassignable. Some fields are narrow fields and some are wide fields. Usually when we have a wide field we rejoice, for we then see masses of truth together, and often get glimpses of relations which we divine rather than see, for they shoot beyond the field into still remoter regions of objectivity, regions which we seem rather to be about to perceive than to perceive actually. At other times, of drowsiness, illness, or fatigue, our fields may narrow almost to a point, and we find ourselves correspondingly oppressed and contracted. (*VRE*, 231)

This description of our mental fields allows us to grasp the "saving" nature of exercising our potential for perspective. In the passage the field originates from within and hopefully widens out toward regions "we seem rather to be about to perceive." These regions exist in the *Varieties* as those "withheld meanings" that seem to haunt the reader. As moments of suspense they are characterized as signs of psychological health and religious growth. They are moments marking conversion, which are not comfortable, but that mean we have not stagnated in our worldview, and the *Varieties* enacts this feeling of suspense and engages us in that epistemological and religious projection of ourselves, even to places we cannot yet "see," but are only vaguely aware of and yet are pointed toward by virtue of an internal "compass-needle" that James argues is always guiding us toward the margin. Much like the central moment of evangelical humiliation in Edwards's figuring of conversion in his *Religious Affections*, the straining toward "something that is seen, that is wonderful" is a mark of spiritual and mental health because it signals the regenerative process of arriving at new truths.

Because this theory of mental fields entails the movement or succession of cen ers, each producing a gravitational pull reorganizing a new set of relations, the feeling of tendency resulting from these interpenetrating states produces margins that generate an individual's sense of disorientation within experience. James, once again, renders this idea of the margin in such a way that provides a vocabulary for actually talking about the feeling:

The important fact which this "field" formula commemorates is the indetermination of the margin. Inattentively realized as is the matter which the margin contains, it is nevertheless there, and helps both to guide our behavior and to determine the next movement of our attention. . . . Our whole past store of memories floats beyond this margin, ready at a touch to come in; and the entire mass of residual powers, impulses, and knowledges that constitute our empirical self stretches continuously beyond it. So vaguely drawn are the outlines between what is actual and what is only potential at any moment of our conscious life, that it is always hard to say of certain mental elements whether we are conscious of them or not. (*VRE*, 232)

Indeed, based on this description, the conversion process not only provides a way of thinking about the indeterminacy of experience, but proposes indeterminacy as the template for conscious (and unconscious) life and makes our actions and behavior at best the testing ground for each stage or "hypothesis." This characterization of experience as highly unstable deems establishing conceptual frameworks for approaching the world seemingly impossible as well as a strange sort of fate: caught up in indetermination, we are never sure of what we are conscious until the invisible, underlying processes of transformation are made visible by the actions that result—the "fruits" as James puts it. In this experiential indeterminacy, the fruits never "prove" anything about the "cause" (because the "cause" is always already part of an indeterminate margin); rather, they legitimate belief in the face of that uncertainty. To be "religious" in this sense means to approach the world as a place wherein theories/beliefs are tested and realized through the fruits of action and behavior.

Basing his pragmatic hermeneutics on the principle of uncertainty allowed James to develop a philosophy foregrounding potential and parity, advocating ever-widening context and perspective, and empowering the individual as interpreter of his or her worldview. In his own philosophical journey, James found the theory of evolutionary biology helpful in structuring an approach to the world, and I would argue that the metaphors and imagery drawn from the physical world serve to reinforce the message that conversion's acts of interpretation reach to all corners of experience. These naturalistic images used to represent mental processes align that imaginative space with a physical environment. More importantly, they underscore the idea of *process*, marrying, imagistically, a method of thinking as processional to the ongoing nature of evolutionary biology. They support the idea that conversion involves the pragmatic hermeneutic approach to every environment we encounter whether it is the truths we are about to perceive over the horizon of consciousness or a species of wildflower we encounter on a hilltop. James's comparison of the conversion process to biological growth through naturalistic metaphors and images expresses his explicit claims that religious experiences, "on account of their extraordinary influence upon action and endurance . . . [must be classed] amongst the most important biological functions of mankind" (*VRE*, 506). Having found the drama of evolutionary biology meaningful, James's translation of it into a redemptive drama widens the context for religious experience in that it includes it among a broader spectrum of encounters that warrant interpretation. In addition, because James construed spiritual growth as a function of biological evolution, he infuses it with a dynamism that finds suitable symbolism in the evolutionary processes of the natural world: "When the new centre of personal energy has been subconsciously incubated so long as to be just ready to open into flower, 'hands off' is the only word for us, it must burst forth unaided" (*VRE*, 210).

Like his predecessors Jonathan Edwards and Ralph Waldo Emerson, James found the flower to be a useful symbol for capturing aspects of spiritual growth. James's flower symbol, however, has the power of conveying the suspense of "incubation" and the spontaneity of the bloom. For James, God is "the finite limit of the field of consciousness."[19] Therefore, the conversion process entails attention to our stream of thought, conceived as a succession of conscious fields. James's flower, like Emerson's, has a more prominent character of individuality, unlike Edwards's "little white flower . . . low and humble on the ground" in his "Personal Narrative." But, unlike Emerson's roses in "Self-Reliance," James's flower has a more defined self-contained internal energy, an energy that does not necessarily extend beyond the individual's own transmarginal field. Emerson's roses, on the other hand, exist with, or in relation to, the divine; they "are for what they are; they exist with God to-day." Because James locates a subconscious region "through which a God *might possibly* communicate with an individual," his emphasis in his characterization of the mind's growth falls on the idea of "incubation" and the incessant regeneration of an individual's "habitual centre" of "personal energy" resulting from personal desire and volition.[20] James explains, with regard to our "field of consciousness," that "whatever it may be on its *farther* side, the 'more' with which in religious experience we feel ourselves connected is on its *hither* side the subconscious continuation of our conscious life," so that there is "the subconscious incubation and maturing of motives deposited by the experiences of life" and "when ripe, the results hatch out, or burst into flower" (*VRE*, 512, 230). In James's symbol of the flower we find an articulation of conversion that captures the beauty and "biology" of the spontaneity that has been associated with Puritan conceptions of spiritual conversion. The idea in James that regeneration is a natural process, and we are merely witnesses to it, retains the mystery of an experience about which, James argues, so much is simply unknown. His characterization of the subconscious as the space of incubation and of emerging truths, where God *"might possibly"* be communicating with us, finally reconciles the process of conversion with the idea that there is no certain way to determine the causes of the effects we experience in that process.

In characterizing the soul, James asserts that it is simply the conglomeration of things that are "hot and vital to us to-day" but could just as easily be "cold" to us "to-morrow" (*VRE*, 195). Soul is merely a matter of our own perspective, or rather *the* matter of our perspective, a grouping of ideas indicating what is important to us "here" and "now" or what is "mine" or constitutes "me." The hot place of man's soul/consciousness is, according to James, *"the habitual centre of his personal energy,"* the "group of ideas to which he devotes himself, and from which he works" (195–196). What James does so faithfully in these chapters on conversion is use a variety of discourses to describe what happens in the mind when new centers of personal energy are created in the course of experience. The result is an intermingling of discursive boundaries revealing the limitations and possibilities each offers for understanding the phenomenon. As a reader, one must become adept at juggling the descriptions each discourse has to offer. In a matter of two pages, he explains that to say a man is "converted" means that "religious ideas, previously peripheral in his consciousness, now take a central place, and that religious aims form the habitual centre of his energy" (*VRE*, 196). Then he calls upon the discourse of psychology to explain *"how* the excitement shifts in a man's mental system, and *why* aims that were peripheral become at a certain moment central," admitting that it cannot, that in the end, we must "fall on the hackneyed symbolism of mechanical equilibrium":

A mind is a system of ideas, each with the excitement it arouses, and with tendencies impulsive and inhibitive, which mutually check or reinforce each other. The collection of ideas alters by subtraction or by addition in the course of experience, and the tendencies alter as the organism gets more aged. . . . But a new perception, a sudden emotional shock, or an occasion which lays bare the organic alteration, will make the whole fabric fall together; and then the centre of gravity sinks into an attitude more stable, for the new ideas that reach the centre in the rearrangement seem now to be locked there, and the new structure remains permanent. (*VRE*, 196, 197)

Immersed in a sea of varying discourses, his audience undergoes the disorientation similar to the experience of reading Emerson's essays. The variety of discourses insures that James's ideas will find the widest possible audience, but it also puts his audience in the position of having to limn meaning from them. We undergo the same interpretative experience he describes. Significantly, the "mutations" of our "instincts" and "propensities" forming new "mental results" (the meanings we construct from the varying discourses he provides) are accomplished, James argues, in two ways: "There is . . . a conscious and voluntary way and an involuntary and unconscious way," what he quotes Starbuck as terming "the *volitional type*" of conversion and the *"type by self-surrender"* (*VRE*, 206).

These two paths to achieving conversion, James notes, are really only two perspectives an individual gains upon the "indivisible event" he conceptualizes as conversion. Quoting Starbuck again, he explains that "self-surrender" provides a perspective viewing the change "in terms of the old self," and one's determination to convert provides the perspective viewing the change "in terms of the new."[21] Both types work in tandem, with the "volitional type . . . building up, piece by piece, . . . a new set of moral and spiritual habits" and the "type by self-surrender" acting as the "vital turning-point" (*VRE*, 206, 210). James presents the process in theological terms, quoting from Starbuck, "Man's extremity is God's opportunity." He also describes it in physiological terms, quoting Starbuck again, "Let one do all in one's power, and one's nervous system will do the rest."[22] Moreover, he reminds his reader that these two paths to conversion are the same as those that were codified and undertaken by New England's Puritans. With such a claim, James conflates the aims he envisions for the pragmatic hermeneutic with the spiritual goals Shepard's saints undertook by using the *ordo salutis*. Both methodologies centralize the role that the perceptual realm plays in the interpretive process and recognize the seemingly dual aspects of searching and surrendering. In addition, both methodologies have as their ends the "assurance and peace which fill the hour of change itself" (*VRE*, 242).

James's argument in *The Varieties of Religious Experience* depends on the emphasis placed on the "incubation" of habits formed through the "indivisible event" of volition and self-surrender. Though he does not go into the particulars of how habits are formed in the *Varieties*, the process he describes in the "Habit" chapter of *The Principles of Psychology*, published twelve years earlier, frames a history of the conversion experience and the methodologies and goals adopted by Shepard, Edwards, and Emerson. As ministers, they would have been especially sensitive to the psychological and physical effects of the atmosphere they created, through their ministrations, at the intersection of an individual's experience of method, perception, and affection.

Recognizing that the brain and spinal cord are "carefully shut up" in "bony boxes," he argues that "the only impressions that can be made upon them are through the blood, on the one hand, and through the sensory nerve-roots, on the other."[23] Therefore, he asserts, the brain is susceptible to the "infinitely attenuated currents," what Emerson would call the "ethereal currents," pouring in through the "sensory nerve-roots." Habits are formed because the "currents, once in, must find a way out. In getting out they leave their traces in the paths which they take. The only thing they *can* do, in short, is to deepen old paths or to make new ones."[24] In this way, the organism can "*form itself* in accordance with the mode in which it is habitually exercised" because "*incessant regeneration*" is the "tendency" of the "Nervous apparatus."[25] Habits, our centers of personal energy, are maintained or created physiologically, James argues, because "every state of ideational consciousness which is either *very strong* or is *habitually repeated*, leaves an organic impression on the Cerebrum."[26] Importantly, these habitual centers of personal energy serve as the "enormous fly-wheel of society, its most precious conservative agent. It alone is what keeps us all within the bounds of ordinance."[27] In James, habits are the register of our experience in the world, a sort of record of our adaptations resulting from a meaning-making process. They are "invisible laws" indicating the ideas to which we devote ourselves:

> We have a thought, or we perform an act, repeatedly, but on a certain day the *real meaning of the thought* peals through us for the first time, or the act has suddenly turned into a moral impossibility. All we know is that there are dead feelings, dead ideas, and cold beliefs, and there are hot and live ones; and when one grows hot and alive within us, every-thing has to re-crystallize about it. (*VRE*, 196–97 [italics added])

In James's formulation, the "real meaning of the thought" in the above quote can issue through the "indivisible events" of self-surrender or voli-tion in the habit forming process. What his formulation articulates is the central role habit forms in the meaning-making process that is conver-sion. We exist as a group of ideas, responding to an environment, and adapting to that environment through adjustments in our "habitual cen-tres" of "personal energy." Our habits indicate the group of ideas "hot" to us, but the moment that an idea becomes cold, either through an emotional shock, for example, or through a gradual buildup of a new habit, our personal "centre of gravity" will "sink into an attitude more stable," our ideas having recrystallized around a new arrangement. As a result, and according to Edwards's formulation of the new spiritual sense being laid in the foundation of the soul, an individual understands that a change has occurred because a *difference* in thought and behavior can be detected, an individual can perceive that, as James describes, "there are dead feelings, dead ideas, and cold beliefs, and there are hot and live ones" that reorient our souls. As noted in the chapter on Edwards, the new habit, though orienting a soul in a new direction, maintains enough of the old set of ideas to insure a continuation of a sense of self, and in his description of the change associated with the work of the Holy Spirit, he attempts to convey the feeling of the recrystallization James speaks of. His language insists on the sense of rebirth at the same time it captures the feeling of continuance.

These recrystallizations signal the moments when we "touch our own upper limit and live in our own highest centre of energy," and in these moments, James explains, "we may call ourselves *saved*, no matter how much higher some one else's centre may be" (*VRE*, 239 [italics added]). Living in "our own highest centre of energy," therefore, is a way of carving our way through life with habit as the response to the stability or rearrangements of the group of ideas making up consciousness. The continuity that these recrystallizations manifest constitutes what James calls "the stream of thought," and in his definition of the "spiritual self" he claims that attention to this stream, or "to think ourselves as thinkers," puts us in touch with this "rather mysterious operation" that is the subjective life. In the chapter called "The Consciousness of Self" in *The Principles of Psychology*, he outlines how "all men" would describe this self if we were to "think ourselves as thinkers":

> They would call it the *active* element in all consciousness; saying that whatever qualities a man's feelings may possess, or whatever content his thought may include, there is a spiritual something in him which seems to *go out* to meet these qualities and contents, whilst they seem to *come in* to be received by it. It is what welcomes or rejects. It presides over the perception of sensations, and by giving or withholding its assent it influences the movements they tend to arouse. It is the home of interest. . . . It is the source of effort and attention, and the place from which appear to emanate the fiats of the will. A physiologist who should reflect upon it in his own person could hardly help . . . connecting it

more or less vaguely with the process by which ideas or incoming sensations are 'reflected' or pass over into outward acts.[28]

As our personal centers of energy change, our spiritual selves seem to
make up what James describes as "the permanent core of turnings-
towards and turnings-from, of yieldings and arrests" forming the contours of our internal lives.[29]

James's articulation of conversion in physiological, psychological, and
spiritual terms allows him to explicate facets of the experience, and of the
concept itself, that clarify its role in Puritan theology and Emerson's literary style. Specifically, each theologian was committed to creating specific habits in his audiences for the purposes of helping them become
more pious or acute interpreters of their experience, thus the role played
by the *ordo salutis*, by Edwards's emphasis on "attention of the mind in
thinking," and by Emerson's transcendental project in *Nature* and literary style. Each of these tools guided perception to that conscious space
where individuals witness the "turnings-towards and turnings-from" of
their experience, fostering the development of that spiritual self who is
attentive, or pious to, the "mysterious process" of crystallization. Each
theologian was also interested in the critical revisioning of culture and
sought to foster a method of thinking that would build a spiritually,
emotionally, and intellectually healthy community, one that would, in
fact, have the best chance at survival. In order to reinstate New England
as a vital means in his preparatory scheme and to establish a church of
covenanting members, Shepard developed an overtly disciplined ministry, preaching the stages preceding conversion emphasizing conviction
and compunction. The *ordo salutis* provided the template determining
for his congregation what parts of their experience they were to turn
toward and what parts they were to turn from, hence the open-ended
narratives. Edwards's theorizing of conversion as the pious attention to
the "mind in thinking" closely resembles James's idea that to develop the
"spiritual self" we need to "think ourselves as thinkers." Emerson, in
turn, writes a transcendental version of the *ordo salutis*, guiding his
readers on a perceptual journey no less directed at inculcating the habit
of becoming aware of, and nurturing, one's own perspectival removes.
All are interested in using their influence to promote what they conceive
to be the most beneficial state of consciousness because, as James would
say, we would be "operating," at "our own highest centre of energy,"
engaged in a process of "incessant regeneration."

Renee Tursi calls the ability of habit to offer secure relations with the
universe in James's thought its "ameliorating force" in that it *facilitates* the

rebirth associated with all of the conceptions of conversion developed by Shepard, Edwards, Emerson, and James.[30] Joseph M. Thomas, in turn, has argued that "habit's trick is to supplant nature by mimicking it, to become, through repetition over time, a virtual or 'second' nature."[31] Indeed, James's descriptions of conversion in physiological terms provide yet another way to understand why the *ordo salutis* was so successful. As a socially prescribed habit, all individual experience was subjected to it. Edwards, on the other hand, was explicit about the fact that the new "spiritual sense" *was* a new habit, and by eschewing orderly preparatory stages, he left the process of acquiring the new habit up to the individual. However, the goal was the same—regeneration—and one's newly acquired habits, cast in the physical terms of "sense," remained "proof" that they were the results of grace. Emerson too was interested in the ameliorative forces of developing the right habits. Particularly concerned about the destructive relations between an individual and history, nature, rhetoric, and language, he developed a literary style compelling his readers and listeners to take responsibility for developing meaning out of the contexts in which they found themselves.

The strength of James's articulation of conversion comes from his ability to describe consciousness as a boundary phenomenon, as a conductive imaginary manifesting the relation between abstract ideas and concrete realities. In providing a sustained rendering of the pragmatic hermeneutic, the *Varieties* illuminates *what happens to ideas* in the course of experience and interpreting the truth.[32] It presents the challenge and complexity that Shepard would have claimed to be the state of fallen man, that our perception and knowledge of God's divinity in the world is seen "but as in a glass," and that the best we can expect of our interpretations of the truth is that they lead us into what James describes in *Pragmatism*, but that Edwards had described earlier, as "satisfactory" relations with the world. Indeed, James's pragmatic method provides the meliorism for the age-old problem of the human inability to see things "as they are." He describes our perceptual fate with an apt symbol:

Hold a tumbler of water a little above your eyes and look up through the water at its surface—or better still look similarly through the flat wall of an aquarium. You will then see an extraordinarily brilliant reflected image say of a candle-flame, or any other clear object, situated on the opposite side of the vessel. No ray, under these circumstances, gets beyond the water's surface: every ray is totally reflected back into the depths again. Now let the water represent the world of sensible facts, and let the air above it represent the world of abstract ideas. Both worlds are real, of course, and interact; but they interact only at their boundary, and the *locus* of everything that lives, and happens to us, so far as full experience goes, is the water. We are like fishes swimming in the sea of sense, bounded above by the superior element, but unable to breathe it pure or penetrate it. We get our oxygen from it, however, we touch it incessantly, now in this part, now in that, and every time we touch it, we turn back into the water with our course re-determined and re-energized.[33]

Indeed, Edwards had devised his new "Logick" with a similar picture of the mind. Most notably, both Edwards's and James's theorizing of a method to interpret the lived experience of uncertainty of the world into truth led them to a valuing of the boundary experience of consciousness and specifically to a conceptualization of the space of the vague. As the space of emergent truths, the space of the vague offers the promise of "consistency, stability and flowing human intercourse" because it is an infinite resource for ideas helping us "to *deal*."[34] Any idea, James argues, that helps us to forge new relations, "whether practically or intellectually, with either the reality or its belongings, that doesn't entangle our progress in frustrations, that *fits*, in fact, and adapts our life to the reality's whole setting, will agree sufficiently to meet the requirement. It will hold true of that reality."[35]

James concludes *The Varieties of Religious Experience* by placing the question of our "fate" at the center of our existence: "however particular questions connected with our individual destinies may be answered, it is only by acknowledging them as genuine questions, and *living in the sphere of thought* which they open up, that we become profound"—to "live thus," James concludes, "is to be religious" (*VRE*, 500 [italics added]). In these concluding words, James returns us to the "genuine" question of Shepard's saints: Am I saved? Launching the saints on a search for a specific experience of belief, the morphology of conversion opened up an epistemological space offering the promise of adaptation to and redemption from their fallen state. Indeed, they lived "in the sphere of thought" that the promise of salvation offered them. That "sphere of thought," what I've been calling a conductive imaginary, is the conscious (and unconscious) space where adaptations in belief and worldview occur through the experience of the gap between a fact and its interpretation. This gap has proven to demand a method of thinking for seeking out relations and finding stability within the uncertainty experienced in the moments of orientation toward new worldviews. All of the authors discussed here undertook not only to theorize a method, but the guide for habituating their audiences to that method as well. *The Varieties of Religious Experience* joins in that effort, by promoting the method of a pragmatic hermeneutic for "living in the sphere of thought" opened up by the questions we constantly need to ask. We are all "saved," James would argue, if we live by trying our best at answering these questions for ourselves.

Notes

Introduction

1. Jonathan Edwards, *Religious Affections* (1746) [hereafter *RA*], ed. John E. Smith, vol. 2, *The Works of Jonathan Edwards*, ed. Harry S. Stout, 26 vols. (New Haven, CT: Yale University Press, 1959), 275.

2. Unless otherwise noted, all quotes by Emerson are taken from *Ralph Waldo Emerson: Essays and Lectures* [hereafter *EL*], ed. Joel Porte (New York: Library of America, 1983), 49.

3. *EL*, 49.

4. *EL*, 301.

5. *EL*, 49.

6. Ibid. (italics added).

7. *RA*, 275.

8. *EL*, 292.

9. William James, *The Varieties of Religious Experience* (1902) [hereafter *VRE*], ed. Martin E. Marty (New York: Penguin, 1982), 197, 196.

10. Ibid., 189.

11. Perry Miller, *The New England Mind: The Seventeenth Century* [hereafter *NEM*] (1939; Cambridge, MA: Harvard University Press, 1954), 21.

12. The term "morphology of conversion" was coined by Edmund S. Morgan and has remained a valuable way to conceptualize the process. *Visible Saints: The History of a Puritan Idea* (New York: New York University Press, 1963).

13. Janice Knight, *Orthodoxies in Massachusetts: Rereading American Puritanism* (Cambridge, MA: Harvard University Press, 1994), 90.

14. William James, *The Principles of Psychology* [hereafter *PP*] (Cambridge, MA: Harvard University Press, 1983), 130–31.

15. Patricia Caldwell, *The Puritan Conversion Narrative: The Beginnings of American Expression* (Cambridge: Cambridge University Press, 1983), 130.

16. Jonathan Edwards, *The "Miscellanies": Entry Nos. a–z, aa–zz, 1–500*, ed. Thomas A. Schafer, vol. 13, *The Works of Jonathan Edwards*, ed. Harry S. Stout, 26 vols. (New Haven, CT: Yale University Press, 1994), 252.

17. *PP*, 1134.

18. *EL*, 60.

19. Lee Rust Brown, *The Emerson Museum: Practical Romanticism and the Pursuit of the Whole* (Cambridge, MA: Harvard `University Press, 1997), 173.

Chapter 1

1. This chapter's summary of revisions to Miller's thesis of the "errand" is a synthesis of Theodore Dwight Bozeman's review of the relevant literature on the topic. It is beyond the scope of this chapter to provide a detailed account of the research surrounding the Great Migration, but Bozeman's article is a good place to start, as are the original texts he cites. Theodore Dwight Bozeman, "The Puritans' 'Errand into the Wilderness' Reconsidered," *The New England Quarterly* 59, no. 2 (June 1986): 231–51.

2. Ibid., 245–46.

3. Ibid., 237.

4. Andrew Delbanco, *The Puritan Ordeal* (Cambridge, MA: Harvard University Press, 1989), 13.

5. Andrew Delbanco, "Thomas Shepard's America: The Biography of an Idea," in *Studies in Biography*, ed. Daniel Aaron, Harvard English Studies 8 (Cambridge, MA: Harvard University Press, 1978), 165.

6. Delbanco, *The Puritan Ordeal*, 14.

7. *NEM*, 5.

8. Ibid., 21.

9. Ibid., 5.

10. *The Will to Believe and Other Essays in Popular Philosophy* (1897; repr., New York: Dover, 1956), 11.

11. Ibid., 29.

12. Norman S. Fiering, "Will and Intellect in the New England Mind," *William and Mary Quarterly* 3rd ser. 29, no. 4 (October 1972): 515–58.

13. Ibid., 517.

14. Quoted in Fiering, "Will and Intellect in the New England Mind," 541.

15. Fiering, "Will and Intellect in the New England Mind," 523.

16. Ibid., 534–35.

17. Quoted in Fiering, "Will and Intellect in the New England Mind," 535.

18. Ibid.

19. Ibid., 540–41.

20. Ibid., 541.

21. Knight, *Orthodoxies in Massachusetts*, 59. For Knight's argument that Ames's influence in England has been overstated in Puritan scholarship see pages 58–59.

22. Delbanco, "Thomas Shepard's America," 160.

23. Knight, *Orthodoxies in Massachusetts*, 177.

24. Ibid.

25. Caldwell, *The Puritan Conversion Narrative*, 124–25. I am greatly indebted to Caldwell for her work on the confessions.

26. Edmund S. Morgan argues that the confessions "demonstrate clearly the familiarity of the narrators with the morphology of conversion, a familiarity produced, no doubt, by a great many sermons on the subject. The pattern is so plain as to give the experiences the appearance of a stereotype." *Visible Saints: The History of a Puritan Idea* (New York: New York University Press, 1963), 90–91.

27. I am borrowing the term "Intellectual Fathers" from Janice Knight, who notes that she is borrowing it from William Haller. I, however, am relying on the distinction Knight makes in *Orthodoxies in Massachusetts* between the "Intellectual Fathers" and the "Spiritual Brethren" to contextualize Shepard's preparatory theology and emphasize the impact of his intellectualism on his ministry. That Shepard belonged to both groups is recognized by Knight and discussed in further detail on pages 55–56. The fact of Shepard's spiritism informs this chapter, but is only referenced in passing.

28. Adrian Johns, foreword to *Ramus: Method, and the Decay of Dialogue; From the Art of Discourse to the Art of Reason*, by Walter J. Ong (1958; Chicago: University of Chicago Press, 2004), ix.

29. Walter J. Ong, preface to *Ramus: Method, and the Decay of Dialogue; From the Art of Discourse to the Art of Reason* (1958; Chicago: University of Chicago Press, 2004), xvi.

30. Ong, *Ramus: Method, and the Decay of Dialogue*, 195.

31. Caldwell, *The Puritan Conversion Narrative*, 140.

32. Knight, introduction to *Orthodoxies in Massachusetts*, 2.

33. Harry S. Stout calculated that the "average weekly churchgoer in New England . . . listened to something like seven thousand sermons in a lifetime, totaling somewhere around fifteen thousand hours of concentrated listening." *The New England Soul: Preaching and Religious Culture in Colonial New England* (New York: Oxford University Press, 1986), 4.

34. David D. Hall, "Toward a History of Popular Religion in Early New England," *William and Mary Quarterly* 3rd ser. 41 no. 1 (January 1984): 51.

35. Delbanco, *The Puritan Ordeal*, 26.

36. Ibid., 26.

37. Caldwell, *The Puritan Conversion Narrative*, 136.

38. Although Delbanco claims that Shepard was "less securely allied" to the preparationists "than has often been presumed," his analysis of the evolution in Shepard's preaching style in New England supports the idea that Shepard adopted a language of discipline in response to the antinomians. They were "jumbling the orderly picture of the mind" and "this was, for him, the first intellectual step to overthrowing all social hierarchies. . . . And so Shepard reasserted a vision of order among the faculties . . . This is why his preaching changed, why the appeal to affections faded from other New England pulpits as well—and gave way to a newly American contemplation of sin as the affections run wild." *The Puritan Ordeal* (Cambridge, MA: Harvard University Press, 1989), 144, 163.

39. Caldwell, *The Puritan Conversion Narrative*, 34.

40. Ibid., 130.

41. After the migration the "true sight of sin," Debanco argues, "has become less a means of grace than an end in itself. Sin, not grace, has become the minister's consuming subject. This shift of emphasis—sometimes subtle, sometimes stark—was among the central spiritual legacies of the Great Migration: these Puritans had discovered that America was the country of the isolated self." *The Puritan Ordeal* (Cambridge, MA: Harvard University Press, 1989), 182–83.

42. William K. B. Stoever, *"A Faire and Easie Way to Heaven": Covenant Theology and Antinomianism in Early Massachusetts* (Middletown, CT: Wesleyan University Press, 1978), 63.

43. Ibid., 44, 45.

44. George Selement, "The Means to Grace: A Study of Conversion in Early New England" (Ph.D. diss., University of New Hampshire, 1974), 56.

45. Ibid., 57.

46. Delbanco, "Thomas Shepard's America," 165.

47. Ibid., 173.

48. Thomas Shepard, *The Parable of the Ten Virgins Opened and Applied* (1659) [hereafter *PTV*], in *The Works of Thomas Shepard, First Pastor of the First Church, Cambridge, Mass. with a Memoir of His Life and Character*, vol.1 (Boston: Doctrinal Tract and Book Society, 1852; repr., New York: AMS Press, 1967), 170.

49. For a calculation of the number of narratives that express disappointment or confusion surrounding New England's effects see Caldwell, *The Puritan Conversion Narrative*, 124–25.

50. Delbanco, "Thomas Shepard's America," 170.

51. Stoever, *"A Faire and Easie Way to Heaven,"* 106.

52. Roger Ward helpfully explains why Jonathan Edwards would later be critical of covenant theology. Ward states, "covenant theology established that what could be trusted was not the soul's appropriation of God's grace, since that was impossible to claim without hubris, but that God had covenanted with a part of humanity to be a peculiar people. The affirmation of God's covenant relationship with the community was sufficient affirmation of one's relation to God." Edwards, as Ward shows, found this ideology of corporate intellectual assent problematic for its tendency to constitute "the goal or telos of preaching and theology," and he "opposed the supposition that a person had the ability to choose God based on coherent grounds presented in rhetorically or philosophically powerful descriptions." Roger Ward, preface to *Conversion in American Philosophy: Exploring the Practice of Transformation*, American Philosophy Series (New York: Fordham University Press, 2004), xvii. The confessions in fact show that one does not need to profess a belief in Christ in order to become a member of Shepard's church and receive the Supper. Shepard's saints were admitted based on their professions of merely a desire to be in the covenant and by their promise to maintain spiritual discipline.

53. Stoever, *"A Faire and Easie Way to Heaven,"* 106, 107. Stoever throws
the faculty of the will in the spotlight in his discussion of the Antinomian
Controversy in *"A Faire and Easie Way to Heaven"* (107), arguing that to deny
the will's activity in closing with Christ, as the antinomians did "deprives
men of proper consent. It is also to imply that that faith by which, alone, a
person is justified is not an act of his own, is not his own faith. These implications suggest . . . that God in regeneration disregards the efficiency proper to
the will as a second cause. Those who argued, with the Hutchinsonians, that
in respect of saving and sanctifying grace a person must 'do nothing' but only
'wait for Christ to do all' seemed to reject the proper activity of second causes
altogether, as they are ordained instruments in the application of redemption."

54. *PTV*, 125.

55. John S. Coolidge, *The Pauline Renaissance in England: Puritanism and
the Bible* (Oxford: Oxford University Press, 1970), 12.

56. Lisa M. Gordis's analysis of the confessions underscores the impact of
ministerial influence on lay interpretive practices. Citing Shepard's exhorta-
tion to his congregants to "make biblical language their own," she argues
that "the convert learns to subordinate his or her subjectivity to the text, the
minister, and most of all the Holy Spirit." In a provocative reading of the
"pronominal confusion" which marks the confessions, she argues that
Shepard's alternations between the first- and third- person in his transcriptions might suggest "the fluidity built into the Puritan sense of the regenerate reader's subjectivity. . . . In these narratives, the voices of Shepard's
congregants blend with the biblical texts they cite and with the voice of the
minister who examines them and records their narratives, just as the
convert's subjectivity was subordinated to the biblical text and to the Holy
Spirit." *Opening Scripture: Bible Reading and Interpretive Authority in Puritan
New England* (Chicago: University of Chicago Press, 2003), 104, 105.

57. *NEM*, 295.

58. Quoted in Miller, *NEM*, 168.

59. In David L. Parker's discussion of the influence of Ramus on Thomas
Hooker and Thomas Shepard he notes that while they both depend on the
Ramist use of dichotomies to make distinctions between preparatory stages,
Shepard inserts an extra dichotomy when he breaks down the stage of
contrition into the two complimentary stages of conviction and compunction, the first of which emphasizes "seeing" sin and the second the "sense"
or feeling of sin. But Shepard doesn't stop there. He also dichotomizes the
stage of conviction associated with "seeing" sin into two kinds of conviction,
"both of which are involved in the Spirit's work upon the understanding":
there is a rational conviction and a spiritual conviction that reveals conviction "really." Shepard demonstrates his Ramism in his method of descend-
ing from the general to particulars, but in doing so he makes the channel of
grace's operations increasingly more difficult to detect within the various
bifurcations that blur the spiritual efficacy of those distinctions. "Petrus
Ramus and the Puritans: The 'Logic' of Preparationist Conversion
Doctrine," *Early American Literature* 8, no. 2 (Fall 1973): 153.

60. Quoted in Miller, *NEM*, 179.

61. Delbanco, "Thomas Shepard's America," 172.

62. Thomas Shepard, *The Sound Believer* (1645) [hereafter *SB*], in *The Works of Thomas Shepard, First Pastor of the First Church, Cambridge, Mass. with a Memoir of His Life and Character*, vol. 1 (1853; repr., New York: AMS Press, 1967), 214.

63. Delbanco, "Thomas Shepard's America," 167.

64. Thomas Shepard, "Thomas Shepard's Record of Relations of Religious Experience, 1648–1649," ed. Mary Rhinelander McCarl, *William and Mary Quarterly*, 3rd ser. 48, no. 3 (July 1991): 462–63.

65. Ibid.

66. Thomas Shepard, *Thomas Shepard's* Confessions [hereafter *TSC*], ed. George Selement and Bruce C. Wooley, *Collections of the Colonial Society of Massachusetts*, vol. 58 (Boston: The Society, 1981), 91.

67. Shepard, "Thomas Shepard's Record of Relations," 448.

68. David D. Hall, "Toward a History of Popular Religion in Early New England," *William and Mary Quarterly*, 3rd ser. 41, no. 1 (January 1984): 52.

Chapter 2

1. Gerald R. McDermott, *One Holy and Happy Society: The Public Theology of Jonathan Edwards* (University Park: Pennsylvania State University Press, 1992), 41 (italics added).

2. Ibid.

3. Ibid., 141.

4. Sang Hyun Lee, *The Philosophical Theology of Jonathan Edwards* (Princeton, NJ: Princeton University Press, 1988), 10.

5. George M. Marsden, *Jonathan Edwards: A Life* (New Haven, CT: Yale University Press, 2003), 90–91.

6. Ibid., 62, 63.

7. Geoffrey Nuttall explains that the distinction between "rational" and "saving" knowledge of Christ reflects the idea that gave birth to the Reformation in that when the Bible became available in the vernacular, Protestants "sought to drink, not only intellectually but spiritually." As Nuttall shows, they found a "rapture" in reading the Bible that they did not experience in other books; the experience was understood as the Holy Spirit at work, "illuminating what was written and enlightening their minds to understand it," inevitably leading to considerations of the authority of scripture. It must be noted here that the Puritans went beyond Luther in attributing the power of scripture to save not only through the power of hearing the preached word but, importantly, through a private reading process as well. This is an early divergence in Protestantism that distinguishes the Puritans. Nuttall argues that at its inception the work of the Holy Spirit was understood in Protestantism as twofold: "the Spirit both inspired its writers and enlightens its readers. Belief in the former of these offices . . . is axiomatic among Puritans. . . . It is over the second of these

offices, the work of the Holy Spirit in the believer, that discussion arises. . . . That the assistance of the Spirit is necessary for the saving knowledge of Scripture is doubted by none: the bare word, the letter of Scripture cannot save by itself. But can the Spirit save, or even speak to, man apart from the Word or Scripture? or is the Spirit tied to Scripture?. . . . How can men know that it is God's Spirit which speaks to them, and not their own fancy? To what in them does the Spirit speak?" *The Holy Spirit in Puritan Faith and Experience* (1946; Chicago: University of Chicago Press, 1992), 21, 22, 23.

8. Smith, introduction to *RA*, 54.

9. William James, "The Moral Philosopher and the Moral Life," in *Pragmatism and Other Writings*, ed. Giles Gunn (New York: Penguin Books, 2000): 242–63.

10. *NEM*, 149.

11. Ibid.

12. Smith, introduction to *RA*, 12.

13. Ibid., 13.

14. Ibid., 24.

15. James Hoopes underscores this point by stating that the "sense of the heart" is a "broad category that includes various experiences of both saints and sinners" and that it is through the experience of conversion and the influx of grace that a saint acquires a new "spiritual sense" after having received "an entirely new and different sort of understanding or intellectual knowledge—the idea of holiness—which follows rather than precedes this new sense." "Jonathan Edwards's Religious Psychology," *Journal of American History* 69, no. 4 (March 1983): 857.

16. Jonathan Edwards, *The "Miscellanies": Entry Nos. 501–832*, ed. Ava Chamberlain, vol. 18, *The Works of Jonathan Edwards*, ed. Harry S. Stout, 26 vols. (New Haven, CT: Yale University Press, 2000), 456.

17. Ibid., 457 (italics added).

18. Perry Miller shows that Edwards's use in his preaching of Locke's idea that words are detached from reality granted him the power to instigate the Great Awakening. He cast society's problems associated with degenerating piety in terms of a language use problem, that if one experienced language in an actual way, one's thinking would generate piety: "[Thinking] can . . . operate entirely with those artificial signs which the mind habitually substitutes for reality. Profitable though the device might be for warfare, business, and speculation, what is it but the supreme manifestation of original sin? It is the negation of life, the acceptance of substitutes, of husks without the corn. Actually to know something, actually to live, is to deal with ideas themselves." *Errand into the Wilderness* (1956; Cambridge, MA: Belknap Press, 1996), 178.

19. Miller, *Errand into the Wilderness*, 185.

20. Philip F. Gura, *Jonathan Edwards: America's Evangelical* (New York: Hill and Wang, 2005), 12.

21. Ibid.

22. Ibid., 14.

23. Jonathan Edwards, *Letters and Personal Writings*, ed. George S. Claghorn, vol. 16, *The Works of Jonathan Edwards*, ed. Harry S. Stout, 26 vols. (New Haven, CT: Yale University Press, 1998), 759, 779.

24. All references to Edwards's text "The Mind" are from Leon Howard's edition, *"The Mind" of Jonathan Edwards: A Reconstructed Text* [hereafter *Mind*] (Berkeley: University of California Press, 1963), 101–2.

25. *Mind*, 54.

26. James Hoopes offers an explanation that may contribute to an understanding of why Edwards abandoned the "Old Logick." He makes the distinction that Edwards "was not in rebellion against faculty psychology, but only against hypostatization of faculties, the assumption that faculties were distinct entities rather than different abilities or functions of a unitary mind." "Calvinism and Consciousness from Edwards to Beecher," in *Jonathan Edwards and the American Experience*, ed. Nathan O. Hatch and Harry S. Stout (New York: Oxford University Press, 1988), 207. This passage recalls the argument that Delbanco made for a strain in Shepard's thought tending toward a more holistic and less compartmentalized picture of the mind. The "Old Logick," ordering the experience of perception according to the performance of each distinct faculty, drained the feeling of immediacy and directness from the experience of God's divinity, not only during the influx of grace, but after one had converted and one's relationship to the world reflected a constant state of virtue.

27. *NEM*, 160.

28. Jonathan Edwards, *The "Miscellanies": Entry Nos. a–z, aa–zz, 1–500*, ed. Thomas A. Schafer, vol. 13, *The Works of Jonathan Edwards*, ed. Harry S. Stout, 26 vols. (New Haven, CT: Yale University Press, 1994), 185.

29. Wallace E. Anderson, introduction to *Scientific and Philosophical Writings*, by Jonathan Edwards, vol. 6, *The Works of Jonathan Edwards*, ed. Harry S. Stout, 26 vols. (New Haven: Yale University Press, 1980), 79.

30. Norman Fiering has shown that Edwards's idealist metaphysics emerged out of truths expressed in the Westminster Confession, that his "belief that existence, or being, implies consciousness seems to have been originally a philosophical amplification of the basic confessional tenet that the purpose of the Creation is the manifestation of the glory of God, with the creation of men and angels supremely important in this scheme. One can follow in Edwards's writings step by step the transformation of this familiar theological dogma into idealist metaphysics." That the "universe does not exist for nothing," Fiering explains, is known through revealed truth, and "whatever the purpose of the universe is, it requires consciousness for that purpose to be a purpose" because "without intelligence to perceive it, the whole concept of 'purpose' is meaningless." "The Rationalist Foundations of Jonathan Edwards's Metaphysics," in *Jonathan Edwards and the American Experience*, ed. Nathan O. Hatch and Harry S. Stout (New York: Oxford University Press, 1988), 82.

31. Anderson, introduction to *Scientific and Philosophical Writings*, 122.

32. Jonathan Edwards, *The "Miscellanies": Entry Nos. a–z, aa–zz, 1–500*, 252.

33. Lee, *The Philosophical Theology of Jonathan Edwards*, 4.

34. Ibid., 132.

35. Roger Ward, *Conversion in American Philosophy: Exploring the Practice of Transformation*, American Philosophy Series (New York: Fordham University Press, 2004), 15 (italics added).

36. *Mind*, 51.

37. Ibid., 101.

38. Edwards and Locke had in common the belief that knowledge either exists in our minds as the experiences of "ideas" of things or as mere representations of things in the forms of verbal symbols, what Edwards called "speculative knowledge." However, as James Hoopes tells us, Edwards was critical of Locke's claim that all knowledge originates in sense experience because this would threaten orthodox doctrines of predestination and efficacious grace: "orthodox doctrine of a merciful, saving change of human nature requires some supernatural influx, rather than a chance encounter between the right ideas and a man willing to attend to them." "Calvinism and Consciousness from Edwards to Beecher," in *Jonathan Edwards and the American Experience*, ed. Nathan O. Hatch and Harry S. Stout (New York: Oxford University Press, 1988), 210.

39. Anderson, introduction to *Scientific and Philosophical Writings*, 128 (italics added).

40. *Mind*, 48.

41. Anderson, introduction to *Scientific and Philosophical Writings*, 128.

42. Jonathan Edwards, *Freedom of the Will*, ed. Paul Ramsey, vol. 1, *The Works of Jonathan Edwards*, ed. Harry S. Stout, 26 vols. (New Haven, CT: Yale University Press, 1957), 137.

43. Ibid., 141.

44. Ibid., 142 (italics added).

45. Edwards, *Freedom of the Will*, 142 (italics added). Claude A. Smith claims that the greatest difference between Edwards and Locke lies in Edwards's determination of the will as the greatest apprehension of good. According to Smith, "Locke's view arises, quite naturally, from his position that man possesses no 'innate ideas,' since his mind is a 'tabula rasa.' Man acts in response to a change in his state. The notion of action as a reflex movement is suggested. Edwards' view, on the other hand, seems to imply a more active view of the mind. It is not simply the 'greatest good' which determines the will, as Locke had stated in the first edition of the Essay. Rather, it is the 'greatest apprehension of Good.' The view of man implied is not that of an inert substance dependent on external stimuli. Instead, the movement of the will depends on man's judgment, as well as on the good apprehended." "Jonathan Edwards and 'The Way of Ideas,'" *Harvard Theological Review* 59, no. 2 (April 1966): 164.

46. David Jacobson, "Jonathan Edwards and the 'American Difference': Pragmatic Reflections on the 'Sense of the Heart,'" *Journal of American Studies* 21, no. 3 (December 1987): 378–79 (italics added).

47. Ibid., 380.

48. Ibid., 383 (italics added).

49. Ibid. (italics added).

50. William James, *Pragmatism* (Amherst, NY: Prometheus Books, 1991), 89.

51. Edwards's section on doctrine in his sermon "A Divine and Supernatural Light" coheres around the idea of conviction in order to expound on the text of Matthew 16:17: "And Jesus answered and said unto him, Blessed art thou Simon Barjona: for flesh and blood hath not revealed it unto thee, but my Father which is in heaven." In dealing with the problem of how one knows whether grace has been experienced, Edwards first describes in the "doctrine" section what the spiritual and divine light is, explaining that it is a "real sense and apprehension of the divine excellency of things revealed in the Word of God." In the second part of the doctrine expounded, after Edwards has described how one may gain a real apprehension of the divine light through a "sense of the heart," he buttresses his interpretation by claiming that the doctrine of convincing truth—through a "sense of the heart"—is "rational." This second part of the doctrine, I would argue, presents (because of the traditional sermonic form) the most explicit defense of the "sense of the heart" on "rational" grounds in his works. In arguing for that sense that indicates divine light, he proves its reliability on grounds that it permits "difference" to be seen: "We can't rationally doubt but that things that are divine, that appertain to the supreme Being, are vastly different from things that are human; that there is a godlike, high, and glorious excellency in them, that does most remarkably difference them from the things that are of men; insomuch that if the difference were but seen, it would have a convincing, satisfying influence upon anyone, that they are what they are, viz. divine." In other words, a will to believe occurs through inclination, or the "sense of the heart" (what James would call "passional grounds") and needs no other proof but its "satisfying" experience. *Sermons and Discourses, 1730–1733*, ed. Mark Valeri, vol. 17, *The Works of Jonathan Edwards*, ed. Harry S. Stout, 26 vols. (New Haven, CT: Yale University Press, 1999), 413, 420.

52. Terrence Erdt looks at the doctrine of the heart's inclination in Calvinism, noting that "Calvin was aware of the danger of a rationalism lurking in the unqualified acceptance of faculty psychology" because the "Scholastics insisted that the authenticity of Scripture rested upon rational proof, but this was no more than an assent of 'cold reason.'" Quoting from the *Institutes*, Erdt argues that for Calvin, faith was a knowledge providing certitude beyond what reason could, "a conviction that requires no reasons . . . in which the mind reposes more securely and constantly then in any reasons; such, finally, a feeling that can be born only of heavenly revelation. . . . I speak of nothing other than what each believer experiences within himself." "The Calvinist Psychology of the Heart and the 'Sense' of Jonathan Edwards," *Early American Literature* 13, no. 2 (Fall 1978), 168, 170, 169.

53. Richard Poirier, *Poetry and Pragmatism* (Cambridge, MA: Harvard University Press, 1992), 42.

54. Jonathan Edwards, *Letters and Personal Writings*, ed. George S. Claghorn, vol. 16, *The Works of Jonathan Edwards*, ed. Harry S. Stout, 26 vols. (New Haven, CT: Yale University Press, 1998), 792.

55. Gura, *Jonathan Edwards: America's Evangelical*, 154.

56. Lee, *The Philosophical Theology of Jonathan Edwards*, 261.

57. Ibid., 258.

58. Ibid., 262.

59. Jonathan Edwards, *Images or Shadows of Divine Things*, ed. Perry Miller (Westport, CT: Greenwood Press, 1977), 69–70.

Chapter 3

1. *EL*, 82.

2. *EL*, 16.

3. *VRE*, 500.

4. Stanley Cavell, *This New Yet Unapproachable America: Lectures after Emerson after Wittgenstein* (Albuquerque, NM: Living Batch Press, 1989), 94 (italics added).

5. Ibid., 77.

6. Ibid., 101.

7. Brown, *The Emerson Museum*, 173.

8. *VRE*, 501.

9. Charles Lloyd Cohen, *God's Caress: The Psychology of Puritan Religious Experience* (New York: Oxford University Press, 1986), 90.

10. Phyllis Cole, "Ralph Waldo Emerson in His Family," in *The Cambridge Companion to Ralph Waldo Emerson*, ed. Joel Porte and Saundra Morris (New York: Cambridge University Press, 1999), 34.

11. Ibid.

12. Ibid., 34–35.

13. Ibid., 41, 44.

14. Perry Miller, *Errand into the Wilderness* (Cambridge, MA: Belknap Press, 1996), 200.

15. Ibid., 195.

16. Ibid., 195–96.

17. Ibid., 196.

18. Ibid., 185.

19. *EL*, 311.

20. Ibid., 273.

21. Ibid., 75, 89 (italics added).

22. Ibid., 124.

23. Brown, *The Emerson Museum*, 88.

24. William James, *Pragmatism* (Amherst, NY: Prometheus Books, 1991), 109.

25. *EL*, 127, 126.

26. Ibid., 125 (italics added).

27. Ibid., 119, 126.

28. Robert Milder, "The Radical Emerson?" in *The Cambridge Companion to Ralph Waldo Emerson*, ed. Joel Porte and Saundra Morris (New York: Cambridge University Press, 1999), 56.

29. *EL*, 76.

30. Ibid.

31. Albert J. Von Frank, "Essays: First Series (1841)," in *The Cambridge Companion to Ralph Waldo Emerson*, ed. Joel Porte and Saundra Morris (New York: Cambridge University Press, 1999), 109.

32. Laura Dassow Walls, *Emerson's Life in Science: The Culture of Truth* (Ithaca: Cornell University Press, 2003), 4.

33. Quoted in Walls, *Emerson's Life in Science*, 12.

34. Ibid., 12.

35. Ibid., 43.

36. Ibid., 45.

37. Ibid., 34, 12, 13.

38. *EL*, 60.

39. *PP*, 245.

40. David C. Lamberth, "Putting 'Experience' to the Test in Theological Reflection," *Harvard Theological Review* 93, no. 1 (January 2000): 72.

41. Ibid., 71.

42. *EL*, 471.

43. Lamberth, "Putting 'Experience' to the Test in Theological Reflection," 72.

44. Ibid., 72.

45. Sampson Reed, *Observations on the Growth of the Mind with Remarks on Some Other Subjects* (1838; Gainesville, FL: Scholars' Facsimiles and Reprints, 1970), 73.

46. Ibid., 74.

47. Ibid., 75.

48. Ibid., 74.

49. Ibid., 75.

50. Ibid., 87.

51. Ibid., 59 (italics added).

52. Walls, *Emerson's Life in Science*, 42.

53. Ibid., 33.

54. John Herschel, *Preliminary Discourse on the Study of Natural Philosophy* (London: Longman, Rees, Orme, Brown, Green, and Longman, 1832), 15.

55. Reed, *Observations on the Growth of the Mind*, 81.

56. Robert D. Richardson, *Emerson: The Mind on Fire* (Berkeley: University of California Press, 1995), 93, 123, 147.

57. Walls, *Emerson's Life in Science*, 58.

58. Ibid., 11.

59. *EL*, 63.

60. Herschel, *Preliminary Discourse*, 49–50.

61. Ibid., 5.

62. Ibid.

63. Antonio Damasio, *The Feeling of What Happens: Body and Emotion in the Making of Consciousness* (San Diego, CA: Harcourt, 1999), 126.

64. Ibid.

65. Ibid.

66. Herschel, *Preliminary Discourse*, 5–6.

67. Ibid., 6 (italics added).

68. Ibid., 6–7.

69. Richardson, *Emerson: The Mind on Fire*, 155.

70. Walls, *Emerson's Life in Science*, 16.

71. Ibid., 25.

72. Ibid.

73. Ibid., 27.

74. Quoted in Walls, *Emerson's Life in Science*, 25.

75. *NEM*, 284.

76. Eduardo Cadava, *Emerson and the Climates of History* (Stanford, CA: Stanford University Press, 1997), 11–12 (italics added).

77. Ibid., 21.

78. Ibid.

79. Ibid., 2.

80. Ibid., 4.

81. Lawrence Buell contributes to this discussion of Emerson's desire to keep ideas in circulation when he argues that the "barrage of aphorisms" found throughout his transcendentalist style, what he calls "catalogue rhetoric," is an "inherently 'democratic' technique" because it "suggests the vast, sprawling, loose-knit country which America is" and that it "also adheres to a sort of prosodic equalitarianism: each line or image is of equal weight in the ensemble; each is a unit unto itself." Considering the arguments that Cadava and Poirier make, that his sentences force us to make sense of words and ideas for ourselves, Emerson's style expresses a population of "loose-knit" individuals employing the creative power of mind to organize chaos into meaning. *Literary Transcendentalism: Style and Vision in the American Renaissance* (Ithaca, NY: Cornell University Press, 1973), 167. In addition, Walls explains that it was the job of society's intellectuals "to stem the advancing tide of skepticism through public interventions—sermons, lectures, articles, essays, books—in a campaign of popular education and recruitment. . . . Moral law directed the flow of energy and imagination away from individual isolation and atomism and toward wholeness and unity, but this flow would disperse into droplets unless everyone was similarly directed, converging through individual instances of active choice toward a society unified in law, . . . [a] democracy without mobs." Walls, *Emerson's Life in Science*, 7.

82. Ibid., 6.

83. Ibid., 7.

84. Ibid., 5.

85. Richard Poirier, *Poetry and Pragmatism* (Cambridge, MA: Harvard University Press, 1992), 22–23.

86. Ibid., 23–24.

87. Ibid., 24.

88. Ibid., 25.

89. Ibid., 40.

90. *NEM*, 133.

91. Poirier, *Poetry and Pragmatism*, 24–25.

92. Ibid., 28.

93. Quoted in Gura, *The Wisdom of Words: Language, Theology, and Literature in the New England Renaissance* (Middletown, CT: Wesleyan University Press, 1981), 91.

94. Ibid., 18.

95. Ibid., 89, 92.

96. Ibid., 92.

97. *EL*, 9 (italics added).

98. Brown, *The Emerson Museum*, 66.

99. Ibid., 67, 66.

100. Ibid., 67 (italics added).

101. Ramist logic set forth in the *Dialecticae* was, in fact, a means of classification, its aim being to arrange in a series, through "dichotomy," the primary relations between arguments whose pattern revealed "a transcript of a unified intellect, a formal description of the image of God." In an ironic twist on the power of a garden, Alexander Richardson translated Ramus's definition of logic, "ars bene disserendi" or "the art of disputing well," as "sowing asunder" because he realized that the Latin gerund "disserendi" was a pun on the idea of "planting seed here and there." Logic could classify, or "sow asunder," "the material of any art, physics or medicine," first by "division of its two component parts, then by a subdivision of each part, and then by continued bifurcations of the subdivisions, until at last . . . the fundamental units, the indivisible 'arguments' would all be enumerated." One could then consult the *Dialecticae* to discover the proper classifications of the arguments. Because the purpose of the classification system of the *Dialecticae* was to provide a "transcription" of the divine plan, man's role in interpreting the material universe entailed no ordering or creative function on the part of man as the cabinets at the Muséum demanded. Man did not look through the material world to the idea behind it. Instead, in Ramist logic, man identified and located arguments and their relations on Ramus's chart, endowing the chart's classifications with the power and authority to, as Walls would say, "look order" into the universe. *NEM*, 125, 127.

102. Walls, *Emerson's Life in Science*, 101.

103. Ibid.

104. Leon Chai, *The Romantic Foundations of the American Renaissance* (Ithaca, NY: Cornell University Press, 1987), 191.

105. Ibid. (italics added).

106. Brown, *The Emerson Museum*, 158.

107. Ibid., 119.

108. *EL*, 10.
109. Brown, *The Emerson Museum*, 125.
110. Walls, *Emerson's Life in Science*, 102.
111. Ibid.
112. Ibid., 103.
113. Ibid., 104.
114. Brown, *The Emerson Museum*, 166.
115. Ibid., 43.
116. Ibid., 51.
117. Ibid., 50.
118. Ibid., 47, 46.
119. Ibid., 166.
120. Ibid., 46.

Chapter 4

1. Quoted in Ralph Barton Perry, *The Thought and Character of William James, Briefer Version* (New York: George Braziller, 1954), 102.
2. Paul Jerome Croce, *Science and Religion in the Era of William James: Eclipse of Certainty, 1820–1880*, vol.1 (Chapel Hill: University of North Carolina Press, 1995).
3. Ibid., 3.
4. Ibid., 230.
5. David Hollinger, " 'Damned for God's Glory': William James and the Scientific Vindication of Protestant Culture," in *William James and a Science of Religions: Reexperiencing "The Varieties of Religious Experience,"* ed. Wayne Proudfoot (New York: Columbia University Press, 2004), 24.
6. Ibid., 25.
7. *EL*, 193.
8. Croce, *Science and Religion in the Era of William James*, 100.
9. *VRE*, 5.
10. Wayne Proudfoot, "From Theology to a Science of Religions: Jonathan Edwards and William James on Religious Affections," *Harvard Theological Review* 82, no. 2 (April 1989): 166.
11. Ibid., 163.
12. Gerald L. Bruns, "Loose Talk about Religion from William James," *Critical Inquiry* 11 (December 1984): 310.
13. William James, *Pragmatism* (Amherst, NY: Prometheus Books, 1991), 99.
14. Charlene Haddock Seigfried, "William James's Concrete Analysis of Experience," *The Monist* 75 (October 1992): 547.
15. Jeffrey Gordon explains that within James's conception of the role that feeling plays in the divination of truth, "we cannot reason our way to passional commitment—except in one circumstance: that the springs of that passion be already flowing before the argument begins, for the argument can then provide the necessary 'clincher,' the reasoning that enables us to

allow that passion rein. This is another way of re-iterating that James intends his argument only for those for whom the religious hypothesis is live, those who have felt in that hypothesis a palpable temptation, those who could feel a religious passion were it not stifled in them by skeptical constraints." In this passage Gordon echoes the problem that Shepard's Puritans faced in attempting to reason their way to the truths about their souls. It was an epistemological process demanding a "passional" response, but to which they responded with the skepticism required by Shepard. "The Rational Imperative to Believe," *Religious Studies* 29 (1993): 19.

16. Bruns, "Loose Talk about Religion from William James," 311.

17. John E. Smith, "The Reconception of Experience in Peirce, James and Dewey," *The Monist* 68 (October 1985): 539, 540.

18. Ibid., 547.

19. Gary Alexander, "The Hypothesized God of C. S. Pierce and William James," *Journal of Religion* 67 (1987): 309.

20. Ibid. Alexander's article makes the argument that James's position helps us "to make sense of religious theism without demanding that belief in God be a requirement for authentic faith" (321). Because God is no longer a requirement for faith, "specific dogmatic beliefs will not last forever and can never be more than hypothetical. The experiences that give rise to such beliefs will, however, remain as long as there are human beings" (321). Cast in this light, we can look back on Calvinist doctrine and especially the *ordo salutis* as merely hypotheses pointing toward a specific spiritual experience. Presented as a way to establish belief about the state of their souls, saints would truly take part in an experimental piety in search of the truth about their election.

21. Quoted in James, *VRE*, 215.

22. Ibid., 210.

23. *PP*, 112.

24. Ibid.

25. Ibid., 116.

26. Ibid.

27. Ibid., 125.

28. Ibid., 285.

29. Ibid., 289.

30. Renee Tursi, "William James's Narrative of Habit," *Style* 33, no. 1 (Spring 1999): 80.

31. Joseph M. Thomas, "Figures of Habit in William James," *New England Quarterly* 66 (March 1993): 9.

32. Grace M. Jantzen notes that James's conception of experience was more inclusive than that found in the British empirical tradition: "Just as our senses are able to perceive material things via ordinary consciousness, so perhaps the margins of our consciousness or our subconscious minds might be the point at which 'higher spiritual agencies,' if there are any, could directly touch us." In the Puritan determination to establish the truth of their perceptions, saints were on the watch for any images that might be the

product of the imagination, the product of the devil's deception. Yet in James, it is because "higher spiritual agencies" could directly touch us that he was "particularly interested in the fringes of consciousness: psychic phenomena, hallucinations, the effects of nitrous oxide and intoxication, and intense or bizarre accounts of religious experience including trances, levitations, seizures, hallucinations, and the like." Having been banished from what could be considered "spiritual" in Puritan doctrine, "fringe" experiences, such as hallucinations, ironically find a home in James's theory of conversion. "Mysticism and Experience," *Religious Studies* 25 (1989): 296.

33. James, *Pragmatism*, 57.
34. Ibid., 95, 94.
35. Ibid., 94.

Index

predestination, 6, 81, 125, 128–29, 169n38
*Preliminary Discourse on the Study of Natural
    Philosophy*, 112–13
preparation theology. *See* conversion process
preparationism. *See* doctrine of preparation
Principles of Psychology, 7, 10, 12, 107,
    153–54, 155–56. *See also* James, William
probabilistic thinking, 138–39
pronominal confusion, 165n56
"Prospects," 132
Protestantism, 16, 19–20, 166–67n7. *See also*
    Calvinism; Puritan Reformed theology
Proudfoot, Wayne, 141
psychic upheaval, 51
purchased deliverance, 60
*The Puritan Conversion Narrative: The
    Beginnings of American Expression*, 8, 21
The Puritan Ordeal, 16, 24
Puritan Reformed theology, 3–6, 11, 15,
    18–19, 22–24, 35, 100, 117, 166–67n7,
    175–76n15. *See also* conversion process

Ramist logic
    compunction, 165n59
    consciousness, 21–23
    conversion process, 21, 34–35, 37, 56, 79
    conviction, 53, 165n59
    demise of, 108–9
    Dialecticae, 174n101
    dichotomies, 22–23, 165n59
    doctrine of preparation, 7, 20, 22–23
    and Edwards, 63–64, 83, 90
    experiential piety, 23
    habit of mind, 75
    and Hooker, 165n59
    invention, 22, 52
    "The Mind," 124
    morphology of conversion, 21, 23
    Parable of the Ten Virgins, 103
    and the promise of America, 8
    Puritan Reformed theology, 22–23
    replacement of, 55
    syllogistic reason, 124
    testimonies, 51
    and truth, 34, 76
rationalists, 97–98
realism, 144
reason, 7, 12–13, 18–19, 34, 40–41, 43, 58–59, 62,
    65, 75, 79, 108–12, 114, 124, 131, 170n51
recrystallization, 155

redemption, 4
Reed, Sampson, 107–12, 117, 125
Reformation, 166–67n7
regeneration
    believing attitude, 87
    "Compensation," 3
    conversion process, 5, 21, 27–28, 37, 40,
        69–70
    and Edwards, 21, 61
    and Emerson, 13, 21
    and experience, 71
    gracious affections, 73
    habit of thinking, 7, 31
    head/heart knowledge, 37
    and human will, 165n53
    and James, 21
    as natural process, 152, 157
    and nature, 110
    in New England, 79–80
    and transparency, 2
Religious Affections, 1, 3, 10, 56, 58–59, 65–75,
    84, 91–92, 96, 99–100, 114, 130, 149. *See
    also* Edwards, Jonathan
religious experience, 13–14, 97, 136, 140–42,
    147–48, 151. See also *Varieties of
    Religious Experience*
repronouncing/renouncing, 95, 121–22
revelation, 61–62
revelation-value, 138–40
Richardson, Alexander, 34–35, 116, 174n101
Rogers, Richard, 5
room of the idea, 11, 60, 67–68, 75–78,
    80–81, 83–88, 90, 112. *See also*
    conversion process; Edwards, Jonathan
rules of reasoning, 80, 83

sainthood, 6–7, 10, 18, 23–24, 26–27, 65, 67,
    69, 88, 164n52, 176n20. *See also*
    conversion process; testimonies
salvation, 4, 6, 23, 26–27, 30–31, 51–53, 60,
    66, 89, 158. *See also* conversion process;
    ordo salutis (order of salvation)
sanctification, 24
Satan, 61
science, 104, 106–7, 112–14, 118, 124, 136,
    142–43, 173n81
*Science and Religion in the Era of William
    James*, 136
Scientific and Philosophical Writings, 64
Second Coming, 54–55